blanet 5copies

L Ⱶ Ⴟ

FOREIGN PROTESTANTISM WITHIN THE CHURCH OF ENGLAND.

Foreign Protestantism within the Church of England:

THE STORY OF AN ALIEN THEOLOGY AND ITS PRESENT OUTCOME.

BY

A. THEODORE WIRGMAN, D.D., D.C.L.,

ARCHDEACON OF PORT ELIZABETH, CANON OF GRAHAMSTOWN, VICE-PROVOST
OF S. MARY'S COLLEGIATE CHURCH, PORT ELIZABETH, SOUTH AFRICA, AND
HON. CHAPLAIN TO H.M. THE KING.

" It is not with anything like a wish to carp at words that I avow
my ignorance of what is meant by the phrase ' *the Protestant Faith.*'
' Protestant ' and ' Faith ' are terms which do not seem to me to
accord together ; the *object* of ' Faith ' is Divine Truth ; the *object*
of ' Protestant ' is human error.   How therefore can one be an
attribute of the other ? "
(Pastoral Letter of Henry Philpotts, D.D., Bishop of Exeter, A.D. 1851.)

" A man is certainly the most perfect Protestant who protests
against the whole Christian religion."
(Edmund Burke, A.D. 1792.)

LONDON:

THE CATHOLIC LITERATURE ASSOCIATION,
13, PATERNOSTER ROW, E.C.

CONTENTS.

INTRODUCTION.

CONTENTS.

CHAPTER I.

LUTHER, ZWINGLI, AND CALVIN, THE FOUNDERS OF FOREIGN PROTESTANTISM.

CONTENTS.

CONTENTS.

CHAPTER II.

THE DOCTRINAL ERRORS OF FOREIGN PROTESTANTISM ON ORIGINAL SIN, JUSTIFICATION BY FAITH, AND PRIVATE JUDGMENT, CONSIDERED WITH REFERENCE TO THE TRUE TEACHING OF THE ENGLISH CHURCH.

CONTENTS.

CHAPTER III.

THE DOCTRINAL ERRORS OF FOREIGN PROTESTANTISM ON
THE SACRAMENTS, CONSIDERED WITH REFERENCE TO
THE TRUE TEACHING OF THE ENGLISH CHURCH
UPON THE SACRAMENTS IN GENERAL, AND HOLY
BAPTISM IN PARTICULAR.

CONTENTS.

CHAPTER IV.

THE DOCTRINAL ERRORS OF FOREIGN PROTESTANTISM UPON THE HOLY EUCHARIST CONSIDERED WITH REFERENCE TO THE TRUE TEACHING OF THE ENGLISH CHURCH.

CHAPTER V.

The Doctrinal Errors of Foreign Protestantism upon the Visible Church, the Apostolic Ministry and the Lesser Sacraments, considered in reference to the True Teaching of the English Church

CONTENTS.

CHAPTER VI.

A BRIEF SKETCH OF THE HISTORY OF "FOREIGN PROTESTANT" INFLUENCE WITHIN THE CHURCH OF ENGLAND UP TO THE CLOSE OF THE EIGHTEENTH CENTURY.

CONTENTS.

CONTENTS.   xix

CHAPTER VII.

INFLUENCE OF " FOREIGN PROTESTANT " THEOLOGY IN THE CHURCH OF ENGLAND IN THE NINETEENTH CENTURY.

CHAPTER VIII.

THE STORY OF THE CUMMINSITE SCHISM.

CHAPTER IX.

The " Liberal " or Latitudinarian Wing of the Foreign Protestant Party.

CONTENTS.

INTRODUCTION.

" *Ut Ecclesia Anglicana libera sit, et habeat iura sua
integra et libertates suas illaesas.*"
                                        Magna Charta.

THE " Ecclesia Anglicana," which was founded by the
mission sent forth by St. Gregory the Great,
and which subsequently absorbed into its
corporate life the noble fruits of Celtic
Christianity in the North and the rem-
nants of the ancient British Church which survived
in Wales and Cornwall, has suffered from traitors
within and foes without. Its ancient liberties, of
which the Great Charter makes mention, suffered a
greater curtailment by the "Submission of the Clergy"
under the iron tyranny of Henry VIII., than under the
hand of the mediæval Papacy at its worst period. Its
ancient laws and privileges were abrogated at will by
the Tudor despotism, and the little fingers of Henry
VIII. and Queen Elizabeth were thicker than the loins
of Pope Innocent the Great.

It is true that Western Christendom needed a Reformation. But the abuses of the Papal Curia formed no
valid excuse for the religious revolution of
Luther, Zwingli and Calvin. Bitterly as
these leaders of revolt were personally and
theologically opposed to each other, the
results of their teaching tended to the same end. They
framed a new religious system of human origin to

The " Ecclesia Anglicana" and the Tudor despotism.

Luther, Zwingli and Calvin framed a new religious system.

I

supplant the Catholic Church of Christ. The cold intellectualism of the Protestant system, as developed on the Continent of Europe, tended to the exaltation of the individual, whose self-centred consciousness of his own personal salvation placed him outside the very idea of the corporate life of the Kingdom of God on earth and caused him to cut himself off from its Apostolic Ministry and Sacraments. The importation of foreign Protestantism into England, during the reign of Edward VI., was an invasion of Zwinglianism, as developed by Calvin, rather than of Lutheranism. It was sanctioned by Somerset and Cranmer, and encouraged by the spoilers of Church property. It was the worst injury which the Church of England has ever received throughout the whole course of her history. The taint of foreign Protestantism remains to this day. This volume deals with doctrinal Protestantism as imported into England from the Continent, and not with political Protestantism in the sense in which Laud and the Caroline Divines used the term. But it may here be noted that the word " Protestant " is absolutely unauthorised in the Prayer Book and formularies of the Church of England.

Influence of Foreign Protestantism under Edward VI.

On February 23rd, 1903, the Russian Holy Synod addressed an Epistle to the Patriarch of Constantinople which dealt with the re-union of Christendom. This letter speaks of Anglicans in the most friendly way as showing "special respect to the Holy Apostolic Eastern Church." It proceeds to deal with Anglican desires for union with the Eastern Church, and as the *Guardian* says (August 24th, 1904) " the question is discussed dispassionately and with considerable knowledge of the English Church. " The Holy Synod says : " First of all it is indispensable that the desire for union with the Orthodox Eastern Church should become the sincere desire, not only of a fraction of Anglicanism

Epistle of the Russian Holy Synod on Re-union in 1903.

(the High Church) but of the whole Anglican com-
munity, that the other purely Calvinistic current

Its view of the which *in essence rejects the Church*, as we
effect of the understand her, and whose attitude towards
Calvinist taint in Orthodoxy is one of particular intolerance,
the Church of
England. should be absorbed in the above mentioned *pure* current."

The Holy Russian Synod clearly perceives the
foreign taint in the Church of England and recognises
the hostility of the " Calvinistic current" in modern
English Church life to any idea of union with the
Eastern Church. This hostility is even more bitter
and pronounced with regard to all efforts
Hostility of the for reunion with the Holy See, which
" Calvinistic
current" to must necessarily be taken into considera-
Catholic unity. tion by every sensible Christian who believes
that it is the will of our Lord that all Christians
should be united in His One Visible Kingdom. The
idea of a reunion of Christendom that takes no
account of the Holy See, and of the majority of
Christians now living in the world who are in communion with it, is contrary to reason and history.
Suppose, for the sake of argument, that Latin Christianity with its historical witness to the Faith, its
ordered discipline and its millions of adherents, was,
at this moment, utterly blotted out and effaced, the
question naturally arises to a thoughtful mind—How
would Christendom, as a whole, face such a loss, and
how long would historical Christianity survive the
catastrophe ?

On the other hand, the idea of union with Lutherans,
Calvinists, and with the confused multitude
Protestants must of other Protestant sects who have des-
accept the Faith
of the Catholic troyed the ideals of historical Christianity
Church as a
condition of is impossible, save on one basis only. The
reunion. Protestants, who deny Baptismal regeneration, who reject Confirmation, who disbelieve in the
Catholic doctrine of the Blessed Sacrament of the

Altar, who deny the Catholic doctrine of the Priesthood and its delegated powers, who reject the Apostolic Succession of the Catholic Episcopate, which
Bishop Lightfoot called "the historic backbone of the
Church," who deny the claims and existence of the
Catholic Church as the Visible Body of Christ; who
reject the authority of her Creeds and Councils;
must be brought to accept these truths of Primitive
Christianity before they can take their places as loyal
members of Christ's Holy Catholic Church.   They
must merge their distinctive individualism into the
corporate life of the Body of Christ, and exchange the
uncertain affirmations of an emotional religion (which
they so strangely couple with the negations of a cold
intellectualism) for the certainties of the Catholic
Faith " once delivered to the Saints."

It would be unworthy to deny or to minimise the
working of God in the hearts of those who
are unconscious of the Incarnation.
Theists like Channing and Dr. Martineau
have been permitted to bear witness to
certain portions of Divine truth, although
their admiration of our Lord's Person does not blind
us to their denial of His Incarnation.   The followers
of Buddha and of Mahomet have borne a similar
witness to certain moral truths, and the Church has
been able to make use of the differing systems of Plato
and Aristotle.

*Theists,
Buddhists and
Mahometans
witness to cer-
tain portions
of Divine Truth.*

We have to be thankful that Reformers of the
Continent originally transferred to the
Protestant sects certain definite portions of
the Creed of Christendom, although their
modern followers have ceased to believe in
many truths which their founders taught.

*Similarly Pro-
testants teach
positively
certain portions
of the Creed of
Christendom.*

The Spirit of God has wrought much in the world
through Protestant teachers, in spite of the defects of
their creed.   It is noticeable, however, that the greatest
leaders and teachers of the Protestants have arisen

amongst those of them who were most logical in their Protestantism, and who did not attempt the impossible task of adapting their tenets to the framework of a Catholic hierarchy and formularies, such as those of the Church of England. Cyril Lucar, the Calvinistic Patriarch of Constantinople in the first half of the seventeenth Century found his position untenable. In like manner the Zwinglian Hooper, in the reign of Edward VI., the returned Marian exiles of Elizabeth's reign, and, in fact, all those who have held the tenets of "foreign Protestantism" within the Church of England, up to the present day, have found themselves aliens to the plain teaching and ceremonial of the Book of Common Prayer, which they were bound to use as the condition of their tenure of office. Men who have perpetually to explain plain words in a non-natural sense, as these persons have had to explain away the doctrine of Baptismal Regeneration in the Baptismal Office, and the *absolvo te* of the Anglican form for private Confession, place themselves in a position of moral and intellectual difficulty which must necessarily minimise such spiritual forces as they possess.

This is the true reason why the great names amongst modern Protestants are necessarily found outside the Anglican Communion. In the nineteenth century the most famous Protestant preachers of the Anglo-Saxon race have been Mr. Ward Beecher, Mr. Spurgeon and Dr. Parker, and the greatest Protestant writers have been Dr. Dale and Dr. Milligan. The key to the influence and power for good which these men have undoubtedly exercised is that they were true to their limitations. They did not attempt to fit themselves into the formularies and beliefs of the Church of England by a forced process of illogical reasoning. They did not make the impossible attempt

Marginal notes:

The most logical Protestants are the best.

It is illogical to fit Protestantism into the framework of a Catholic hierarchy and formularies.

Thus the most able and spiritual of the Protestants are found outside the Anglican Communion.

to minister under conditions that required perpetual explanation, conditioned by silence as to awkward facts that could not be explained.   They stood aloof from the organisation and formularies of the Catholic Church in the honesty of their Protestantism, and for this reason their witness to such portions of Catholic truth as they retained and taught was strong and powerful.   The position of a convinced Pro-

The position of foreign Protestantism within the Church of England has involved perpetual controversy.

testant of the foreign type within the Church of England is so strained and impossible that the history of " the Calvinistic current " in the Anglican Communion has been from the first a tacit ignoring of the true sense and theological balance of our formularies, coupled with occasional strenuous efforts to get them altered in a Protestant sense.   This struggle began with Hooper and was continued by the returned Marian exiles under Elizabeth in the form of Puritanism within the Church, which found further expression in the Millenary Petition to James I., and obtained the definite result of a temporary victory under Cromwell, when the Church was supplanted by the Presbyterians and Independents, and King Charles and Archbishop Laud were judicially murdered for their faithful loyalty to the Church.   The struggle was continued at the Savoy Conference and in the abortive Revision of the Prayer Book in 1689, and its principles animated Lord Ebury's Prayer Book Revision Society of the middle of the nineteenth century.   And it is with us even to-day.

Men who are thus perpetually plunged into controversy on an illogical basis have no space to be great.   The well-known story of a prominent Anglican Protestant leader describing himself as " a great and good man " in an anonymous letter to the Press (which he subsequently admitted that he had written) shows a pathetic consciousness of littleness and of a weak cause which invites our pity rather than our smiles.

We can justly honour the memory of the pious "Evangelical" clergy of the eighteenth Century, who carried into the pulpits of the Church of England some of the fire of the spiritual revival of Whitfield and the Wesleys. They were not aggressive controversialists. The Catholic traditions of the Prayer Book had been almost lost to the Church of England by the secession of the Non-Jurors, and the few who maintained them were powerless in the face of the Whig-Hanoverian policy of repression and calculated stagnation in all matters concerning the true life of the Church.

The early leaders of the " Evangelicals " in the eighteenth century deserve honour for their zeal and piety.

Venn, Cecil, Romaine, and Newton were prominent types of this pious Protestant school of thought. They did not value the historical continuity of the Church of England because they never understood that the visible Church was the Body of Christ. They regarded the Church solely as a "National Establishment" which gave them the opportunity of proclaiming from its pulpits certain portions of the Gospel of Christ which they had found precious to their own souls. The Establishment did not trouble them by forcing them to face the question of the inherent discrepancy between their own teaching and certain forgotten doctrines of the Prayer Book, so that their ministry was not tarnished by controversy, or assailed by doubts as to the validity and honesty of their own position within the Church of England. They kindled real sparks of devotion and life when the Church was suffering from the dry rot of Sir Robert Walpole's policy, and evoked some " enthusiasm " in days when decorous and semi-pagan moral essays took the place of sermons and when men like Bishop Lavington condemned the " enthusiasm " of Wesleyans and Roman Catholics alike. But their successors during the first half of the nineteenth century did not inherit their self-sacrifice and religious

Their limitations.

Degeneracy of their successors.

earnestness.   They gradually became powerful and
fashionable, and consequently claimed a
They claim a
monopoly of
"the Gospel" in
the Church of
England. monopoly in the Church of England.   They
framed the religious phraseology and de-
fective theology of their predecessors into
a rigid system of catchwords and unreal
" shibboleths " which they called the " Gospel."   They
claimed for themselves the monopoly of the sacred
title of " Evangelical," by which term they virtually
substituted their own narrow and imperfect conception
of the " Gospel " for the breadth of the true Gospel of
Christ.   They became self-satisfied and self-sufficient,
and began to condemn all those who differed from
them in a spirit of uncharitable exclusiveness
begotten of theological ignorance.   The Catholic
movement of 1833 filled them with terrified
Their alarm at
the Catholic
Revival of 1833. amazement.   The revival of the teaching
of the Caroline Divines and the Non-
Jurors was an echo from an almost forgotten past, which shewed them that their capture of
the Church of England would be seriously disputed.
They found that the Prayer Book, which they had
hitherto used with a freedom which disregarded
teaching they did not like, (viewing, as they did,
its ritual and ceremonial from Calvin's well-known
standpoint as *tolerabiles ineptiae*), was a formidable
and irresistible weapon in the hands of the Tractarians.

Their very position was threatened by the plain
words and rubrical directions of the Book
Their discovery
that the Prayer
Book was a
stronghold of
"Tractarianism." which they were solemnly pledged to use
in their public ministrations.   They faced
their unpleasant situation with a cry of
" No Popery " and became furious and
illogical controversialists.   They set themselves to vindicate their own position by making the position of the
Tractarians impossible.   They determined to get the
Prayer Book altered to suit their views, and when
Lord Ebury's Society for this purpose was formed

in 1854 its promoters did not realise that their
Their desire for
its revision. action was self-condemnatory. To continue the use of a book which taught Baptismal Regeneration, and other doctrines which they repudiated with equal energy, whilst at the same time they agitated for its revision, deprived their Protestantism of its moral backbone. They patronised Dissent from the superior social standpoint
Their consequent
illogical position of the Establishment, and marvelled that men of robust common sense amongst the Dissenters did not reciprocate their appeal for aid and sympathy in the warfare against the Tractarians. Mr. Spurgeon in later days considered these self-styled "Evangelicals" out of place in the Church of England. Dr. Parker some years ago said that the Prayer Book "was drenched in Popery," by which he meant that it taught plain and simple Catholic doctrine in a way which no honest Protestant could accept.

If the "Evangelicals" had abstained from controversy, and had been content to teach quietly their own defective beliefs without attacking the Tractarians, the anomalous nature of their religious ancestry and position within the Church of England would have escaped strict historical scrutiny. But they
They sanction
a policy of
" Militant
Protestantism " sanctioned a policy of militant Protestantism which has resulted in riot, blasphemy and disorder. The Exeter surplice riots and the outrages at S. George's in the East in the early sixties were unparalleled in the history of Christianity in England for their blasphemous profanity. And the elements of riotous blasphemy were let loose again in the closing years of the nineteenth century. We have seen services indecently interrupted, crucifixes smashed, and crosses over graves broken down by the iconoclastic fury of our modern militant Protestants. S. Paul's Cathedral and Westminster Abbey have both been the scene of Protestant outrages.

The advocates of foreign Protestantism would have
won respect if they had logically and loyally accepted
A true logic   the consequences of their opinions.   If
would have led   they had possessed the fine discipline and
them to secession.
courage of their Scottish co-religionists of
the Disruption, they would have left the Church of
England *en masse*, and appealed to the nation upon a
basis of honest Protestantism that need not be perpetually explaining away the Book of Common Prayer.
Probably they might have organised and led the forces
of Protestantism in England to a Pyrrhic victory over
the Church in matters temporal, which would have
despoiled it of its property and severed its connection
with the State.   It would have emerged from the
storm with increased spiritual power.   It would have
been freed from its Erastianism and its " Calvinistic
current," and would thus have been able to speak with
a living voice that would be at least intelligible and
coherent.   Its membership would have involved the
reality of self-sacrifice.   As things are, the Protestant
and alien element is not strong enough to pose as the
Their remaining   sole arbiter of the policy and life of the
has caused   Church of England.   It is however capable
confusion and   of making enough dissentient and discord-
disorder.
ant clamour to prevent the true voice of
that Church from finding its definite expression.   It
has caused the Church of S. Augustine and S. Gregory
the Great to become a city of confusion.   It has
invaded the missionary enterprise of the Church
of England and destroyed that corporate unity
of effort which is an essential condition of true
missionary work by employing party societies with
their consequent disintegrating tendencies.   The story
of the early days of Bishop Copleston's episcopate in
Ceylon some thirty years ago, when the clergy of the
Church Missionary Society were actively disloyal, and
the sharp line drawn in the Indian mission-field
between the missions of the Church Missionary Society

whose clergy declined to accept the same Missionary Bishop as was appointed for the missions of the Society for the Propagation of the Gospel, alone suffice to demonstrate the disunion caused by the alien Protestant element which has obtained a foothold within the Church of England. One of the most disgraceful episodes in the history of militant Protestantism is the fanatical outburst occasioned by the recent controversy upon the " King's Declaration." The inconceivable malignity of the abuse poured forth upon the Church of Rome by heated partisans has been a disgrace to English civilization.

Count Le Maistre, in an oft-quoted passage, considered that the Church of England was capable of being a central rallying point for the reunion of Christendom, because she contained a Protestant as well as a Catholic element. But he did not realise the facts of the case. The presence of a foreign Protestant element in the Church of England does not constitute an attraction to Protestants outside her communion, but rather the reverse. A Protestant who is drawn to the Catholic faith finds the need of definiteness and unity.

The mistake of Le Maistre.

The presence of this Protestant element within the Church of England repels outsiders.

He finds neither the one nor the other in the present chaos of conflicting factions which constitutes the English Established Church. He is more likely to pass by the Church of England altogether, as the late Lord Bute did when he passed from Presbyterianism to the Church of Rome. The Protestant element in the Church of England is thus a positive hindrance to the movement (strangely called "Home Reunion") which aims at the re-absorption into the Church of England of the various sects of English-speaking non-Episcopal Christians who have departed from her communion. These people can very clearly see the illogical position of militant Protestantism within the Church of England and it does not fascinate them.

They also realise that the Protestants within the
Church unconsciously consider themselves, socially
and otherwise, superior to their brethren outside the
pale of the Establishment. This irritating assumption
of superiority is not veiled by condescending appear-
ances of Protestants of the Establishment alongside
of their so-called " Free Church " brethren upon the
common platform of " Evangelical Alliances," or
" Keswick Conventions," or at the opening of Dis-
senting places of worship. Count le Maistre was very
far from the truth when he imagined that the alien
Protestant element within the Church of England
could attract Protestants to itself from outside. The
sole attractive power of the " Ecclesia
Anglicana " lies in her Catholic Hierarchy,
her valid Sacraments and her adhesion to
historical Christianity as expressed in the
Creeds. A Protestant who desires to become a
Catholic may join her with safety, and rest upon the
fact that God has left to her the priceless heritage of
valid Sacraments administered by a valid Apostolic
Ministry. He can rest upon these facts, and hope for
the time when she will see *peace through the truth*
within her own borders, and cease to endeavour to
make room for elements within her which are foreign
to her historical Christianity.

The late Canon Liddon wrote some plain words of
warning against this Anglican comprehensiveness. " The doctrine of the ' Three
Schools ' in the Church of England, all
interesting and admirable, is hard to reconcile
with the nature and obligations of a Revelation
from God. It cannot be equally agreeable to Him
to say that Baptismal Regeneration, for instance, is a
Truth which He has revealed, and that it is a falsehood
which obscures the true sense of His Revelation. The
attempts to combine contradictories as ' two sides of
Truth,' only result in injuring the sense of truth in

The real attractive power of the " Ecclesia Anglicana."

Canon Liddon's warning.

those who make them." (*Liddon's Life* by G. W. E. Russell, page 146.)

The Anglican Communion in America most certainly gained by the secession of its extreme Protestant party more than thirty years ago under Bishop Cummins. The body which he founded under the name of the "Reformed Episcopal Church" showed by its formularies and procedure what its ideals were, and how unnaturally those alien ideals had endeavoured to graft themselves upon the American Church. The "Cumminsite schism" deserved the respect of all honest men at its formation, for those who formed it felt that their Protestantism could no longer submit to the unnatural restraints imposed upon it by the Catholic creeds and formularies of the Anglican Communion in America. The subsequent effect of this exodus of foreign and militant Protestantism has been that the American Church has drawn to its communion a very large number of the ministers and members of the various non-episcopal Protestant bodies. It is not hampered by the harmful social prestige of a State Establishment, and it can administer its discipline without the Erastian intervention of the secular courts of law. In like manner, the Anglican Communion in South Africa and the Scottish Church have been proved capable of holding their own in the face of enormous Protestant majorities, because their poverty in material resources is more than counterbalanced by their unity of doctrine and their freedom from State control.

The Scottish and the South African Church are alike free from the militant Protestant element. It has attacked them both and failed in its attempt to

assimilate them to that condition of practical confusion which exists in the English Establishment. In
the face of poverty and many trials, both these
Their consequent witness to Anglo-Catholic ideals. Churches have set before the world the ideal of the Church of England, as she appeared to the minds of Laud and the
Caroline divines, taking her stand upon the Creeds
and Œcumenical Councils of Christendom and fearlessly claiming her full heritage of Catholic truth and
Apostolic order.

The exodus of the alien element of militant and
aggressive Protestantism from the Church of England
would set her upon the same basis as the Scottish
and South African Churches. She would cease to be
a city of confusion, and she would be able to purge
herself from the vague theology of her "Modernists,"
and seek reunion with the rest of Christendom upon
the intelligible and reasonable basis of historical
Christianity.

It would be manifestly uncharitable and untrue to
Militant Protestantism not to be confused with subjective piety. confuse militant and aggressive Protestantism with that subjective temper of
mind which is a natural characteristic of
many eminent Saints, and which finds
abundant scope for its special excellences and graces
within the broad bosom of the Catholic Church.
There are Anglicans of this type of subjective piety
who are loyal to the Church, and whose only error of
policy is that they do not openly and publicly
dissociate themselves from the disloyal faction of
aggressive and militant Protestantism which desires to
Subjective piety of the early "Evangelicals" in intention loyal to the Church. turn the Church of England into a Protestant sect. The personal fervour and piety
of the "Evangelicals" of the eighteenth and
early nineteenth centuries could readily
have adapted itself loyally to the broad sym-
pathies of Catholic life and order, if they had realised
the true teaching of the Book of Common Prayer.

INTRODUCTION. 15

The spirit of these good men would never have been in real harmony with the destructive violence of Hooper and the Edwardian Reformers. They were, unconsciously, out of touch with the disloyal narrowness of the Elizabethan Puritans who had attempted to reduce the Church of England to the model of

And unconsciously out of touch with militant Protestantism.

Geneva by carrying out in secret the Calvinistic regimen, whilst outwardly conforming to the rule of Episcopacy and to the use of the Prayer Book. These early "Evangelicals" had no real sympathy with Cromwell's "Puritan Revolution." Neither, although their beliefs were defective with regard to the Visible Church and its sacramental life as the covenanted sphere of God's grace, would they have been in sympathy with the bitter, aggressive and disloyal temper of the militant Protestant faction which disturbs the Church of England at the present day. The worst outburst of

They had no sympathy with "No Popery" riots.

militant Protestantism of their own day was manifested in Lord George Gordon's "No-Popery" riots in London. It is impossible to prove that any of the Evangelical leaders of that time expressed the slightest sympathy with the rioters.

But their successors have not been equally guiltless. There was no earnest protest from the mid-Victorian Evangelical leaders against the blasphemous pro-

Their successors failed to protest against Protestant mob violence.

fanities of the riots at St. George's-in-the-East. In like manner we cannot acquit the Evangelical leaders of a later date from complicity with the policy of persecution which resulted in the imprisonment of clergy for conscience sake some twenty-eight years

And tacitly approved a policy of persecution against Catholics.

ago. The policy of persecuting Ritualists was only dropped because it aroused public sympathy for them. The Islington Clerical Meeting of 1883 denounced it as "a disastrous policy." But this Evangelical protest against it lost its force because it was made *after* the "persecution policy" had proved a failure, and not before it had done its worst in the prolonged and scandalous imprisonment of the Rev. S. F. Green of Miles Platting, in whose case the usually tolerant Bishop Fraser became the tool and dupe of militant Protestantism.

Policy of modern Evangelicals dictated by their "left wing."

For the last thirty years "Evangelicals" have allowed their policy to be dictated by their disloyal "left wing," who are the inheritors of the foreign Protestant traditions and doctrinal errors which this volume is meant to trace and explain. The intention of the writer is to promote the peace and unity of the Church of England by appealing to the more learned and pious Evangelicals to dissociate themselves effectively from the militant Protestant party. He cannot make this appeal to men of the type of Bishop Chavasse of

The learned and pious Evangelicals have not formally discouraged their extreme men.

Liverpool and the late Bishop Thorold of Rochester, without mentioning the fact that the passive aid lent to the forces of militant Protestantism by men of wide reading such as Dr. Griffith Thomas and the late Mr. Dimock, and devout scholars like Bishop Moule and Bishop Drury on its doctrinal side, has been most disastrous. The task of identifying the doctrinal teaching of

Certain of them have published books which have encouraged Protestant errors.

these pious and devout men with certain distinctive errors of foreign Protestantism is not a pleasant one, although unhappily it is not very difficult.

Certain salient points of doctrine will be dealt with in the following pages. The teaching of foreign Protestant formularies will be compared with certain doctrinal statements put forth by the late Bishop Ryle, Bishop Moule and others of the same school of thought, and then the whole will be compared with the official formularies of the Reformed Episcopal Church of America

Their doctrinal teaching will be compared with "foreign Protestant" and "Cumminsite" formularies.

which was founded by Bishop Cummins in 1873. The

immediate cause of the secession of Bishop Cummins was the protest of the Bishop of New York against his taking part in an "Inter-Denominational Communion Service" organised at a meeting of the Evangelical Alliance, held at New York in 1873. The detailed history of his action and its consequences will be dealt with in a separate chapter, which will give the reasons why the Lambeth Conference of 1888 endorsed the decision of the American Church which regarded the consecration of "Bishops" and ordinations performed by him as null and void. The thirty-five "Cumminsite" Articles of Religion were adopted in 1875.

There is no desire to suggest conscious disloyalty on

No desire to impute conscious disloyalty to these writers

the part of the Bishops who have assimilated their teaching to the standards of "foreign Protestantism." They have for the most part forborne to carry it out practically, as the Bishop of Newcastle has by his public actions and as the Bishop of Carlisle has by his curiously bitter polemics. But for all that, they are personally responsible for direct encouragement of the doctrinal errors of the "left wing" of their followers. They have thrown their weight and influence upon the side of that alien "foreign Protestant" element in the Church of England which finds its legitimate expression in the "Cumminsite" formularies.

It is impossible to examine in detail the voluminous and learned writings of Mr. Dimock. And the same

The volume called "English Church Teaching" is a doctrinal manifesto, issued by responsible authors.

applies to the works of Bishop Ryle, Bishop Moule and Bishop Drury. But in 1897, Bishop Moule, Bishop Drury and Canon Girdlestone put forth a joint doctrinal manifesto under the auspices of the National Protestant Church Union. The book is called "English Church Teaching," and at the time of writing it the three authors occupied a responsible position amongst Evangelicals. Canon Girdlestone had been Principal of Wycliffe Hall, Oxford,

Dr. Moule was Principal of Ridley Hall, Cambridge, and the Rev. T. W. Drury was Principal of the Church Missionary College at Islington. Thus two of them were directly responsible for the training of candidates for Holy Orders and one of them had not long ceased to occupy a similar post. Two of these Theological Colleges were intended to train men for work in England and the other College for the missionary work of the Church. Their joint manifesto of Protestant theology must necessarily have been written with a deep sense of personal responsibility. The Colleges whose teaching they directed were representative of their school of thought. In the following pages quotations will be made from the teaching contained in this volume and from other books of the same school of thought, which will be compared in certain definite points with the doctrinal formularies of foreign Protestantism and with those of the "Cumminsite" sect of Reformed Episcopalians in America. The comparison with this latter body is quite fair and equitable, for Bishop Cummins and the Reformed Episcopalians seceded openly and honestly

Character of the Cumminsite formularies

from the American Church because they could not accept the Catholic doctrines of the Book of Common Prayer. They revised the Prayer Book and Articles upon the lines demanded by Lord Ebury's "Prayer Book Revision Society" of forty years ago, and, unless the Church of England is

Dangers of Prayer Book Revision from a Protestant or Rationalist standpoint.

very careful, we are in danger of concessions like those of 1689 being suggested to please the "left wing" of the Evangelicals as well as concessions to satisfy the partisans of so-called "Liberal Christianity," if we do not resolutely stand by the Prayer Book as it is. The Cumminsite "Declaration of Principles" and Articles of Religion show us the alien "foreign Protestant" element in the Anglican Church freed from compromise and saying exactly what it wants and what it means.

It may fairly be suggested that Bishop Moule and

The writers of the book "English Church Teaching" have not receded from their position. Bishop Drury would not now endorse their published teaching as it stands in the book they put forth in 1897. In a letter published in the *Guardian* in 1905, Canon Girdlestone resolutely stood to his guns. He had nothing to modify or retract in his own share of the book and he openly defended his colleagues. He put forth the bold claim that the book fairly represented " English Church Teaching " and one object of the following pages will be to show that it does not do so. With regard to the Bishop of Durham, there is no possibility of his having altered his views. One of the crucial denials of Catholic doctrine in " English Church Teaching " is the utter rejection of the Catholic doctrine of the Real Objective Presence of our Lord in the Blessed Sacrament *sub speciebus panis et vini.* Dr. Moule wrote this part of the book,

The Bishop of Durham's approval of Mr. Dimock's doctrine of the " Real Absence." A. D. 1910. and in 1910 he wrote a commendatory Preface to Mr. Dimock's book on " The Lord's Supper " in which he uses the remarkable words with regard to the author: " Remember your guides, who spoke unto you the Word of God, whose faith follow, considering the end of their walk of life." These words constitute a plain endorsement of Mr. Dimock's teaching, which is distinctly enough expressed on p. 23 of his book where he says that " the great chasm of cleavage in the matter of Eucharistic doctrine is that which separates between the doctrine of the REAL ABSENCE, and the doctrine of the REAL PRESENCE in or under the form of the consecrated elements considered in themselves." We are thankful to Mr. Dimock for this clear issue between the foreign Protestant invention of the " Real Absence " and the Catholic doctrine of the " Real Presence." Mr. Dimock's whole volume is devoted to proving the doctrine of the " Real Absence," which he does with a strangely perverted show of learning.   And this is the teaching endorsed by the Bishop of Durham, who bids us " remember your guides," of whose number Mr. Dimock is the one whom his Preface specially recommends.

The teaching of the " Real Absence " is enforced by Mr. Dimock with much devout and pious verbiage, but there it is.   It is the doctrine of Zwingli, which neither Hooker nor Waterland considered to be allowable in the Church of England, although defective Eucharistic doctrine, such as theirs, has been tolerated amongst us.   It contradicts the teaching of Holy Scripture, as interpreted by the consentient voice of the Catholic Church for more than eighteen centuries.

Mr. Dimock's teaching is purely Zwinglian.

The actual words in which Zwingli taught the " Real Absence " are too long to quote here. They are to be found in chap. iv., vol. ii., of Darwell Stone's *History of the Doctrine of the Holy Eucharist*, and as Archbishop Temple plainly asserted in his Primary Charge (p. 6) the Zwinglian heresy of the " Real Absence " is not tenable within the Church of England,

Archbishop Temple's denial that " Zwinglianism " is tenable within the Church of England.

Dr. Colenso was condemned by Bishop Gray in his trial before the Court of the Metropolitan, for holding the Zwinglian doctrine on Baptism and the Holy Eucharist.   This formed "Charge III." in the " Articles of Presentment" against him, and it must be remembered that Bishop Gray's judgment and sentence of deposition were endorsed by Archbishop Longley of Canterbury and both Houses of Convocation, as well as by the American, Canadian and Scottish Churches.   The point here emphasised is that the Colenso judgment was the formal and official condemnation of the "Real Absence " as taught by Zwingli, Dr. Colenso, and Mr. Dimock, in his book on " the Lord's Supper."   It is conceded that Bishop Moule has used different phraseology from that used by Dr. Colenso.   But the fact

Dr. Colenso was condemned for " Zwinglianism."

remains that he has commended Mr. Dimock's book, which teaches the "Real Absence" not less clearly, though in a more pious form, than the crude assertions of Zwingli and Dr. Colenso.

It is readily admitted that theories of a "Virtual" Presence, and the "Receptionist" doctrine taught by Bishop Bull and others, have been tolerated in the Church of England, although they do not represent the full teaching of her formularies. But to teach Zwinglianism on the Holy Eucharist contradicts the Prayer Book and Articles. *Sunt certi denique fines.* There is a limit of toleration on the Protestant side, which the upholders of the errors of foreign Protestantism have over-passed when they find themselves in agreement with the reformed Prayer Book and Articles of the "Cumminsite" sect rather than with the teaching of the Anglican formularies which they have sworn to maintain.

Other defective Eucharist theories are tolerated.

Once more it is needful to say that the writer of these pages does not desire to undervalue the subjective tendency in religion, which has developed a very real type of piety in the minds of many, in all ages of the Church. But the subjective tendency must be carefully guarded lest it lead people away from the objective truth of the Sacramental life of the Holy Catholic Church as the Body of Christ.

A. T. W.

CHAPTER I.

LUTHER, ZWINGLI, AND CALVIN, THE FOUNDERS OF FOREIGN PROTESTANTISM.

THE epigram which bluntly stated that the Lutheran doctrine of Justification produced a Solifidian Antinomianism which practically made "every man his own Tetzel," contains a considerable amount of truth.   The sale of indulgences, as preached by Tetzel, was a scandal to every spiritually. minded Catholic in Germany.   But the reaction against the penitential and doctrinal system of the Catholic Church, which Luther headed, carried him and his followers to the opposite extreme of a self-absolving individualism which found its logical outcome in the gross immoralities of John of Leyden and the Anabaptists of Münster.   It was in vain that Luther himself attempted to control the forces of religious anarchy that his movement had evoked.

Luther taught a "self-absolving" individualism which caused. religious anarchy.

After the Diet of Worms in 1521, the Elector of Saxony concealed Luther in the Castle of Wartburg to preserve him from his enemies. But when he came out of his seclusion in the following year and returned to Wittemberg, his original centre of action, he found that his disciples were beyond his control. Carlstadt had destroyed the images in the Church of All Saints and inaugurated a religious anarchy which afterwards bore fruit in the chaos of Protestant sects

His followers got out of hand and caused the Rebellion of the peasants and the loss of 100,000 lives.

which sprang from the Lutheran principle of individual private judgment. Munzer, the Anabaptist, and the crazy enthusiasts known as the Prophets of Zwickau, preached social anarchy and communism. They set the peasants aflame with the spirit of revolution and in 1524 thousands of them flew to arms in open revolt against the feudal Princes of Germany. Luther drove Carlstadt and Munzer from Wittemberg and thus precipitated the revolt which was the indirect result of his own teaching. He got alarmed at the storm he had raised, and urged the Princes of Germany to smite and spare not. The insurrection was crushed at the cost of 100,000 lives. Carlstadt soon deserted the cause and saved himself for further disputations with Luther, but Munzer was captured and executed, having first recanted his heresies, and received the Viaticum of the Church after confession and absolution.

Erasmus wrote plainly to Luther on the Peasants' Revolt. " You see that we are now reaping the fruits of what you sowed. You will not acknowledge the rebels; but they acknowledge you, and they know only too well that many of your disciples who clothed themselves in the mantle of the Gospel have been the instigators of this bloody rebellion. In your pamphlet against the peasants you in vain endeavour to justify yourself. It is you who have raised the storm by your publications against the monks and the prelates, and you say that you fight for Gospel liberty, and against the tyranny of the great! From the moment that you began your tragedy, I foresaw the end of it." (Menzel, *Neuere Geschichte*, Vol. I., p. 174.)

View of Erasmus and of a modern historian on Luther's conduct.

A thoughtful and impartial modern historian writes as follows of Luther's attitude with regard to the Peasants' Revolt : " Yet terror, and his proximity to Thuringia, the scene of the most violent and dangerous form of the revolt, while they may palliate cannot excuse Luther's efforts to rival the brutal ferocity of

Munzer's doctrines. He must have known that the Princes' victory, if it came at all, would be bloody enough without his exhortations to kill the peasants like mad dogs, and without his promise of Heaven to those who fell in the holy work. . . . It is almost a commonplace with Lutheran writers to justify Luther's action on the ground that the Peasants' Revolt was revolutionary, unlawful, immoral, whilst the religious movement was reforming, lawful, and moral; but the hard and fast line which is thus drawn vanishes on a closer investigation . . . . The distinction between the two movements has for its basis the fact that the one was successful, the other was not. . . . Luther in fact saved the Reformation by cutting it adrift from the failing cause of the Peasants, and tying it to the chariot wheels of the triumphant Princes. If he had not been the Apostle of Revolution, he had at least commanded the army in which all the revolutionaries fought. He had now repudiated his left wing and was forced to depend on his right." (Cambridge Modern History, vol. ii., pp. 193-194.) Luther had stirred up the spirit of socialistic revolution by preaching a gospel of unfettered individualism. His " left wing " will be heard of again, although he clung to the skirts of the Lutheran Princes who formed his "right " with such servile tenacity as to develop ultimately the Erastian doctrine that the Prince, or Head of the State, was *ipso facto* the *summus episcopus* of the Lutheran sect in his dominions. His repudiation of the Catholic Church had bred anarchy and his sole refuge from the spirit of lawlessness which he had raised was in the formal and abject subjection of German Protestantism to the Civil Power which continues to this day. The Augsburg Confession crystallised Luther's Erastianism in the formula, " Cuius regio eius religio," which involved the right of each Prince to dictate the religion of his subjects. When Luther saw a chance of scoring

Luther's Erastianism.

a point in favour of his views, his sense of personal importance made him as reckless of consequences as the careless Kafir herdsman who, in the dry season in South Africa, lights his pipe and throws down his smouldering match to burn and destroy acres of " veld " and bush as the result of a moment's thought-

The secret influence of Hussite fanaticism. lessness. The Hussite revolt, as finally developed in the lurid fanaticism of Ziska and the Taborites, had been finally crushed by Sigismund in the year 1435, when Ziska's successor, Procopius, was defeated after the Council of Basle. But the socialistic ideas of Wycliffe, and his revolt against Catholic doctrine on the Apostolic ministry and the Sacraments, which had been sedulously propagated in Bohemia by Huss and Jerome of Prague, survived and spread after the Taborite revolt had been crushed. It can hardly be doubted that the German peasants who had certain grievances against feudalism, which Luther admitted, were secretly imbued with the ideas of the Taborites, and Luther's attack upon the established order of the Church gave them a convenient pretext for a gospel of anarchy. The crazy Anabaptist prophets of Zwickau were true Taborites, but they would never have become the leaders of revolt if Luther's movement had not stirred them to action, and if they had not previously joined

The left wing of Luther's movement. the " left wing " of his followers. The horrors of the Peasant revolt and its suppression did not give pause to Luther's assault upon the doctrines of the Church. Whilst it was still raging he preached his famous—or rather infamous—sermon " On Marriage " at Wittemberg in

Luther's attack on celibacy and the Catholic doctrine of marriage. 1522. The universal enforcement of clerical celibacy had produced grave evils, owing to the degeneracy of the priesthood, which resulted from the Papal Schism and the corruptions of the Roman *curia*. The idea of personal self-sacrifice had vanished from the minds of many of the secular clergy, and the monastic life was invaded by a loss of high ideals which bred corruption. A Reformation was needed on primitive lines of duty and self-sacrifice. The celibacy of priests, monks, and nuns needed a restoration on the true basis upon which S. Paul placed it. But Luther attacked all celibacy as an evil *per se*. To him the primary duty of every man and woman in the world was to "be fruitful in procreation of children." " Crescite et multiplicamini" was the text of his sermon. He left no room whatever in his theory of sexual relationship for the Pauline idea of a voluntary and consecrated celibacy whereby men and women could "serve the Lord without distraction." (I Cor. ix., 35.)

To Luther the man who was not a father and the woman who was not a mother had failed to fulfil the primary law of their being. The late Professor J. B. Mozley has well been described as the "Butler" of the nineteenth century. His predilection for the Augustinian doctrines of grace carried him some distance in sympathy with Luther's views and even with the merciless development of them by Calvin.

Professor Mozley on Luther's doctrine of marriage. His *Essay on Luther* (vol. i., *Essays*, p. 321) is the most masterly and lucid monograph on the views and character of that Reformer which has ever been written. For this reason it is most instructive to quote his words on Luther's sermon *De Matrimonio*. " *Crescite et multiplicamini*. In this sentence he saw the whole of the Divine law, advice, and recommendation upon the subject of marriage collected. Here, he said, is a universal command and statute under the action of which the whole human race comes. It is quite evident therefore that everybody is intended to marry, and that everybody should marry. . . . In accordance with this new speculative movement, society was, with respect to the general rules and regulations of marriage, thrown back upon the Old Testament Code as distinguished from the subsequent legislation of the New. The temper of a sterner and purer dispensation was disregarded, *the forbidden degrees were largely thrown open*, Luther countenanced even more flagrant violations of the Christian code, and his sermon *De Matrimonio*, delivered at Wittemberg in the year 1522, *gave licenses from which the natural conscience of a heathen and savage would recoil.*" (*Essays*, vol i., p. 401.)

Luther's permission of adultery.

We fear that it is necessary to our historic investigation of Lutheran Protestantism to be more explicit than Professor Mozley has been. In the Sermon *De Matrimonio* Luther directly counselled the commission of adultery under certain circumstances. If a wife had no children by her husband Luther authorised her to ask her husband's permission to commit adultery with one of his near relatives in order that she might fulfil woman's destiny and have a child. The man whose wife was barren was advised by Luther to use a similar license. Luther cites the example of Ahasuerus. A man may take "Esther" while "Vashti" is still living.

Gross language of his sermon.

A man may take his wife's handmaid according to Old Testament liberties. And this sermon, whose gross language cannot be quoted in English, was preached *in German* before a mixed congregation at Wittemberg by Dr. Martin Luther, and subsequently published by him in the collection of his sermons which was given to the world in 1544. (*Martini Lutheri de Matrimonio, sermo habitus Wittembergae, Anno 1522. Tom. V. Opp. Lutheri Wittembergae, 1544. p. 19 et seq.*) Professor Mozley well says "that such a theoretical movement on the subject of marriage should produce some awkward practical fruits was not surprising.

Some of its results.

So fierce and naked an appeal to original rights was likely to set men speculating very freely and largely as to what their rights were." (*Ib.* p. 401.)

The terrible bloodshedding which marked the ending of the Peasants' revolt had not quelled the fierce spirits or the fantastic doctrines of the Anabaptists.

In 1533 Rottman, the Lutheran minister of Münster, adopted Anabaptist views and brought The Anabaptists. John of Leyden and his fanatical followers into the city. Luther's sermon on Marriage not only abolished it as an indissoluble sacramental union, but opened the door to the license of these Anabaptist sectaries who preached the abolition of marriage as well as of property and social order.

The Anabaptist leaders openly adopted polygamy John of Leyden in Münster, and thus anticipated the adopts modern development of Mormonism from polygamy. a debased form of American Protestantism. John of Leyden became " King of Münster" and appeared in public with his crown and a harem of " queens." He issued an edict that no books but the Bible could be permitted to exist, and he ordered the priceless library of Greek and Latin manuscripts which Langius had collected to be committed to the flames. Münster was captured after a long siege in 1535, and John of Leyden, with his accom- His capture and execution. plices, was executed. Before his execution he argued with one Corvinus, a Court preacher of Philip, the Landgrave of Hesse, who re- minded him that S. Paul said, " Let every man live with his *wife*, not with his *wives*." " Ah," His argument with Corvinus. said John. " S. Paul did not speak of *all* wives, but of each in particular. The first is my wife, I live with her; the second is my wife, I live with her ; the third is my wife, I live with her; that is very simple. Besides is it not better that I should have several wives than several concubines ?"

Corvinus appears to have taken this last argument back with him to the Landgrave's Court. We shall hear of it again. Meanwhile it is remarkable that the English Anabaptists very soon repudiated the pernicious doctrines of their German spiritual ancestors and became a respectable sect of the ordinary Puritan type about the middle of the seventeenth century.

Luther's onslaught upon the Catholic doctrine of marriage influenced princes as well as peasants. Philip, Landgrave of Hesse, was a dissolute soldier-Prince who favoured the doctrines of Luther from political motives.

Philip of Hesse desires to commit bigamy with a dispensation from Luther.

He had been married for about sixteen years to Christina, daughter of George Duke of Saxony, who had borne him eight children, but he had been continuously unfaithful to her throughout his married life. He became politically useful to Luther, and his Lutheran Court chaplains wished him to partake of the Lord's Supper after the Lutheran rite. He scrupled at this on account of his frequent acts of adultery but said that he declined to reform his life. He became enamoured of Margaret de Saal, maid of honour to his sister Elizabeth, and he promised the Lutheran divines that if they would give him a dispensation to commit bigamy with her he would cease from promiscuous adulteries and content himself, as a pious Protestant Prince, with two wives and no more.

Bucer draws up his case.

Bucer, who married a renegade nun, and afterwards played a prominent part in England as Regius Professor of Divinity at Cambridge under Edward VI., came to the aid of Landgrave Philip. He drew up his case for him to submit to Luther and the Wittemberg divines. In this document Bucer permits the Landgrave to speak for himself. He appeals to the example of Abraham, Jacob, David, and Solomon, and adds "S. Paul has never excluded from heaven him who has two wives." He repeats John of Leyden's argument that he had better have two wives than keep concubines, and adds, "I know that Luther and Melanchthon have advised the King of England not to divorce his first wife but to take a

Luther's advice to Henry VIII. to commit bigamy.

second." This statement throws a curious side-light on the divorce controversy of Henry VIII., who preferred the facile decrees of nullity of his successive marriages granted him by Cranmer to the cruder counsels of Luther and Melanchthon.

The reply of the Lutheran divines was a dispensation, divided into twenty-four articles, *The Lutheran dispensation.* giving the Landgrave *permission* to commit bigamy, but requesting him *to conceal* his marriage from the world. It was signed by Luther, Melanchthon, Bucer, Philip's Court chaplain Corvinus, and four other leading Lutheran preachers. In the *Strange wording of the marriage contract.* " marriage contract " the Landgrave declares that he takes Margaret de Saal to wife, "because without two wives it would be impossible for him to live godly and to merit Heaven."

On the 4th of March, 1540, the bigamous "marriage" of Philip of Hesse and Margaret de Saal *The bigamous "Marriage" takes place in the presence of Bucer and Melanchthon.* took place in the presence of Bucer and Melanchthon. The Landgrave's conscience was quieted by the Lutheran dispensation. He appeared in public with his two wives, walked with them to Church, and sat between them at his table. He had six sons by Margaret de Saal, and had two more sons and a daughter by his first wife Christina, subsequent to his bigamous union with Margaret. Luther's position in the matter was plain enough from his sermon *De Matrimonio.* He overthrew our Lord's teaching on marriage, as enforced under the New Covenant by the unanimous voice of the Catholic Church. The words used in Philip's Dispensation are conclusive : " For that which is permitted concerning marriage in the law of Moses is not forbidden in the Gospel." (See text of the Dispensation in Hare's *Mission of the Comforter*, p. 834.)

Professor Mozley says : " Now this act of Luther's *Professor Mozley on Luther's action.* does not appear one we need hesitate to judge. It is the act of deliberately permitting a Christian to have two wives, and thus deliberately violating the Christian code with respect to marriage. Marriage is by original institution monogamy; departure from that institution was allowed afterwards, in condescension to man's weakness and hardness of heart, but Christianity reverted to its and enforced it as an inviolable law; and of this law Luther deliberately sanctioned the transgression." (*Essays* vol. i., p. 404.) Luther's desire that Philip's bigamous union should be concealed from the world was in vain. "The news soon leaked out. Melanchthon quailed before the public odium and nearly died of shame, but Luther wished to brazen the matter out with a lie. 'The secret *yea*,' he wrote, must for the sake of Christ's Church, remain a public '*nay*.' He alleged the analogy of the confessional, a good confessor must deny in court all knowledge of what he has learnt in confession. The moral effect of this revelation upon the Lutheran cause was incalculable. Cranmer wrote from England of the pain which it caused to the friends of the Reformation and the handle it gave to the enemy. John Frederic (Elector [of Saxony) and Ulrich of Würtemburg refused to guarantee Philip immunity for his crime, the legal penalty for which was death; and the Landgrave, seriously alarmed, sought to make his peace with the Habsburgs, and possibly with Rome. . . ." (*Cambridge Modern History*, vol. ii., p. 241.)

Luther counsels concealment of the bigamy.

Opinion of Cranmer.

We leave this crime of Luther and his chief followers to the judgment of all Christians worthy of the name with a sense of relief. But Luther's attack on Christian marriage did not stop short at the licensing of bigamy. He allowed divorces and relaxed the forbidden degrees. Succeeding generations of Lutherans enlarged his laxity, and in 1794 the Prussian Legislature allowed marriages between uncle and niece, nephew and aunt, brother-in-law and sister-in-law. In one German town of about

Luther's relaxation of the forbidden degrees.

4,000 inhabitants no fewer than 171 divorce suits were
pending at the same time and in Transylvania two-
thirds of the women married were divorced
German
divorces,   within the year.   A German professor
stated to the Royal Commission on the
Marriage Laws that "the state of marriage in Germany
makes a German cover his face with his hands for
shame."   The laxity of Lutheran Germany infected
the Swiss Reformers.   The present condition of the
Protestant Cantons of Switzerland with regard to
marriage and divorce is as bad as that of Germany
and the laxest States of the American Union (see
Luckock's *History of Marriage*, p. 223).

The destruction of Holy Matrimony as an indissoluble sacramental union was naturally followed by
looseness of morals amongst the followers
Effect of Luther's
ideas upon the   of Luther, Zwingli, and Calvin.   Statistics
morals of
Protestants.   prove that the illegitimate births in
Lutheran and Calvinistic countries far
exceed in number those in Catholic countries.   Some
years ago the illegitimate births in Calvinistic Scotland
were ten per cent. as against three per cent. in Ireland,
and even this low Irish average was mainly furnished
by the Protestants of the North.   The Celts of Ireland
have never allowed the English Divorce Act to apply
to them and are as moral as the Calvinistic Celts of
Wales are the reverse, and the laxity of the Calvinistic
Lowland Scots is equally notorious.   The destruction
of all true ideals of marriage as a sacrament, which
has infected Protestants throughout the world, began
with Luther.   His fanatical hatred of monastic vows
and clerical celibacy led him in mature life to marry
a renegade nun.

Bishop Creighton says : " Luther on his part was
determined to show how irreparable was
Bishop Creighton
on Luther's   his breach with the past, and how entirely
marriage.   he was free from old traditions.   On June
13th, 1525, he married a runaway nun, Katerina von

Bora, whom he had for some time sheltered in his house. It was a bold act, which created a great sensation and struck dismay even into the hearts of many of Luther's friends, who thought that such a step was unworthy of a religious leader." (*History of the Papacy*, vol. v., p. 264.)

Professor Mozley says : "The step lowered him in his own estimation. No theory could make the marriage of a monk and a nun not ignominious ; no theory could make it necessary for Luther to marry at all. . . . She came in his way and he married her, feeling all the time the deep blow to his self-respect. The stars were unusually brilliant one evening when he and Katharine were walking in the garden. ' *What a brilliant light!*' said Luther, as he looked upward ; ' *but it burns not for us.*' '*And why are we to be excluded from the Kingdom of Heaven?*' asked Katharine. ' *Perhaps*,' said Luther, with a sigh, '*because we left our convents.*' Katharine— ' *Shall we return then?* ' Luther—' *It is too late to do that.*' (*Essays*, vol. i., p. 422.)

Professor Mozley on the same.

Erasmus received the news of Luther's marriage with the remark that it was popularly believed that "Antichrist would be born of a monk and a nun," and further hinted at a scandalous cause for the marriage itself. But Erasmus and the Humanists were no friends to Luther and his movement, and Luther's marriage was evil enough *per se* without giving historical credence to Erasmus on the subject.

Erasmus on Luther's marriage.

The Lutheran doctrine concerning the Apostolic Ministry of the Church and the authority of Holy Scripture naturally follows from the root heresy of Luther on Original Sin and the Justification of Man. Professor Mozley's acute analysis of Luther's teaching is brilliant and masterly, but is too long for quotation. We may summarise it as follows. Luther suffered from religious depression and melancholia.

The Lutheran doctrine of the Ministry.

A summary of Luther's teaching.

3

He was morbidly self-contemplative and restlessly introspective. He fled from German student life and its activities into the dulness of a monastery and his undisciplined nature hated its disciplined routine. His monastic vows galled him from the very first, and he sought for some panacea of his own to cure his religious melancholy and give him peace. The Pauline spirit of watchfulness lest an Apostle and teacher should "become a castaway," the very idea of doubting his own ultimate salvation and working it out "in fear and trembling," was utterly abhorrent to him. He had nothing in common with the spirit of the author of the "Imitation of Christ." He wanted absolute personal assurance of his own salvation once for all, and given in such a way that if his conscience should question his conduct at any future time he might deaden its voice, and say to his inner consciousness of wrong-doing, Peace, be still! He wanted his salvation to be assured by a single action of his intellect, and the Pauline idea of "working it out" by a life-long process of conversion and sanctification had no place in his scheme of life. He had no real grasp of the Incarnation, and the power of the risen life of Christ, sacramentally interwoven with the lives of the baptised, as the source of their holiness and as the ultimate means of the destruction of sin within them. He invented a new religion based on his own exaggerations and distortions of the theology of S. Augustine. The wise decisions of the Council of Orange, held under Caesarius of Arles in A.D. 529, had been accepted by the whole of Western Christendom as a reduction of S. Augustine's unbalanced statements on grace, freewill and predestination to a series of propositions which embodied the truth of Scripture as interpreted by the Catholic Church. These decisions of Catholic theology were despised by Luther, who invented Calvinism. The strife between the German and Swiss Reformers, which was subsequently perpetuated by the separate organisations of Lutheran

The Council of Orange.

Its decisions a correction of Augustinianism.

and Calvinistic Presbyterianism, has obscured this fact,
concerning which Professor Mozley observes:
"It is of course wrong historically to call
Luther a Calvinist, because Luther preceded
Calvin, and was the original discoverer of
that set of ideas which Calvin only compacted and
systematised. But among ourselves, in consequence of
our acquaintance having lain more with the Genevan
than the German branch of the Reformation, these ideas
are associated with the name of Calvin, and therefore
amongst us Luther's theology may be designated as
Calvinism." *(Essays,* vol. i. p. 350.)

Luther despised them and was the real author of Calvinism.

Luther's new religion was a modified form of Gnostic
Dualism. "The Law" revealed a world of
absolute evil, "Christ" a world of absolute
good. "The Law" and "Christ" represent
irreconcilable principles. The idea of the Catholic
Church, as expressed by S. Thomas Aquinas, that the
Gospel was a "new law" of Love, was passionately
denied by Luther, whose "Pecca fortiter," uttered to
Melanchthon, embodied his hatred of the idea of men
working out their own salvation by the law of the
Gospel, which is a faith "that worketh by love."
According to Luther's doctrine of "Original Sin,"
human nature is *totally* and *absolutely*
corrupt and there is *no difference* between
fallen human nature and the nature of
devils. The Atonement of Christ was an
arbitrary act whereby the elect amongst these "men-
devils" should be saved, in spite of their evil deeds, by
an abstract motion of the intellect which he called
"Faith." This "Fides informis" of Luther's imagina-
tion is, as Professor Mozley says, "an *extra-moral*
faith," external to all human conduct.

The Religion of Luther was a "Dualism."

His doctrine of the total corruption of human nature.

When a man had said "I believe," the righteousness
of Christ was immediately "imputed to him,"
and became his own and there was no more
scope in him for the accusing voice of
conscience whatever his conduct might be subsequently.

His error of imputed righteousness.

We shall deal later on with Luther's strange and unscriptural expression of assurance, " *Let the con- science sleep joyfully in Christ.*" These words accu- rately describe the function of the conscience in Luther's system. The Lutheran dogma of "justification by faith" was the solvent of Luther's doubts and

The Lutheran dogma of Justification by Faith.

religious melancholy. But it contradicted S. Paul just as much as it contradicted S. James, whose Epistle Luther rejected from his Canon of Scripture, and it made every man virtually " his own Tetzel."

Professor Mozley accurately defines it as follows :

Professor Mozley's definition of it.

" The faith which was the medium in Luther's process of justification was thus a pure and abstract faculty of confidence, which was efficacious in and out of itself. Believe that you are absolved and you *are* absolved—never mind whether you deserve absolution or no. He that *believes* is better than he that *deserves*. Always be sure that you are pleasing to God ; if you are *sure* you are, you *are*. Feel yourself safe ; if you *feel* safe, you *are* safe. The task of the Christian was to work himself up by strong effort to the belief that he himself was personally saved, was a child of God, was in a state of justification. If the believer asked why, or how, he was to believe, he was told again, Believe ; *make* yourself believe ; believe *somehow or other*. He was urged with arguments enough, addressed to his mere will and sense of personal advantage ; was threatened and promised ; was told he would be intolerably wretched if he did not believe so, unutterably happy if he did, but *ground of reason there was none*. Assurance, thus left to assure itself as it. could, became an anxious struggling and fluctuating gift. It rose and it fell with the state of the spirits and even state of the body. These struggles, or agonies, occupy a prominent part of the practical or devotional department of Luther's theological system . . . Genuine faith is wide and social in its object, looks forward to the ultimate triumph of virtue over vice, to the great Day of Judgment and the restitution of all things. But Luther's faith, as it narrowed its basis, narrowed its object too. Withdrawing from the wide ground of reason and nature, the unsupported faith of mere will—*choosing* to believe because it *wished* to do so—as it derived all its strength from the individual, interested itself about the individual only ; and faith became, in its whole scope and direction, *personal*." (*Essays*, vol i., pp. 346, 349, 350.)

Luther's system is "foreign Protestantism"—a distinct departure from "The faith once delivered to the Saints"—as wide in its essentials from Pauline Christianity as the Gnostic and Manichæan heresies from which it borrowed its leading ideas.

Luther's system the basis of foreign Protestantism.

The Swiss Reformers, Zwingli and Calvin, added nothing to Luther's new religion save that they materialised it into a rigid and consistent system. Luther believed in the Real Presence in the Mass and only rejected the doctrine of the Eucharistic sacrifice. There was no logical place in Luther's system for his doctrine of the Real Presence. Carlstadt had shown Luther that the true Protestant spirit of free inquiry and unrestricted private judgment could not put up with his adaptation of the Catholic doctrine of the Eucharist. The famous disputation on the subject between Luther and Carlstadt in 1524 had wide issues. It showed that Luther's system was based upon a rejection of the voice of Catholic antiquity, and that his Eucharistic doctrine was a useless excrescence upon his central dogma of Solifidian Justification. Zwingli saw this and swept the Mass out of his Swiss adaptation of Lutheranism. Calvin was more conservative in his language than Zwingli, but his teaching led to practically the same results. The Eucharistic controversy between the Lutherans and the Zwinglians is

His Eucharistic doctrine illogical.

most barren and unreal. Both the Lutheran and the
Swiss Reformers had substituted a man-
made ministry of preachers for the Apostolic
Priesthood of the Catholic Church. The dis-
putants on either side had thus cut themselves
off from the possibility of a valid Eucharist, which
requires for its due celebration a priest validly ordained,
so that the controversy became absolutely nugatory.
Foreign Protestantism needed no valid ministry.

His rejection of the Apostolic Ministry was followed by the Swiss Reformers.

According to Luther every baptised man was
his own priest. To quote Professor Mozley
again : " This theory at once supplied
Luther with the power of making a Church.
Baptism was all he wanted and baptism he had. Every
baptised person could, so far as principle went, administer the sacraments and perform all the offices of
a priest. What members of the baptised body should
perform such offices was indeed a grave question of
external order : and the founder of a Church was
obliged to secure order. He could only secure order by
authority, and therefore he had to fix upon some
authority. But the only authority he wanted was one for
this external purpose ; and such an authority
seemed ready made for him in the State.

Professor Mozley on Luther's theory of the Ministry.

His Erastianism.

He made the State this authority and the
whole question was settled. . . . A society is the
natural keeper of an idea, and Luther, full of the truth
of his own idea of Justification, of which he considered
himself the all but inspired teacher, made a society in
what way he could. The established channels of
Ordination, the Episcopacy, the Apostolic Succession, a
whole system of external Church appointments which
was coeval with Christianity, went for nothing in
comparison with the necessities of a new doctrine
demanding some mode of establishing and transmitting
itself. . . . The new Lutheran Church rose up because
the Lutheran doctrine wanted it and appealed to no
other sanction or right." (*Essays*, vol. i., p. 383.)

The essential and fundamental idea of the ministry amongst foreign Protestants is utterly opposed to the threefold Apostolic Ministry of the Catholic Church in its orderly succession as deriving its authority from our Lord and not from the congregation.

Dr. Lindsay, the Free Kirk Professor, takes precisely the same view in his contribution to the " Cambridge Modern History." In his analysis of Luther's "Appeal to the Christian Nobility," he summarises the Lutheran view of the ministry as follows : " The clergy were distinguished from the laity, not by an indelible character imposed upon them in a divine mystery called ordination, but because they were set in the commonwealth to do a particular work. If they neglected the work they were there to do, the clergy were accountable to the same temporal Powers that ruled the land." (*C.M.H.*, vol. ii., p. 137.)

Dr. Lindsay on Luther's view of the Ministry.

To assert, as Bishop Drury does in the volume already mentioned called " English Church Teaching " (p. 187), that the " Continental Reformers had no desire to break away from the ancient constitution of the Church, had it been possible to obtain reformation and at the same time not forfeit Episcopal order," is an untrue presentment of historical facts for which there is no excuse. It is useless for Bishop Drury to quote an abstract phrase from the Augsburg Confession, or from Melanchthon, Beza, or Calvin, *ostensibly* in favour of Episcopacy. Men are judged by their deeds, which express the true meaning of their words. The ancient Catholic Episcopate of Denmark was abolished, and Luther's emissary Bugenhagen, a Lutheran minister, purported to ordain seven other Lutheran ministers to take the place and title of the Danish Bishops. The name " Bishop " was no more objectionable to the Lutherans than it is to the Methodist Episcopal body in America. It was the *reality* of Episcopal jurisdiction and Apostolical succession which the new Lutheran

Bishop Drury's mistaken assertion on Luther's view of the Ministry.

Luther abolishes the Episcopate of Denmark.

His objection to any valid Episcopal jurisdiction.

society declined to recognise. The Scottish Presbyterians went so far as to "re-ordain" as ministers
of their schism any Catholic priests who joined them,
whilst at the same time they allowed the title "Bishop"
to the unconsecrated superintendents who sat
in the seats of the ancient Catholic hierarchy
of Scotland, until these "Tulchan" Bishops, as

The "Tulchan"
Bishops in
Scotland.

they were derisively called, were superseded by the validly
consecrated Hierarchy which was restored by James I.

Bishop Drury is historical scholar enough to know
that when Lutherans and Calvinists talk
about *Episcopacy* they mean "a name" only
and not the Catholic Hierarchy with its
lawfully derived succession and jurisdiction.

Bishop Drury's
denial of the
necessity of the
Episcopate.

It is to be feared that Bishop Drury's own doctrine of
the ministry resembles that of the Lutherans and
Calvinists. He *denies* that the historic and Apostolic
Episcopate is necessary to valid ministrations within the
covenanted sphere of God's grace. *(English Church
Teaching*, p. 186), and he has the hardihood to assert that
this denial is the true teaching of the Church of
England, notwithstanding the plain words of the
Preface to our Ordinal, and of Article XXXIV. which
endorses the Ordinal itself. At all events he ought to
have known what so accurate and carefully balanced an
historian as Bishop Creighton said on Luther and
Episcopacy. "On May 14th, 1525, amid the
tumult of the Peasant war, Luther laid his
hands on the head of his secretary Georg
Röser, and conferred on him the title of

Bishop
Creighton on
Luther's
rejection of a
valid Episcopate.

Deacon. Georg von Polinz, Bishop of Samland, had
adopted Luther's teaching, and Luther, *had he chosen*,
could have followed ecclesiastical tradition in the call of
new ministers. But he was so convinced of his own
inherent capacity to reform the Church that he did not
think of recognising any superior authority."
(History of the Papacy, vol. v., p. 265.)
Bishop Creighton gauged Luther's motive

His accurate
estimate of
Luther's views

correctly. He would own no superior authority to his own in the new religion he had founded. He deliberately and of set purpose broke the historic and Apostolic succession of the Danish Episcopate (see *Church Quarterly Review, April, 1891*). When he confuted Carlstadt and the prophets at Wittemberg he said : " I am the *only person* you should listen to. Martin Luther is the *first man* of the Reformation, others come after him, he therefore should

Luther, a Protestant Pope. *command*, and you should *obey*. It is your lot. *I am the man to whom God has revealed His word.*" (*Mozley's Essays* I. p. 387.)

It was not likely that Luther, who adopted the standpoint of a Protestant Pope, could tolerate Episcopacy. In 1522 he wrote his book against the Hierarchy. Here is his opinion of Apostolic Episcopacy :

His coarse abuse of the Hierarchy. " Listen, ye Bishops, ye hobgoblins of the devil, Doctor Luther will read you a Bull and a reformation which you will not like to hear . . . Whosoever shall lend aid, and assist with person, means or reputation, so that the Episcopal order be laid waste, and government by Bishops abolished, these are the beloved sons of God, and true Christians who observe the precepts of God and oppose the ordinations of the devil." The violence of this language is the remote but authentic origin of the subsequent fanaticism of the Covenanters against Prelacy, which resulted in the deliberate murder of Archbishop Sharp in 1679 by zealous assassins of this sect—a deed which evoked the covert sympathy of the bulk of Scottish Presbyterians. Luther not only abolished the threefold Apostolic Ministry and the whole character of

Luther assails the Authority of Holy Scripture. Historic Christianity. He proceeded to assail the authority of those very important portions of Holy Scripture which conflicted with his theory of justification. No more misleading *dictum* was ever pronounced than Chillingworth's famous sentence, " The Bible, and the Bible only, is the

religion of Protestants." The idea of supplanting an
infallible Church by an infallible book occurred to the
minds of certain of the foreign Reformers. It also
became a favourite theory of the Scottish and some
English Protestants. It formed no part of Luther's
system. If the Bible was in his way, the Bible had to
make way for the teaching of the *first man of the
Reformation*, to whom God, as he said, " had revealed
His word."

The New Testament contained moral precepts, and
our Lord unveiled the perfect Moral Law in
the Sermon on the Mount. To teach morals,
according to Luther, was an *accidental* part
of the Gospel, only introduced to emphasise
the fact that good works could not be done by man even
with the aid of the grace of God. " Homo præcepto
impossibili monetur," said Luther, " ut videat suam
impotentiam." " In this way," Professor Mozley says,
"the whole system of law and precept which confronts
us on the very surface of Scripture was reduced, by a
method of esoteric interpretation, into a mere husk and
outside ; the external fabric of the deeper truth that
there was no law. . . . The Gospel language was only
a pious fraud; and the issue showed the real meaning."
(*Essays*, vol. i., p. 394.)

Luther found it impossible to apply this perverted
interpretation to the Epistle of S. James,
therefore he cast it out of the Lutheran
Canon of Scripture. He says of S. James
that " he undertakes to put down those who trusted to
faith only without works. He wrests Scripture, and
what is more, contradicts Paul and all the Scriptures,
seeking to effect by inculcation of the law that which
the Apostles effect by incentives to love. For these
reasons *I will not have him in my Bible in the list of
canonical books*." (Luther's *Preface to the Epistle of
S. James*, ed. 1522.)

He thus relegates the Epistle of S. James to the

Luther's hatred of the idea of the " New Law " of Christ.

Luther rejects the Epistle of St. James.

position of a New Testament " Apocryphal " book and in his general Preface to the New Testament he calls it *epistola straminea*—" an epistle of straw." His ignorance of ordinary Biblical questions is manifested by his statement that it is spurious, because S. James was slain by Herod *before* the martyrdom of S. Peter and S. Paul, and *this author must have lived after them!* He had apparently not heard that Church authority and tradition attributes the Epistle to S. James, the Bishop of Jerusalem. Luther's free handling of the Holy Scriptures has borne fruit in his followers. The birth-place of the " Higher Criticism," in its most extravagant modern developments is Lutheran Germany, and Luther is its true father. Sir H. Howorth, dealing with the " *Bible Canon of the Reformation*," thus quotes Luther's definition of Catholicity : " *What does not preach Christ, that is not Apostolical, whether Paul or Peter preached it. On the other hand, what preaches Christ, that is Apostolic, even if Judas, Annas, Pilate or Herod wrote it.*"

Sir H. Howorth, a witness from the Protestant side, well says " It would assuredly be difficult to find a more elastic, uncertain and arbitrary Rule of Canonicity." (January Number of *International Journal of the Apocrypha*, p. 7.)

But the most serious heresy of Luther was his semi-Nestorian view of the Incarnation. Instead of the Catholic statement that "the Person of the *Son* united within itself the two natures," he said that " the Divine and human natures were so united with each other that *Christ* was but one single Person." " Christ," according to Luther, is *not* the Person of "the Word made flesh," but a *tertium quid*, resulting from the union of the Divine and human natures. In the words of the modern Lutheran divine Dorner, Luther " looked to the full actual existence of the Divine-human Person as resulting from the

Luther's Nestorianism.

completion of the growth of the Divine-human life."
(Dorner, *Person of Christ*, vol. ii., p. 79.)

In other words, he did not believe that God and man
were united in the Person of God the Son by the action
of the Holy Ghost in the womb of the Blessed Virgin,
but that the *completion* of the growth of our Lord's
manhood was necessary to the union of the two natures,
which formed the being whom he called " Christ," a
species of Nestorianism that varied little from the
heresy that the Blessed Virgin only bore the Infant,
Who when He grew up was united to the Logos.
This variation of the Nestorian heresy has been since
very common amongst Calvinists and has caused them
to shrink from the title " Theotokos" as applied to the
Blessed Virgin by the Council of Ephesus.

Luther also held the heresy of the ubiquity or
omnipresence of our Lord's glorified Manhood. He derived this heresy from the
speculations of Scotus Erigena, and it is
admirably refuted by Hooker. (E.P. Bk. v., 55.)
Primarily he applied it to justify his theory of Consubstantiation, which was a false doctrine of the Real
Presence in a Eucharist which involved no
sacrificial Oblation and needed no Priest to
consecrate it, since Luther had abolished the
Apostolic Ministry and Priesthood. His
" Ubiquity " theory practically absorbed the Manhood
into the Godhead and thus involved Eutychianism,
which was a strange graft upon his semi-Nestorian
tendencies, which the Calvinists approved, whilst they
opposed his view on " Ubiquity." He interpreted the
κένωσις in Philippians ii. 7, as being the " emptying"
of our Lord's *Manhood*, which he considered to be
clothed with all the Divine attributes, instead of the
emptying or humiliation of the "Word " by the fact of the
Incarnation. His speculations on the κένωσις resulted in
the Protestant heresy of our Lord's ignorance as Man,
which, as subsequently developed by Dr. Colenso and

Marginal notes:

Luther's interpretation of the κένωσις.

Luther's heresy of the ubiquity of our Lord's glorified Humanity.

Professor Godet, has infected large portions of nineteenth century Protestantism and has tainted the theology of certain modern Anglicans. When Luther was reminded that his view of the κένωσις was in direct conflict with the interpretation of the Fathers of the Catholic Church, he characteristically replied that " the Fathers have often enough erred. It is enough that we do not cause them to be pronounced *heretics*." (Quoted by Dorner, *Person of Christ*, vol. ii., p. 391.)

We may sum up the development of the heresies of Luther as follows :—

Summary of Luther's heresies.
i. Solifidianism, whereby *fides informis* justifies the elect, who are predestined by irresistible grace, a heresy which produced the Antinomianism of Agricola and the Anabaptists, as well as the Calvinism of Geneva.

ii. Denial of the threefold Apostolic Ministry of the Catholic Church and the substitution of the heresy that every baptised person can administer the Sacraments and that a settled ministry is constituted by the Civil Power.

iii. Abolition of the Sacrament of Marriage, sanction of divorce and polygamy amongst Christians, and laxity with regard to the forbidden degrees.

iv. Denial of the Canon of Scripture as accepted by the Catholic Church, which ultimately produced heretical as contrasted with legitimate Biblical criticism.

v. Semi-Nestorian heresy on the Person of Christ and semi-Eutychian assertion of the ubiquity of · His Glorified Manhood.

In thus summarising the leading heresies of Luther, the writer expressly disclaims any idea of minimising the necessity of a reform in the Catholic Church of his day and time, or of forming a harsh judgment upon Luther's peculiar temperament.

No attempt is here made to give a consecutive history
of his opinions or of the external and
internal causes which led him to form them.

Limits of this
work.

To do so would be to write a history of the
Continental Reformation in its successive phases which
is already available in Bishop Creighton's unsurpassed
and masterly "History of the Papacy," supplemented as
it now is by the Reformation volume of the " Cambridge
Modern History."   The sole aim of these pages is to
trace to their Continental sources certain heresies
which have exercised a potent and most dangerous
influence in the Church of England for the past
three hundred years. It is therefore unnecessary
to trace the origin of the corruptions and abuse in
Western Christendom which were reformed by the
Council of Trent, or to unravel the tangled web of
European politics in the sixteenth century, with which
the course of ecclesiastical affairs was inextricably
involved.   The narrow limits of our inquiry also hinder
any examination of the Renaissance in Art and Letters
or of the influence of Erasmus and the Humanists.   The
history of the alien thread of Protestant heresy, which
became definitely interwoven with the life of the Church
of England in the reign of Edward VI., must be told in
reference to past and present facts and consequences.
The student of causes in relation to effects has plenty
of material upon which to base his conclusions in the
larger historical works already mentioned.   It will be
necessary, however, to deal briefly with the religious
revolution at Zurich and Geneva, for the heresies of
Luther were modified and developed in various directions
by Zwingli and Calvin before they infected the Church
of England.

Zwingli was a Swiss republican and a Humanist.
He was the personal friend of Erasmus, and
although he professed independence of
Luther he was profoundly influenced by
his revolt.   He realised very early in his career as a

The religious
system of
Zwingli.

Reformer that Luther's reform was illogical in destroying the Catholic doctrine of the Ministry and at the same time retaining the doctrine of the Real Objective Presence in the Holy Eucharist.

Luther said, " No Catholic Church, no Bishop, no Priest, but a Mass (without the Sacrifice) ministered by a preacher appointed by the authority of the *Prince*. Zwingli said more logically, " No Catholic Church, no Bishop, no Priest, no Mass, but a social meal of commemoration, presided over by a preacher appointed by the authority of the *people*." Calvin's subsequent organisation at Geneva developed Zwingli's democratic principles into an orderly system which grew in Scotland, as well as at Geneva, into a theocratic despotism of a temper so autocratic and tyrannical, that the proverb passed amongst Protestants that " new Presbyter was but old Priest writ large."

More logical than Luther's

Calvin's development of Zwinglianism.

The republican and democratic character of Zwingli's " reformation " at Zurich did not suit the German Princes, who were using Lutheranism as a political force to break up the German Empire under Charles V. Philip of Hesse, their leader, was more than a mere voluptuary. He was an astute diplomat and an able leader. He had seen Luther part from the original " left wing " of his movement in the Peasant and Anabaptist revolt. He saw Zwingli developing a theological "left wing" to Luther's movement, and he foresaw a split which would weaken Protestantism as an anti-Imperial factor in German politics. Hence he arranged a conference between Luther and Zwingli at Marburg in September, 1529.

Republic and democratic character of Zwinglianism.

Philip of Hesse arranges Conference at Marburg.

In April of the same year he and certain other German Princes had presented a " Protest " at the Diet of Spires against the enforcement of the Edict of the Diet of Worms against

The "Protest" of Spires.

Luther and his followers. The name " Protestant " was given to these Princes, who also protested against saving Christendom from the invasion of the Turks when they laid siege to Vienna. Philip of Hesse openly declared that the Turks were the allies of the Protestant Reformation (*Cambridge Modern History*, vol. ii., p. 207). History repeated itself in this particular at the outbreak of the Crimean War, for certain leading English Protestants welcomed the Turkish alliance as a means of furthering their scheme for converting the Eastern Christians to Protestantism. But the friendship of the Turks was not enough for Philip of Hesse. He desired to unite Luther and Zwingli. The effort was

Failure of Marburg Conference.

vain and the Conference at Marburg came to naught. Zwingli, as a politician, desired to meet Luther half-way. He signed fourteen out of the fifteen articles of concord drawn up by Luther and Melanchthon, but Zwingli, Œcolampadius, and Bucer, would not sign the fifteenth article, which asserted the Real Presence in the Eucharist. Luther chalked on the table round which the Conference met, " This is My Body: " and declined to accept Zwingli's figurative view of the Eucharist as the bare commemoration of an absent Christ. Zwingli adduced to prove his view the figurative passages "I am the door," " I am the true Vine," which illustrations Bucer must have brought with him to England. They have become naturalised amongst English Zwinglians even to the present day. We find that a scholar so distinguished as Bishop Moule holds the figurative view of the Holy Eucharist, and denies categorically the doctrine of the

Bishop Moule's teaching Zwinglian.

Real Presence : a denial which he inaccurately asserts to be the true doctrine of the Church of England. He refers to Bullinger's " Decades " to confirm his erroneous sacramental views, apparently forgetting that the teaching of Zwingli's successor at Zurich cannot be reconciled with the Scriptures as interpreted by the continuous witness

of historical Christianity. *(English Church Teaching,*
pp. 96, 114-128.)

The result of the Conference of Marburg was the
final separation of the German and Swiss

Luther's abuse
of Zwingli.

Protestants. The Lutherans and the
" Reformed," whose sceptre passed from
Zwingli to Calvin when the former was killed at the
Battle of Kappel in 1531, became two hostile organisations, who gave themselves cordially to mutual recrimination and abuse. Luther called Zwingli "a false
prophet, a mountebank, a hog, and a heretic " (Luther

Final breach
between
Lutherans and
Zwinglians.

De Cœna); and wrote, a few days after the
Marburg Conference, that the Zwinglians
were "not only liars but the very incarnation of lying, deceit, and hypocrisy."
(Cambridge Modern History, vol. ii. p. 209.)

The Zwinglians were angry, but did not copy
Luther's generous wealth of invective. Œcolampadius
wrote to Zwingli " thanking the Lord who aided His
servant against the crafts of Luther, who now holds
his peace. His *ape* Bugenhagen *(Bugenhagius illius
simius)* takes his place." Zwingli contented himself

Zwingli on
Luther's
Eucharistic
teaching.

with remarking that the Lutheran doctrine
of the Eucharist as expressed in the
" Syngramma," with Luther's own preface,
" was inspired by the devil " *(ut illorum
halitus Satanam ubique spirat).*

It was significant that Zwingli appeared at Marburg
in a military cloak with a sword at his

Zwingli the
author of
militant
Puritanism.

side. His modern statue at Zurich represents him with a sword, and his death
in battle was typical of his life of action
as a political and social revolutionist. Zwingli was
the real author of militant Puritanism. He was the
true forerunner of Cromwell's " Ironsides," and of that
curious survival of seventeenth century Calvinism
which took shape in the Transvaal Republic under
Paul Kruger, at the close of the nineteenth century,

Zwingli's teaching on the Ministry may be summed up as follows:—(i) Every Christian is at liberty to preach. (*Non unius aut alterius de Scripturæ locis pronunciare, sed omnium qui Christo credunt.*—Works, i., p. 143.) (ii) "Holy Orders," which they say impresses a certain *character* upon the soul, is a *human figment*. Whosoever ministers the Word is a Bishop—i.e. the act of preaching and teaching makes a man, *ipso facto, a Bishop* (*Ordo sacer, quem perhibent animæ characterem quendam infligere, humanum figmentum est. Qui ergo administrat verbum "Episcopus" est.* (Zwingli, *De Vera et Falsa Rel.*, ii. p. 217.)

Summary of Zwingli's teaching on the Ministry.

The subsequent Calvinistic and Presbyterian doctrine of the "parity of Ministers" which oppugned the Threefold Order of the Apostolic Ministry, thus originated with Zwingli, who would have none of Luther's idea of a Lay Prince as "summus Episcopus."

Zwingli naturally denied the *potestas clavium* which our Lord conferred upon His Apostles and their successors in the Catholic Church. The power of " binding and loosing " was to Zwingli the mere preaching of the Gospel. He was more consistent than Luther, who abolished the Apostolic Ministry who are alone commissioned to absolve the penitent, whilst he allowed the retention of a system of Confession and Absolution, empty of all validity. Zwingli's consistency in this point was followed by Calvin. "*Claves sunt pascere,*" said Zwingli, " the pastoral office means preaching the gospel which whosoever has believed is saved—is *loosed* ; whilst he who has not believed is *bound* " (*De V. et F. Rel.*, ii. 196). Upon the Sacraments Zwingli was again consistent with his arbitrary and novel premises. Sacraments do not convey grace, " they are signs and ceremonies by which a man proves to the Church that he is a soldier of Christ (*quibus se homo Ecclesiæ probat militem esse Christi.*") (Op. cit., ii. 198).

His denial of the "power of the Keys."

Baptism does not *make* sons of God, but those who are *already* sons of God receive a token (or *seal*) of sonship (Ib. ii. 477). Baptism does not take away sin (Ib. p. 121). The Baptism of Christ and His Apostles was the same as the baptism of John (Ib. p. 68). He interprets " Hoc est corpus Meum " as follows : "This *is*, that is, *signifies*, My Body. Which is to be explained further, as if a matron showing the ring of her husband left to her by him, should say ' Lo ! this *is* my husband ' (*Hoc est, id est, significat, Corpus Meum. Quod perinde est, ac si quæ matrona coniugis sui annulum ab hoc ipsi relictum monstrans*, ' *En ! coniux hic meus est*,' *dicat* " (Ib. ii. p. 293).

The Zurich liturgical forms very carefully expressed Zwingli's views. The baptismal form omits all mention of baptismal regeneration, or of the Nicene teaching that Baptism is " for the remission of sins." There is a prayer that the child, as he grows up, may have the light of faith, and that is all. The Catholic *doctrine* of Holy Baptism is totally eliminated, although its *form* and *matter* remained. The same is true of the Catholic doctrine of the Eucharist. The Zurich formulary is so studiously, and of set purpose, antagonistic to the Catholic Liturgies of the Church that the common charge of narrowness levelled against Catholics for denying the validity of Presbyterian and other non-episcopal ministrations must fall to the ground. The Zurich form consists of the reading of the words of Institution by the " Antistes " or " president of worship," as a *Lectio*, or lesson read to the assembly, and illustrated by the partaking of some bread and wine. The very idea of any consecration of the elements is most studiously avoided, or of anything more than what Canon Liddon called " a bare memorial of an absent Christ." The Zwinglian and Calvinistic " Lord's Supper " does not pretend to be the Holy Eucharist of the Catholic Church.

[marginal note:] Expression of Zwingli's views in the Zurich formularies.

[marginal note:] Zwinglian and Calvinistic " Lord's Supper " a new rite.

It is a new rite, unknown for fifteen centuries
of Christendom, and it is not in the least degree
uncharitable on the part of Catholics to say
that this Zwinglian ordinance is not the Holy
Eucharist, or (to use the expression of the Prayer Book
of 1549) the " Mass " of the Catholic Church. The
Zwinglians and Calvinists of set purpose abolished the
Mass and set up their new rite in its place. When we
say that their rite is invalid, and that it is not the
Blessed Sacrament as ordained by Christ, we are
simply in agreement with their own view of it. Their
new rite involves a " Real Absence " instead of a
" Real Presence." It conveys no grace. It involves
no Eucharistic Sacrifice. It demands no Priest to
celebrate it, and requires no Altar on which to offer it.
Zwingli and Calvin substituted for the Catholic
Church a religious republic without a
priesthood and without sacraments, save
Baptism which the Church could reckon
as lay baptism, administered by preachers
without valid ordination. The Swiss Protestants
framed a religion which, on the whole, was preferable
to Lutheranism, as it was absolutely logical and consistent. It was more honest to begin
absolutely *de novo*, and to sweep away
every vestige of Catholic order and Sacramental validity than to keep, as Luther
did, the husk of the Catholic Sacramental system
when he had destroyed the kernel. Continental
Protestantism, as a whole, kept the Christian name by
the sole channel of the Form and Matter of Baptism,
which was validly administered in most cases by the
ministers of the various Protestant sects, whose
administration of Baptism can be accepted on the
basis of the validity of Lay Baptism which the
Catholic Church admits.

It is necessary to touch briefly upon the system
and career of John Calvin. He was a
Frenchman. He was trained as a lawyer,

Marginal notes:

A religious Republic substituted for the Catholic Church.

Avoidance of Lutheran inconsistencies.

Calvin.

and he possessed to the full the French faculty
of compelling the whole universe to fit in with
the precise definitions of his own logic. His link with
Lutheranism was the Lutheran Melchior
His link with Wolmar, who taught him the Greek
Luther.
language and literature. Calvin was a
brilliant classical scholar, and a great admirer of
Erasmus and the Humanists. In 1532 he published
his first work—an able classical commentary on
Seneca's *De Clementia*. Shortly after this date he
read some of Luther's sermons, and appears to have
imbibed the Lutheran doctrine of irresistible grace.
He ceased to be a Catholic and fled from Orleans,
where he had been practising law, to Basle, which had
become a Zwinglian city under the influence of
Œcolampadius. Here he met Bullinger, and shortly
afterwards, at the age of twenty-six, wrote
Publication of his *Christianæ Religionis Institutio*. This
his Institutes.
was the first edition of his world-famous
"Institutes," which ultimately became the text-book
of the Genevan discipline and dogma. In 1536 he
settled at Geneva, and made that city the seat of the
strange lay-papacy which he ultimately established.
Geneva was the centre of his influence, and the scene
of his life work until his death in 1564. His orderly
and logical mind could not be satisfied with the
chaotic inconsistencies of Lutheranism, or the barren
negations of Zwinglianism. He was the founder of
Knox and an intellectual Puritanism whose foremost
Milton his example amongst Englishmen was John
successors.
Milton, and whose most narrow and bitter
exponent was the Scotsman, John Knox. The vagueness and inconsistencies of foreign Protestantism took
shape under his legal and logical mind, and he formu-
lated his new religion with a completeness of system
Intellectual and orderliness of detail which left no
completeness of points untouched, and few loopholes for
his system and
its unifying controversy or disunion open. The subse-
force.
quent controversies amongst his followers

arose from the rejection of parts of his system, but for those who accepted it as a whole it possessed a binding and unifying force second only to that exercised by Mahommedanism.

The parallel between the Arabian camel driver and the French lawyer can be drawn very closely. Both were fatalists, both had a clear conception of the unity and the sovereignty of God, and both believed in propagating their opinions by the power of the sword. The active tyranny of Mahomet and his followers finds its parallel in the intolerant rule set up by Calvin at Geneva and by John Knox in Scotland. The Solemn League and Covenant was enforced by the sword in the same spirit as the Mahommedan formula, "There is one God, and Mahomet is His prophet."

Parallel between Calvin and Mahomet.

A further parallel is afforded by the fact that Calvinism, in its logical developments, is as far removed from the Catholic Faith, as revealed by our Lord and His Apostles, as is Mahommedanism. The Christ of Mahomet is a great prophet and teacher of humanity. The Christ of Calvin is supposed to be incarnate for the strange and inadequate purpose of redeeming a certain number of persons who have been elected by God to be saved, and who therefore could not be lost, even if there had been no Incarnation at all. The Christ of Calvin bears no relations whatever to the mass of mankind, who are created for eternal damnation. To teach people who are born to be damned is of course a waste of time, and therefore Calvin did not consider our Lord to be a prophet or teacher of humanity as Mahomet did. Calvin, like Luther found no place for Christian ethics in his system. It is useless, according to Calvin, for born reprobates to attempt to cultivate Christian morality. It is unnecessary for the elect to concern themselves primarily with morals and conduct. As Luther practically said, Our Lord did

But Calvin's Christ no teacher of Humanity.

Christian ethics no primary concern in Calvinism.

not come to *teach* the world, or to lay down a *code of morals* for the world, but to redeem the elect by a formal judicial process, conducted *outside* themselves and bearing no relations whatever to Christian conduct. Calvin's famous "five points" show plainly that his system cannot logically be interpreted otherwise than has just been done. They are as follows :

Calvin's Five Points.

i. The Election of certain persons to be saved, and the consequent choice of others for damnation.
ii. Christ redeemed the elect alone, and did not die for all.
iii. Man has no free will to choose right or wrong.
iv. God's grace, given to the elect, is absolute and irresistible.
v. The Elect will finally persevere to salvation, whatever their conduct may be.

Fortunately Calvin's followers were not as logical as their master. Calvin burnt Servetus for heresy, but this cruel punishment for false opinions was a characteristic of the age. The tyranny of the Scottish Covenanters and the fierce intolerance of the New England Puritans, who persecuted to the death those who differed from their religious polity, was not approved by the milder natured Calvinists. But these men were better than their creed, and preferred to be illogical rather than consistent. It is fortunate for the peace and progress of the world that the followers of Luther, Zwingli, and Calvin to some extent declined to endorse the crude heresies of their leaders. The various Protestant "Confessions of Faith" show traces of a modification of the views of the leaders of the Continental Reformation. It will be the object of the next chapter to examine how far this modification extended, and what were the chief departures from "the Faith once delivered to the Saints" which were involved in the doctrinal formularies of Foreign Protestantism.

Calvin's teaching modified by his followers.

CHAPTER II.

The Doctrinal Errors of Foreign Protestantism on Original Sin, Justification by Faith, and Private Judgment, considered with reference to the true teaching of the English Church.

The pathology of the physical diseases of man forms a most important branch of medical science.
The pathology of spiritual disease. The pathology of spiritual disease or the careful investigation of the causes and sources of the various heresies that from time to time have arisen amongst Christians, is a no less important branch of the science of Theology. At the outset we must carefully notice a fundamental difference between the " sound doctrine " of the " Faith once delivered to the Saints " (S. Jude 3) and the erroneous doctrines of heresy.

The Catholic Faith was delivered by our Lord and His Apostles to the whole body of the
The Catholic Faith is not the creation of individuals. *fideles.* We cannot point to any special dogma of the Creed, and say that S. Peter, or S. Paul, or S. James, or S. John, was the creator, or even the foremost champion of it.

S. Athanasius did not *create* the ὁμοούσιον neither did S. Cyril *invent* the term Θεότοκος which was the watchword of the Church against the heresy of Nestorius. The doctrines of the Catholic Church form an interdependent and harmonious whole. The function of the Œcumenical Councils was to preserve the true balance of the Faith as a whole and to maintain the due proportion of its various parts. What appears at first sight to be a development of doctrine, or a novelty of definition, is really no more than an illumination or illustration of the original deposit of dogma. The great Teachers and Doctors of Catholic Theology never attempted to formulate original doctrines of their own. Their aim was Pauline. We preach not ourselves, but "Christ Jesus the Lord" (II. Cor. iv. 5). The Catholic Church does not tolerate the unbridled individualism of human teachers. However powerful an individual may be in his personality and gifts of leadership, he has no right to formulate original opinions, or doctrines, and teach them to others as a part of the Catholic Faith. The most brilliant intellects and the most powerful leaders in the Catholic Church have ever rejoiced in consecrating their gifts to the strengthening of the corporate life, and the illuminating of the corporate Faith, of the "Body of Christ"—the Kingdom and City of God upon earth. If it were not so—if the factions of Corinth had not been condemned by S. Paul as flagrant contradictions of the Catholic ideal— if men had been allowed to call themselves the followers "of Paul, of Apollos, of Cephas," the Body of Christ would indeed have been divided (I. Cor. i. 12).

The Catholic Church casts the gifts of her leaders into the common treasury of her corporate life

The Church of the first century would have anticipated the sectarian confusion of the Protestant Reformation, and we cannot conceive of the possibility of its victory over persecution in the first three centuries, and its subsequent triumphant emergence from the conflict with heresy during the Council period, if it had lost its corporate unity, and had been split up into warring fragments, such as have destroyed the corporate life of Teutonic Christianity since the Reformation. It is idle to parallel the struggle with heresy during the Council period with the struggles of rival sects of Protestants since the Reformation. The great

Necessity of corporate unity.

Councils represented the corporate life of the Catholic
Church, and the leaders of heresy were condemned
by them as perverters of the "Faith once delivered."
But the post-Reformation Protestant sects have
emancipated themselves from all vestiges
of allegiance to the authority of the
Catholic Church. Their nomenclature
stands self-condemned in the light of
S. Paul's condemnation of human leadership. The
very names of "Lutheran," "Calvinist," "Sweden-
borgian" and "Wesleyan" are an avowal of revolt
against the visible corporation of the "One Gospel"
and the "One Faith."

(margin note: Human leadership, a note of Protestantism.)

Three hundred years of religious discord amongst
English-speaking Christians have dulled
our spiritual perceptions, and caused us to
view our Lord's prayer "*ut omnes unum
sint*," in a spirit of neglect which borders
on irreverence, as if unity involved a visionary and
impracticable ideal. We content ourselves with our
surroundings, and take refuge in the idea that God
has *allowed* this weltering chaos of sectarian anarchy,
which has resulted from the teaching and principles
of the Protestant Reformation, without ever venturing
the further thought that God has *permitted* this
disunion as a punishment for national sins, and that
it is our duty to strive for the undoing of what has
thus been done that we may fulfil that ideal of unity
which is in accordance with the Will and Prayer of
our Blessed Lord Himself. Our first step must be to
diagnose the diseases of foreign Protestantism, and
find out what is wrong with it, especially with regard
to the alien influence it has exercised within the
" Ecclesia Anglicana."

(margin note: Three hundred years of sectarian division and its consequences.)

If we can say of the Catholic Church, after each
great period of trial in her history, "*Merses
profundo pulchrior evenit*," we can also say
with good truth that the reason of her successive

victories is that her leaders were true Catholics, *" Nullius addicti iurare in verba magistri."* They followed no leader but our Blessed Lord—King and Captain in His own Kingdom. They did not fall a prey to those strangely opposing errors which lie at the root of Protestantism as a whole—namely, an overweening confidence in human leadership, coupled with a no less ill-balanced trust in the illuminative guidance of the private judgment of each individual. The combination of these mutually incompatible principles has caused Protestantism to be instinct with the spirit of division. A leader arises and sets forth a creed of his own fashioning. Whilst he lives his personality will for the most part hold his followers together, but when he dies the principle of individualism finds its natural outcome in the dividing of his inheritance. Thus sects beget fresh sects, and the process of division and sub-division is only stayed by the civil Power, as in Germany and Scandinavia. Where this disintegrating process has free course, as in the British Empire and America, it runs riot, and finds its sole restraint in the sense of weakness which it engenders, and the consequent efforts of thoughtful Protestants to unify rather than divide. The pathos of these efforts consists in the fact that their authors have not grasped the true principles of the solidarity of Christendom, and have not sought to return to the corporate unity of the Catholic Church. We are conscious of a like pathos in contemplating the numerous doctrinal formularies of Continental Protestantism. They bear strong traces of a desire to combine fidelity to the leadership and novel opinions of Luther, Zwingli and Calvin, with the further purpose of conciliating the private judgment of individuals, so as to hold together as many persons as possible within the net of each organization for

Margin notes:

Protestant divisions are caused by the cross-currents of human leadership and private judgment.

The doctrinal formularies of Foreign Protestantism combine Novelty and Opportunism.

which they were framed. They therefore combine the
Note of *Novelty* with the Note of *Opportunism*. The
Catholic Creeds, on the contrary, declare in plain and
uncompromising terms the Revelation of God in the
Gospel of our Lord Jesus Christ.

The standard work on the Protestant Confessions of
Faith is Dr. P. Schaff's " History of the Creeds of
Christendom." "A Harmony of Protestant Confessions"
was published in Latin at Geneva in 1581. An
English translation of this work was
published at Cambridge in 1586, and a
new edition of this English version was
published in 1842 by the Rev. Peter Hall,
an Anglican Zwinglian, as a counterblast
to the theology of the Tractarians. His notes are
fiercely polemic and violent, whereas Dr. P. Schaff's
great work is distinguished for its candour and
moderation. Writing as a Calvinist of the American
" German Reformed " body, Dr. Schaff candidly admitted " the leaning of the Lutheran Christology to
Eutychianism, and the leaning of the 'Reformed'
(i.e. Calvinists) to Nestorianism." (Vol. i. p. 217.)
He also admitted that the " Reformed," although
the producer of Puritanism, Congregationalism,
Methodism, etc., " is ever in danger of multiplying
sectarian divisions, over-ruling the principle of
authority by private judgment, and disregarding the
lessons of history." (Vol. i. p. 219.) We may well
say of this great Calvinist scholar, who has now
passed to his rest, *utinam noster esses !*

Dr. P. Schaff's " History of the Creeds of Christendom " is reliable and accurate.

The Lutheran formularies of chief importance are
the Augsburg Confession of 1530 and
the " Formula Concordiæ " of 1577. The
Lutheran sect in its controversies, which
were bitter and interminable, centred itself so completely upon the personal teaching of Luther that it is
not too much to say that it placed Luther on a level

The Lutheran formularies.

with our Blessed Lord Himself. The "Formula of
Concord" was devised to exalt Luther's
teaching by making his speculations and
errors the test of German Protestant orthodoxy. Andreæ, a leading Lutheran and
Chancellor of the University of Tubingen, wrote on
July 24th, 1576, with regard to the efforts of the Elector
Augustus of Saxony to preserve Luther's "gospel"
unpolluted, that the Elector's intention was "*ut
Lutheri doctrina—pura et sincera in scholis et
ecclesiis restituatur, adeoque Lutherus, hoc
est Christus, cuius fidelis minister Lutherus
fuit vivat.*" And he adds that the Torgau
Convention, which preceded the "Formula of Concord,"
did its work "*iuxta spiritum Lutheri, qui Chirsti est.*"
No human teacher, since Mahomet, had ever been
thus exalted by the adulation of his followers. Even
at the present day German Rationalism identifies
Christianity with Lutheranism. We have seen how
Luther exalted himself as the first man of the
Reformation. He wrote to Melanchthon on September
15th, 1530, in approval of the draft of the Augsburg
Confession, which for the time being suited
the politics of his Princely patrons, and
used the following remarkable words:
"*ego canonizabo vos, ut fidelia membra Christi, et
quid amplius quæritis gloriam*"*!* A man who had so
far lost the balance of his own personality as to offer
to "canonise" his friend as a saint, and to ask him
"what greater glory he can desire" than such a
"canonisation" at the hands of a renegade monk
must have at times hovered on the borderland of
mental disease. And this is the most charitable way
of regarding the heresies, profanities and indecencies
which Luther undoubtedly perpetrated. Moehler, a
most charitable and broad-minded theologian, writing
of the *individualism* of the Protestant leaders, says:
"In Luther it was the inordinate pretension of an

Luther is exalted unduly by his followers.

The intention of the "Formula of Concord."

Luther's strange self-exaltation.

individuality which wished to constitute itself the arbitrary centre round which all should gather—an individuality which exhibited itself as the universal man in whom everyone was to be reflected—in short, it was the formal usurpation of the place of Christ." (*Symbolik*, p. 9.) This must be carefully borne in mind in considering the Lutheran Confessions of Faith. The Augsburg Confession reflects Luther's mind less than the others. Political exigencies drove the Lutheran Princes who signed it to keep Luther in the background in order to embarrass Charles V. by a show of moderation. It was therefore drafted by Melanchthon, whose mind was naturally conciliatory. In the Augsburg Confession Melanchthon approximated as far as he could to the Catholic Faith. At a later period he deserted Luther's doctrine of the Real Presence, and temporised with the Zwinglian party. Finally, when his mother was dying, and she asked him whether she should cling to Protestantism, or turn to the Catholic Faith in which she had been brought up, he replied, "Mother, the new faith is the most *convenient*, the Catholic Faith is the most *secure*" ("Dieses ist zwar annehmlicher, der Catholische aber sicherer.") (vide Ægidius Albertinus in Audin's *Life of Luther*, vol. ii. p. 360). A man of this type would naturally present Luther's opinions to the Diet of Augsburg (A.D. 1530) in the most Catholic form possible. The line of the Augsburg Confession was, "our teaching is practically Catholic, why cannot the Catholic Church make room for our peculiarities?" Peace undoubtedly might have been made if the Pope, the Emperor, and the German Princes, had not been playing at cross-purposes. But when negotiations were broken off, the Augsburg Confession became a convenient rallying point for the Lutherans, who edited and re-edited it, and finally supplemented it by the "Formula of Concord." It is

The Augsburg Confession is moderate for political reasons.

Melanchthon's varying views.

well known that Luther was hostile to its modes of expression and only assented to it for political purposes. On some crucial points it positively denied his teaching, and on others it modified the crudeness of his heresies. But his followers were able to read into it some of Luther's worst errors, acting upon the principle that a Lutheran "Confession of Faith" was intended to reflect the mind of Luther. The four Saxon "Visitation Articles" of 1592 are in accord with the "Formula of Concord," but are worth mentioning because they were used as a means of drastic persecution against the Calvinists of Saxony. All pastors, school-teachers, and officers of the Government had to subscribe to them on pain of dismissal. Chancellor Crell, the leader of the Saxon Calvinists, was imprisoned under these Articles, and finally executed under circumstances of some barbarity. The Lutheran ministers scoffed at his prayer on the scaffold, whereupon he prayed that their mocking might not be turned into mourning. After the axe fell the executioner held the severed head aloft and said, "This was a Calvinistic stroke." (G. Frank, *Geschichte der Protest. Theologie*, vol. i. p. 297.) Thus the Reformation devoured its own children, and thus arose the Saxon proverb, "Rather a Papist than a Calvinist."

Luther's qualified assent to the Augsburg Confession.

The four Saxon "Visitation Articles" were devised against the Calvinists of Saxony.

We turn now from the Lutheran to the "Reformed" Confessions of the Zwinglians and Calvinists. We have first in order the "Sixty-seven Articles" of Zwingli, which expressed his personal aberrations from the creed of Christendom, and were put forth in 1523. Then come the "Ten Theses" of Berne, which were prepared by Zwingli, and which united the three Protestant Cantons of Berne, Zurich and Basle. We have next to deal

The Reformed Confessions.

The Sixty-seven Articles of Zwingli

The Ten Theses of Berne.

with the " First Helvetic Confession " of 1536,
and the " Second Helvetic Confession " of 1566, the
interval between them being filled with
the theology, politics and personality of
Calvin. Lastly we shall note briefly the
" Heidelberg Catechism," which is still
most extensively used as a moderate compromise between Lutheranism and Calvin-
ism, and has become the chief authorised formulary of
the Dutch Reformed body in South Africa. The
"Gallican Confession " of 1559 and the "Belgic
Confession " of 1561 are of the same type of doctrine
as the other documents we have mentioned. The
easiest method of pursuing our inquiry will be to state
the Catholic Faith on each several point
with which we deal, and then state the
various errors and heresies upon that point
which are revealed in the Lutheran,
Zwinglian and Calvinistic formularies. It is necessary to examine first of all the Catholic doctrine of
" Original Sin." The phrase itself does not
occur in the Bible, but the doctrine is
Scriptural. The Church teaches that the
Fall of Man has injured the soul and body of everyone born of human parents—save that we may believe
in our Lord's special Redemption of His Blessed
Mother, of whom S. Augustine (*De Nat. et Grat.*
c. xxxvi.) says, "*propter honorem Domini nullam
prorsus, cum de peccatis agitur, haberi volo quæs-
tionem.*" The Pelagian controversy in the fifth
century caused S. Augustine to oppose Pelagius with
divers unbalanced statements which the
Catholic Church never endorsed. From
the further exaggeration of Augustinianism,
coupled with an infusion of Mohammedan
fatalism, sprung the heretical anthropology of Luther
and the anti-Christian logic of Calvin.

The Catholic Church set a true balance to the

The side-notes:

The First and Second Helvetic Confessions, the Heidelberg Catechism, the Gallican and Belgic Confessions.

The comparison of Protestant formularies with the Catholic Faith.

The Catholic doctrine of the Original Sin.

S. Augustine opposed Pelagius with unbalanced statements.

Augustinian theology in the final condemnation of
Pelagian tendencies in the Second Council
of Orange (*De gratia et libero arbitrio*)
which was held A.D. 529 under Cæsarius
of Arles. Its decrees were those of a
Provincial Synod only, but their acceptance by Pope
Boniface II. and consequent authoritative circulation,
led Canon Bright to say very truly that "this little
Gallican Council earned the respect and gratitude of
ages for having brought a great question to a comprehensive settlement and preserved the Christianity of
Western Europe from a one-sidedness baneful to its
soul-attracting power." (*Anti-Pelagian Treatises of
S. Aug.* Introd., p. lxvi.)

Final settlement of Pelagian Controversy by Second Council of Orange.

The First Decree of the Council of Orange is to the
effect that the soul, as well as the body,
has been injured by original sin, and
adduces, as Scripture proofs, Ezek. xviii. 20.
Rom. vi. 16, and 2 Pet. ii. 19.

The decrees of Orange correct Augustinian theology.

The Second Decree states that Adam's sin did not
harm himself only, but passed on to his posterity,
quoting Rom. v. 12, in proof of the statement.

In its Twenty-fifth Decree the Council denies categorically the Augustinian doctrine of *absolute predestination* of certain persons to eternal life, and its
complement, the absolute reprobation of others.
S. Augustine's doctrine differed from Calvin's in leaving
space for the grace of the Sacraments, and for the
corporate life of the Church as a visible body. But
Calvin's fatalistic logic denied the corporate life of the
Visible Church and limited the grace of the Sacraments to those whose absolute predestination already
made them the recipients of "irresistible grace."

The exact words of the Council of Orange on this
subject must be quoted as the verdict of the Church
of the sixth century against the future heresy of Calvin
(derived in the first instance, as we have seen, from
Luther) in the fifteenth century. "We believe that

5

this also is in accordance with the Catholic Faith,
namely that *all* the baptised, having received grace
through Baptism, with the help and co-operation of
Christ, are able and ought to fulfil those things which
belong to the soul's salvation if they will to work with
faithfulness. But that some are predestined by Divine
Power for evil, we not only refuse to believe, but also
we pronounce anathema with all detestation upon
those, if there be any such, who desire to believe in so
great an evil. (*Hoc etiam secundum fidem Catholicam
credimus, quod accepta per Baptismum gratia, omnes
baptizati, Christo auxiliante et co-operante, quæ ad
salutem animæ pertinent possint et debeant, si fideliter
laborare voluerint, adimplere. Aliquos vero ad
malum divina potestate prædestinatos esse, non solum
non credimus, sed etiam si sunt qui tantum malum
credere velint, cum omni detestatione illis anathema
dicimus.*" Conc. Arausican ii. 25.)

This question of absolute predestination and reprobation assumed so large a space in the scheme of
foreign Protestantism that we allude to it here, as
indirectly linked with the doctrines of the Fall and its
consequences.

But to return to the Catholic doctrine of Original
Sin. It is a deprivation, an injury, and
an inherited taint which influences our
freedom of will in the direction of evil,
so that the discords thereby brought into our nature
can only be harmonised by the grace of God's
Redeeming Love in Christ. Bishop Forbes, in commenting upon Article IX. thus carefully defines the
donum supernaturale of which Adam was deprived by
the Fall : " The relation of Adam to God
was caused by a supernatural gift of Divine
Grace superadded to the endowments of
Nature . . . . Luther's cardinal error was,
that he mistook the distinction between
the *natural* and the *superadded* gifts, maintaining

*Original sin is a
deprivation
and a taint.*

*Bp. Forbes on
the donum
supernaturale
and Luther's
error on the
Fall of Man.*

that Adam's acceptableness with God was *natural*, and an integral constitutive part of his nature. He failed to distinguish between the nature itself of the mind and will, created by God alone without us, and the virtue and uprightness which are perfected by our co-operation with the grace of God. Divines called the former the *image*, and the latter the *likeness* of God. The importance of the distinction is obvious. Moreover, Luther and many of his followers denied the freedom of the will in fallen man."

Abp. Trench quotes P. Lombard on "Image" and "Likeness." (Bp. Forbes, on the Thirty-nine Articles, pp. 141, 142.) Archbishop Trench draws the same distinction as Bishop Forbes with regard to *image* and *likeness*. He quotes P. Lombard (*Sent*. ii. *dist*. 16): *Imago secundum cognitionem veritatis, similitudo secundum amorem virtutis*. He also notes that Baxter, following the usual erroneous Protestant theology, calls this distinction a "groundless conceit." (*N. T. Synonyms*, p. 49.)

S. Thomas Aquinas couples with the deprivation of the "donum supernaturale" the evil taint of " a disordered disposition resulting from the dissolution of the harmony of original righteousness." (*Est enim quædam inordinata dispositio, proveniens ex dissolutione illius harmoniæ in qua consistebat ratio originalis institiæ*. (*Summa Theol*. I. ii. Q. 82, A. i.)

S. Thomas Aquinas on Original Sin.

Bishop Harold Browne summarises the Decree of the Council of Trent upon Original Sin with fairness and accuracy, as follows: (i) "That Adam by transgressing lost holiness and justice, incurred the wrath of God, death, thraldom to the devil, and was infected both in soul and body. (ii) That Adam derived to his posterity death of body and sin of soul. (iii) That sin, transmitted by generation, not by *imitation*, can be abolished by no remedy but the death of Christ, and that the merit of Christ is applied

Bp. Harold Browne's summary of the Tridentine doctrine of Original Sin.

to children in Baptism as well as to adults.   (iv) That newly born children ought to be baptised as having contracted sin from Adam."   (*Browne, on Thirty-nine Articles*, p. 236.)

The Eastern Church lays stress upon the *temporal* consequences of Original Sin, which it calls "a hereditary burden."   It emphasises "labour, sickness and death," but says that mortal sins are the outcome of " our depraved choice contrary to the Divine Will," and denies the total corruption of human nature.   [Decree vi. of *Synod of Bethlehem* (against the Calvinists) 1672.]

The Eastern Church on Original Sin.

The Ninth Article of the Church of England was drawn up by the Elizabethan Divines with a view to conciliate all parties.   It must be remembered, in dealing with the Articles, that they do not form a Creed or " Confession of Faith," and that the Lambeth Conference decided in 1888, that the " whole of the Articles," as being " coloured in language and form by the peculiar circumstances under which they were originally drawn up," could not be imposed upon the Colonial and Missionary Churches as a condition of communion with the See of Canterbury.   The Articles also cannot be interpreted in a sense contrary to the teaching, explicit and implicit, of the Catholic Creeds, the Decrees of Œcumenical Councils and the Book of Common Prayer.   Dr. Field, Dean of Gloucester, may be regarded as a link between the more Churchly Elizabethan Divines, and the Caroline theologians of the type of Laud and Andrewes.   His words on " Original Sin " form an interesting and almost contemporary comment on Article IX., showing that he considered it to teach Catholic doctrine.   He said : " If we speak of Original Sin *formally*, it is the *privation* of those excellent gifts of Divine Grace.   . . . which Adam had and lost."   (*Field on the Church*, App. to Bk. iii., c. 5.)

Article IX.

True value of the Articles.

The Lambeth Conference of 1888 on the Articles.

Dean Field on Original Sin.

But the Ninth Article needs no apology or explanation. It is a plain exposition of the Catholic doctrine of " Original Sin," and is commended for its balanced language by the greatest German Catholic theologian of the nineteenth century. (See Möhler, *Symbolik*, p. 79.)

The Bishop of Gloucester says that the " quam longissime " of the Latin Article must be interpreted by the " very far gone " of the English Version, and in proof of this he points out the important fact that the Westminster Divines in 1643 published an emendation of the Article to bring it into accord with Protestant Theology. (Bp. Gibson on Thirty-nine Articles, p. 370.)

The Bishop of Gloucester on Article IX.

The Westminster Assembly amended Article IX. as follows:—" Original Sin standeth not in the following of Adam as the Pelagians do vainly talk, but *together with his first sin imputed*, it is the fault and corruption of the nature of every man that naturally is propagated from Adam; whereby man is *wholly deprived* of original righteousness," etc. And it ends with substituting for the cautious Tridentine phrase " *ratio peccati* " as a definition of concupiscence, the stringent words, " concupiscence and lust *is truly and properly sin.*"

The Westminster Assembly amends Article IX.

Protestant theology could not tolerate in Article IX. (i) its omission of the heresy of the *imputation* of Adam's sin; (ii) its cautious " very far gone " instead of " wholly deprived," which expresses the heresy of the *total* depravity of human nature; and (iii) its careful avoidance of the heresy that concupiscence is " truly and properly sin." This avoidance on the part of the Elizabethan Divines is more marked, because the Thirteen Articles drawn up in 1538, in an abortive attempt at concord between Henry VIII. and the Lutherans, contained this heresy. The identification of the word " renatis " in the Latin form of Article IX. with

Identification of " renatis " with the " baptized."

" baptised " in the English form has always been an impassible barrier against the Protestant heresy that Regeneration is identical with Conversion, and therefore cannot be inseparably connected with Holy Baptism. We have thus shown that the Church of

Article IX. is Catholic in its teaching.

England teaches in the Ninth Article, as well as in her formularies (where he who runs may read it), the Catholic doctrine of Original Sin, and Baptismal Regeneration as its remedy.   We shall recur to the latter point again.   Meanwhile, before examining the heresy of the Protestant Confessions on this subject, it may be remarked in passing that persons who hold and teach Protestant heresy on this or other matters of faith, have no legitimate standing ground within the Church of England, or within any of her daughter Churches who are in communion with Canterbury.

It is necessary to examine the Lutheran " Confessions " on " Original Sin " in their order.   The Augsburg Confession was intended to conciliate.   And yet it says, "they (i.e. the Protestants)

The Augsburg Confession on " Original Sin."

teach that after Adam's Fall, all men who are engendered according to Nature, are born in sin—that is to say, without fear of God, without confidence in Him and with concupiscence."

The " Formula of Concord " (A.D. 1576) says that " Original Sin is no trivial corruption, but

The " Formula of Concord " an Original Sin.

is so profound a corruption of human nature (*tam profundam humanæ naturæ corruptionem*) as to leave nothing sound, nothing incorrupt in the body and soul of man or in his mental and bodily powers."

The Lutheran doctrine of Original Sin, as expressed in these formularies, involves the total

Lutheran doctrine of " Total Depravity."

depravity of human nature just as plainly as Luther's own coarser expressions teach it.   The Calvinistic Confessions teach the same heresy. The Second "Helvetic Confession" was

The "Second Helvetic Confession" on Original Sin.

compiled by Bullinger, Zwingli's successor at Zurich, and was an embodiment of the teaching of Calvin and Zwingli. In cap. viii. it defines Original Sin as that " by which we are plunged into evil desires, turned away from good, inclined to every kind of evil, and filled with every kind of wickedness, faithlessness, contempt and hatred of God so that we can do no good thing of ourselves or even contemplate it." The Eighth Question

The Heidelberg Catechism.

of the " Heidelberg Catechism " of 1563 asks, " Are we so depraved that we are *wholly* unapt to any good and prone to all evil ? " The answer says, " Yes." The " Gallican Con-

The Gallican Confession.

fession " of 1559 states that Original Sin caused man to fall from grace " so that his nature is totally corrupt " *(en sorte que sa nature est du tout corrumpue)*. The " Belgic Con-

The " Belgic Confession."

fession of 1561 defines Original Sin as " a corruption of the whole nature." The Scotch Confession " of 1560 states that Original Sin is that by which " was the Image of God utterly defaced in man."

The heresy of the *total* depravity of man by reason of the Fall is thus placed in the forefront of Foreign Protestant teaching. It invaded England both from the Continent and from Scotland, but it cannot be honestly fitted into the framework of the Anglican

The heresy of the Total Depravity of man in the " Cumminsite " 7th Article.

formularies. The formation of the " Re-formed Episcopalian " body by Bishop Cummins in 1873 has already been men-tioned. It was an honest secession of the Ultra-Protestant party from the American Church and thus deserves respect. Naturally we find in its Seventh Article an assertion of the *total* depravity of human nature. It follows the wording of Article IX. of the Anglican Church with the significant substitution of the phrase "*wholly* gone " for " very

far gone," from original righteousness. It is impossible to acquit the pious Evangelicals of the close of
the eighteenth century from the charge of using far too
strong language on this subject. Canon Overton says
The Evangeli-   "that all who were connected with the
cals of the   Evangelical Revival insisted upon the *total*
eighteenth
century fell   *depravity* of human nature. They held
into this heresy. that the Image of God was not only defaced
but effaced by the Fall." (*The Evangelical Revival in
the Eighteenth Century*, p. 187.)

The same teaching has been dogmatically asserted
by the extreme Protestant "left wing" of the Church
of England at the present day. The "Cumminsite"
alteration of Article IX. in order to make it teach the
total depravity of human nature is intelligible. But
" English   the assertion (on p. 37 of " English Church
Church   Teaching ") that the Articles " teach plainly
Teaching" also   the *total* depravity of human nature " is a
asserts it.   *suggestio falsi* which points to a non-
natural interpretation of Article IX. for which men of
the calibre of Bishop Moule, Canon Girdlestone and
Bishop Drury ought not to have been jointly responsible. Canon Girdlestone's excuse (published in the
Guardian of November 7th, 1905) that "it is
impossible to put all one's theology into a shilling
book," is no valid answer to a published criticism of
inaccurate statements put forth in the volume aforesaid.
The size and price of a book have nothing to do with
the truth or falsity of the statements contained in it.
On p. 219 of the same volume we have the statement
that the "total depravity of human nature" was one
Bishop Ryle's   of the leading doctrines of the Evangelical
" Knots Untied." Revival. The late Bishop Ryle republished,
when he was Bishop of Liverpool, a book
called " Knots Untied " (under the auspices of the
" National Protestant Church Union ") which is
redolent of a special dogmatic infallibility, aptly

conveyed by its title. The book is full of theological
misconceptions and unproven assertions
and assumptions. It has been a sort of
text book for " militant Protestantism."
He counsels laymen to forsake their Parish Churches
if the Clergy do not teach what he calls " the Gospel."
(*Knots Untied*, p. 452.) He says that the Primitive
Church of the earliest ages forsook Scriptural teaching,
and started " a new system," " a region where the
malaria of idolatry has begun to arise" (Ib., p. 494).
He calls the Blessed Virgin Mary " one of our fellow
sinners" because she says " My spirit hath
rejoiced in God my Saviour " (Ib., p. 497),
quite oblivious of the fact that the Catholic
doctrine of her sinlessness has always regarded the
fact that she was sinless, as the first fruit of the
Redeeming Love of Him Who deigned to be " born of a
pure Virgin," and that " without spot of sin." *The*
Homily of Repentance says that our Lord was incarnate
" *of her undefiled substance.*" His encouragement of
" militant Protestantism " is open. He advocates
a policy of fighting Catholics " even if a secession of
our antagonists is the consequence." He advocates
their " untiring exposure by the pulpit, the platform,
and the press." He urges " lawsuits wherever there
is a reasonable hope of success " (Ib., p. 29). He
permitted this latter policy, as Bishop of Liverpool,
with the result that one of his clergy (Mr. Bell Cox)
was imprisoned as a Confessor of the Catholic Faith. We
have digressed thus far to emphasise the character of
his book. We now come to his teaching
on " Original Sin," which is as contrary
to Article IX. as the corresponding
" Cumminsite " Article VII., and the passages from " English Church Teaching " which have
already been quoted.

The Bishop says that " In consequence of Adam's
Fall all men are as *far as possible* gone from original
righteousness. They have no will to serve their

Maker, no love to their Maker, and no meetness for Heaven " (Ib., p. 5).   He explains his view further as meaning *the total corruption of human nature*— a radical and universal corruption of man's will, intellect, affections and conscience " (Ib., p. 410). This is practically what Luther meant by his doctrine of "men-devils."   Bishop Ryle's teaching is the doctrine of the Westminster Confession and of the various foreign Protestant formularies.   It is *not* the doctrine of the Prayer Book and Articles of the Church of England, which teach clearly and plainly on this point the Scriptural and Catholic doctrine of Original Sin, as expressed in the first and second Decrees of the Council of Orange.   It is impossible for an honest man to teach this "foreign Protestant" heresy of the "total depravity" of human nature, and at the same time to claim to be a loyal member of the Church of England. This is a crucial and fundamental issue.   Out of this un-Catholic and un-Scriptural doctrine of the "total depravity" of human nature as the direct consequence of the Fall, the whole fabric of "foreign Protestant" error has been built up, which has so grievously affected the Church of England.

He taught the error of Luther and of the Westminster Confession.

This heresy of " foreign Protestantism " is incompatible with the Anglican formularies.

And it has also caused a most dangerous " Liberal " reaction in the direction of positive unbelief.   As a specimen of this we have the utterances of two well-known Cambridge Professors.   Dr. Inge has said, " We must frankly take our choice between the Pentateuch and modern science—between the theory of a *ruined human nature* and the theory of a gradual development from lower forms." (*Guardian*, April 17th, 1907.)

It has caused a dangerous " Liberal " reaction.

Dr. Inge confuses the Catholic doctrine of Original Sin with the "ruined human nature" theory of Luther and Calvin.   He would derive all human tendencies to sin from the theory of man's evolution from lower

Original Sin, as taught by S. Paul, denied by Dr. Inge and Professor Burkitt.

forms of animal life, and would call it the survival
of the brute in man. He utterly rejects the Apostolic
authority of S. Paul's teaching of the " two Adams,"
quite oblivious of the fact that modern biological
science tends more and more to confirm the
belief that the whole human race has a common
origin, and that the First Adam, on the accepted
principles of heredity, would transmit to his posterity
the taint of Original " *Sinfulness* "—a more accurate
term than " *Sin*." Dr. Inge, by implication, denies
that our Lord, as the Second Adam, is the Restorer of
fallen humanity. And we have worse things from
Professor Burkitt. At the Manchester Church Congress, speaking, as he necessarily must, with the
fullest sense of responsibility, he said, " We may accept
S. Paul's Epistles as genuine, as being really letters of
Paul of Tarsus, the great Apostle who brought the
Gospel into Europe. But even if they be genuine,
can we accept to-day the views they champion about
the origin of evil, and the primitive fall of man?
You know we can do nothing of the kind. There is
no use shirking the plain fact ; we do not now
receive S. Paul as an authority upon the origin of
sin and death." (*Manchester Church Congress Report*,
p. 48.)

Thus " foreign Protestantism " is devoured by its
own direct offspring. A recoil from its unnatural
perversion of the Catholic doctrine of Original Sin,
has led to a Rationalist rejection of the teaching of
the New Testament. The unbalanced dogma of
" verbal inspiration," and the untrue assertion of the
dogma that the Bible is the *sole* and *infallible*
dogmatic authority, apart from the Church, as the
witness and keeper of Holy Writ, and the " pillar and
ground of the Truth," has destroyed the legitimate
teaching authority of the Holy Scripture, as defined
by the consentient voice of Christendom, and as
expressed in the Anglican Sixth Article of Religion.

The " foreign Protestant " element in the Anglican
Communion is not only disloyal to
its teaching and formularies in its
own peculiar sphere of negative and
positive error, but it is the fruitful
parent of every other species of misbelief
amongst us, from the heresies of Benjamin Hoadley in
the eighteenth century to those of Dr. Colenso, Dr.
Cheyne, and the nebulous " Liberals of our own time."

The " Foreign Protestant " errors are responsible for Broad Church as well as " Evangelical " misbelief.

We now come to our second crucial point in considering the doctrinal errors of "foreign
Protestantism." In the previous chapter
the Lutheran doctrine of " Justification by
Faith " was explained, according to the
carefully balanced and accurate analysis of the
late Professor Mozley. Lutheranism made it the
" articulus stantis aul cadentis ecclesiæ " so it is
justifiable to regard it as the central
doctrine of "foreign Protestantism." It
arose from the special circumstances of
the early fifteenth century. The Papal
Schism, the transient effect of the reforming Councils
of Constance and Basle, the rise of Humanism, and
the lowered ideals of the Clergy, tended
towards a semi-Pagan philosophy amongst
the educated, and towards formalism
amongst the mass of the people. The revival of
learning, and the political revolt against Feudalism,
which simmered beneath the surface, when it did not
cloke itself under the form of quasi-religious revolts,
caused a social, political, and religious unrest which
demanded a real revival of spiritual religion within
the Church. Reform was needed, and not revolution.
But the unbalanced mind of Luther made him a
leader of revolution rather than reform.
His revolt from historical and corporate
Christianity was centred upon the individual. His system left no room for

The Lutheran heresy on the Justification of Man.

The central doctrine of foreign Protestantism.

The contributory causes of this error.

Luther inaugurated Revolution instead of Reform.

personal and corporate religion to develop concurrently in the Visible Church, whose "note of holiness" is infused into the individual lives of its members. Luther's new religion made each individual the final arbiter of his own righteousness before God. "A man is justified when he believes himself to be justified." The mildest expression of Lutheranism, carefully refined by Melanchthon, and by the political exigencies of the German Princes, was, as has already been stated the Augsburg Confession. It says: "Men are justified freely through faith, *when they believe that they are received into favour (quum credunt se in gratiam recipi).'* (Article VI.) This heretical statement is repeated in Article XX., which says that "We obtain remission of sins, grace and justification, by faith only *(credentes quod propter Christum recipiamur in gratiam.")* Bishop Gibson traces this same heresy in five other places in the Augsburg Confession, while Bishop Forbes calls it "the peculiar symbol of Lutheranism." The Anglican Article XI., "Of the Justification of Man," has expressly rejected this Lutheran substitution of a man's subjective consciousness of his own belief for the *fides formata* of Catholic theology, which is aptly paraphrased by the *"fides vera et viva"* of our Article XII. The rejection is all the more remarkable because Article XI. owes some of its phrases to the Confessions of Augsburg and Würtemberg, and further because, in 1538, a Conference of Anglicans and Lutherans agreed upon certain Articles, the fourth of which, "De Justificatione," contained the heretical statement with which we have been dealing. Its affirmation in 1538, and its rejection in 1571, is evidently quite deliberate. It is the outcome of Luther's confusion of faith (*fides*) with trust (*fiducia*).

Margin notes:

He teaches the self-justification of the individual.

The Augsburg Confession teaches the same error.

Article XI. expressly rejects it.

"Fides formata" in Article XII

The " Cumminsite " Article XI. defines "justifying faith " as " the reliance or dependence on Christ which accepts Him as the sacrifice for our sins." This, of course, is a paraphrase of the Lutheran heresy that *fiducia* justifies us, and that this *fiducia* operates to justify a man when, by a subjective and internal process, *he believes himself to be justified.*

The " Cumminsite " and the Anglican Article are doctrinally irreconcileable. The late Bishop Ryle stated, with a positive dogmatism peculiar to his personality, that Anglo-Catholics " are ever thrusting upon the public their favourite *Diana of the Ephesians,* their darling notion that the Prayer Book, and not the Articles, is the test of a Churchman. I am going to say, and to prove that the Articles and not the Prayer Book are the first, foremost and principal test of a true Churchman." (*Knots Untied,* p. 82.)

It is self-evident that the Articles are not the Anglican " Confession of Faith," and we have already stated that their acceptance has been declared by the Lambeth Conference of 1888 to be unnecessary for Colonial and Missionary Churches as a condition of communion with the See of Canterbury. The Japanese Church has rejected the Thirty-nine Articles, because it declines to be entangled with the controversies (peculiar to the Tudor Reformation in England) with which they deal. But although the Articles will not—and were not intended—to bear the stress laid upon them by Bishop Ryle and his followers, he appealed to the Articles and by them his doctrine shall be judged. Bishop Ryle gave his unqualified assent to the teaching of Luther on Justification in the following words : " The key to all his success was his constant declaration of Justification by Faith without the deeds of

Marginal notes:

The " Cumminsite" Article XI.

Doctrinally in conflict with our Article XI.

Bishop Ryle on the Articles.

The Articles are not a " Confession of Faith."

Bishop Ryle held Luther's heresy on Justification.

the law. This was the *truth* which enabled him to break the chains of Rome, and let light into Europe." (*Knots Untied*, p. 434.)

This is an absolutely unqualified statement. There is no hint to show that Bishop Ryle did not hold the Lutheran error of confusing *fides* and *fiducia*. There is no hint to show that he did not hold the heresy of the Augsburg definition "that men are justified freely through faith, *when they believe that they are received into favour*"—a statement which substitutes a man's own *belief* of *what he believes*—a mere personal issue—for the true *fides formata*, "the faith that worketh by love." It may even be said that Luther substituted a *trust* in a man's own belief that he is saved, for the Atoning Work of our Lord Himself, as if faith, *per se*, had some special efficacy.

To quote Bishop Ryle again. "For the truth's sake Luther broke the unity of the Church in which he was born, denounced the Pope and his ways, *and laid the foundation of a new teaching*. And who shall dare to say that Luther was wrong?" (*Knots Untied*, p. 450.) Bishop Ryle hit the mark here when he admitted that Luther's teaching was *new*. It was unheard of from the Apostle's days to his own. He set S. Paul against S. James, and grossly perverted the teaching of both these Apostles. Article XI. is not Lutheran, as we have already shown. The words of the Article, "We are justified by faith only," are not Lutheran, because the Article refers us to the Homily, which practically defines justifying faith as "*fides formata per charitatem*" (Aquinas: Summa iii. Q. xlix. Art. 1). "Faith does not shut out repentance, hope, *love*, dread, and the fear of God to be joined with faith in every man that is justified," says the Homily. Luther's heresy, which asserts that a barren assent, or belief (*fides informis*), justifies, finds no place in the teaching of the Anglican

Bishop Ryle admitted that Luther's teaching was "new."

Article XI. is further explained by the "Homily of Salvation."

Articles.   The "justifying faith" of Article XI. is not
only explained by the Homily, but is expressed and
explained most clearly by the " true and lively faith "
of Article XII.   This "*vera et viva fides*" is a synonym
for the " *fides formata* " of S. Thomas Aquinas, which

Bishop Ryle
held that
"fides informis"
justifies us.

Luther rejected with his usual coarse vehemence.   But Bishop Ryle held Luther's
" new teaching."   He held by " *fides informis*," which he called " *simple faith*."
He said : " All religious systems which put anything
between the heavy-laden sinner and Jesus Christ the
Saviour, except simple faith, are dangerous and un-

To him "*fides
formata*" was a
" complicated
faith."

scriptural."   He evidently considered *fides
formata*, (*faith that worketh by love*, Gal.
v. 6) a *complicated* faith, and said, " all
systems which make out *faith* to be anything *complicated*, anything but a simple childlike
dependence—the hand which receives the soul's
medicine from the physician—are unsafe and poison-
ous systems.   All systems which cast discredit upon
the simple Protestant doctrine which broke the power
of Rome, carry about with them a plague spot, and
are dangerous to souls."   (*Knots Untied*, p. 460.)

It is evident from this somewhat violent language
that the late Bishop of Liverpool must have found it
very difficult to work with, or deal fairly by, the large
number of clergy in his diocese who were loyal to the
Anglican definition of Justification, and who rejected
what the Bishop called, very rightly, the "new
teaching " of Luther.

" *De mortuis nil nisi verum* " would have been Bishop
Ryle's rendering of the well-worn adage, and though
silence with regard to his forceful dogmatic utterances

This teaching
endorsed by
him as Bishop
of Liverpool
in 1896.

would have been welcome, two things must
not be forgotten.   The volume from which
we have quoted was reissued by him, as
Bishop of Liverpool in 1896, and in the
Preface we find the words: " I find nothing to retract,

cancel, or withdraw. I wish my readers to understand that the views which I held as a presbyter I still hold as Bishop."

And the second thing is that this volume is still largely circulated as a chief text-book of that "militant Protestantism" which derives its inspiration from Luther, Calvin and Zwingli, and is alien to the true teaching and spirit of the Articles and Prayer Book of the Church of England.

The same Lutheran error on Justification appears in Bishop Moule's portion of "English Church Teaching." He begins with contrasting the "Covenant of Works" with the "Covenant of Grace," and says that "the first Covenant has for its watchword : Do God's Law, and claim life." The second has for its watchword 'Accept God's Christ, and claim life.' The first says ' Do this and live by thy merit.' The second says 'Trust Him and live,' and in that life do His Will by His Spirit." (*English Church Teaching*, p. 59.)

Bishop Moule teaches the same Lutheran error in "English Church Teaching."

This is a very unreal and dangerous antithesis. It implies that God set impossible and impracticable conditions before the Israelites under the Old Covenant, and it is redolent of Luther's perversion of S. Paul's Epistle to the Galatians. The object of that Epistle was to preserve the broad basis of the Catholic Church from the narrow theory of Judaising Christians who desired to impose the Mosaic ceremonial law upon Gentile Christians. S. Paul's argument demanded that he should show that the Mosaic law was temporary, and not permanently binding, save in the fulfilment of its moral precepts by our Lord's revelation of perfect morality in His Sermon on the Mount, and in His own perfect obedience to the law of righteousness. Mr. Dimock, of whose writings Bishop Moule says (in his commendatory notice of their recent re-issue) : " I owe mental and spiritual debts to

His unreal antithesis between the Old and New Covenant.

Mr. Dimock avoids this error.

Mr. Dimock far greater than I can specify in words,"
is, upon this point, a wiser author than Bishop Moule.
He says : " We must not also fail to bear in mind that,
in speaking of the Old Covenant or the Covenant of the
Law as considered *by itself*, we are speaking of that
which, in historical fact, never did stand *by itself*. The
promise of the good things to come had gone before.
It told of a Covenant older than *the Old*. The Law was
a schoolmaster to prepare men's hearts to lay hold of the
promises of the Messiah given to the Patriarchs—
promises older than the foundation of the world. And
these promises were unfolding before the faith of the
pious Israelites while they were living under the Law."
(Ritual, Its Use and Misuse, p. 41.)

Luther, and the foreign Protestant Reformers generally, fell into the grievous error of treating the
" Covenant of the Law " *by itself*, in sharp antithesis to
the " Covenant of Grace." Mr. Dimock rightly says
that it never did stand " *by itself*."

Professor Mozley is an impartial witness. His
published work on Baptismal Regeneration

Professor
Mozley on
Luther's false
antithesis
between the
Two Covenants.
is a denial of Catholic doctrine upon the
subject. We may therefore quote him with
confidence with regard to Luther's crude
antithesis between " the Law " and " Christ,"
—the " Covenant of Works," and the " Covenant of
Grace." Luther " pictured miserable man vainly
fighting with a stern and inexorable impossibility. The
insatiableness of the law, the law of conscience, was a
grievance in the constitution of things ; *the more you try
to fulfil it the more you transgress. Una lex gignit
alias decem* : one law begets ten more, till they mount
up to infinity. With a Manichean intensity he insisted
upon the absolute evil of all visible and perceptible
nature. *In man and in the devil spiritual things were
extinct.* Do what thou wilt ; *tu es in hoc seculo nequam.*
This world which *is* darkness, not is *in* darkness but *is*
darkness itself. In his book *De servo arbitrio* he

describes the Deity as *though not making sin*, yet as if it were the next thing to it, *not ceasing to make and multiply natures vitiated by sin, natures from which He has withdrawn His Spirit.*" (*Licet enim Deus peccatum non faciat, tamen naturam peccato, subtracto Spiritu, vitiatam non cessat formare et multiplicare, tanquam si Faber ex ligno corrupto statuas faciat.*"—Luther *De Servo Arbitrio*, Op. ii. p. 459.)

"Upon the dogma of the absolute evil of man's goodness a great difficulty immediately arises with respect to the doctrine of Justification. How was man ever to be justified and become acceptable to God being, as he was, simply evil? The Church has always admitted good works into a regular place in the process of Justification. But the Church has been enabled to do this from the circumstance that she has never annihilated the goodness of human works on account of their imperfection. The Church has therefore been enabled to maintain

Professor Mozley on Justification.

with respect to man's Justification all the teaching of natural religion, and the whole language of reason ; such as, that all who do their duty according to their light, please God in their degree." (*Essays*, vol. i. pp. 336-338.) Professor Mozley here lays down the Catholic doctrine that *fides formata* justifies us—the *vera et viva fides* of Article XII. But Luther enunciated the heresy that *fides informis* justified us, and in his commentary on the Galatians says : "What the senseless sophists have taught respecting *fides formata* is mere idle talk. Therefore we

Luther's denial of "fides formata."

must beware of this doctrine and regard it as a very diabolical and hellish poison, and conclude with S. Paul that we are justified by faith only, and not *per fidem formatam caritate*. But to return to Luther's view of the Covenants.

Luther denied the existence of human goodness.

Luther denied all human goodness because at its best it is imperfect. This unScriptural and unreasonable heresy was expressed by him as follows : " Every work

of a righteous man is damnable and a mortal sin, if it
is judged by God's judgment." *("Omne opus justi
damnabile est, et peccatum mortale, si judicio Dei
judicetur."—Opera.* Tom. ii. 325-6.)

"The law was abolished, the whole law : moral as

Professor
Mozley on
Luther's theory
of Justification.

well as ceremonial—and had no place or
existence in the scheme of reconciliation.
Luther had answered his question how man
should be justified, and the difficulty of
absolute evil on man's part had a complete and
triumphant solution in the doctrine of absolute Imputation on God's. The righteousness of man, then, being
a simply *imputed* one in contrast with an *actual* state
of absolute sin, the next step in the Lutheran system
was to say that man individually appropriated that
righteousness to himself, or was individually justified,

Luther put the
conscience to
sleep.

when the idea of that imputed righteousness wholly expelled and effaced the sense
of that actual sin. *Let the conscience* (said
Luther) *sleep joyfully in Christ without the least sense
of the law of sin and death. Conduct thyself altogether
as though thou hadst never heard of the law of God.
Beyond and above the light of law and reason doth the
Gospel take us into the darkness of faith where the law
and reason have no business. Let the pious remember
that in conscience they are free before God from the
curse of the Law.* The meaning is, under every form
and turn of language, exactly the same. Our con-

Luther's Gnostic
Dualism.

science must be conscious alone of that
which it does not see in us—righteousness ; totally unconscious of that which
alone it does see in us—sin. Such are the two Lutheran
worlds, or natures of *utter* evil and *absolute* good ;
a perceptible and actual state of evil, an unperceived and
imputed state of good, whereof the latter must wholly
annihilate in idea and feeling the former in order for
the individual to be justified. The 'Law' and 'Christ,'
for these are respectively their two names, are antagonist

principles opposed to each other with the intensity and fierceness of the two principles in the Eastern Dualistic philosophies—two contraries in irreconcileable war with one another—and the triumph is when the former is destroyed. The 'Law' is *horror, blackness, quaking, pallor, sadness, and despair.* To this legislatorial principle *Christ* is the antagonistic. *Christus gigas potentissimus sustulit legem.* Christ does not legislate, but kills Law. He says to the Law, *Ego ligabo te : I will bind thee Captivity I will lead thee captive.*" (*Mozley's Essays*, vol. i. pp. 339-343.)

Bishop Moule's antithesis between the " Covenant of Works " and the "Covenant of Grace " is not expressed in Luther's unbalanced rhetoric. But it is Lutheran in its essence nevertheless. And we find him *totus Lutheranus* when he says, " Salvation is thus by faith ; that is to say, it is ours by personal *accepting trust.* The knot of the Covenant is actually tied from our view-point when the sinner, with eyes opened by the grace of God, *sees the Son, and believes on Him. . . .* Faith is the *empty hand* which receives the full Christ." (*English Church Teaching*, pp. 62-63.) This a plain declaration of the Lutheran " new teaching," as Bishop Ryle has aptly called it. It is an assertion that we are justified by Luther's *fiducia*, the *fides informis* of the " empty hand," the *fiducia* of " accepting trust." There is practically no doctrinal difference between Bishop Moule and Bishop Ryle upon Justification by Faith. Both hold the Lutheran doctrine which Bishop Ryle defended with Luther's vehemence of speech, whilst Bishop Moule reminds us more of the gentler methods of Melanchthon. But the same radical error is manifest in both of them, and Bishop Moule shows it plainly when he puts the Sacraments of the Gospel in a *subordinate position* to the Covenant of Grace instead of being its initiation and fulfilment in us. He says :

[Marginal notes:]

Bishop Moule's Lutheran views.

He upholds Luther's "new teaching" of Justification.

Bishop Moule asserts that "fiducia" justifies us.

He subordinates the Sacraments to the Covenant.

" It is a mistake to think of the Sacraments first and the Covenant after. Much mental and spiritual confusion may result. This let us avoid. Let us search God's Word first about His *Everlasting Covenant* of Peace, sealed with the Blood of the *great* Shepherd of the Sheep. Then shall we better understand the work of the precious Sacraments of Covenant Grace." (*English Church Teaching*, p. 64.)

This is an extraordinary theological *bouleversement.* He regards the If we regard the Sacraments of the Gospel Covenant apart from the Zwinglian-Calvinist view as the from its "seals." " Seals " of the " Covenant," and—to carry the simile further—regard the " Covenant " itself as a " Deed " or " Instrument " conferring salvation upon us, what sane person would accept a " document " *per se* as valid, till he had examined the " seals " which attest its reality and the genuineness of its signatures ? The genuineness of the " seals " is the sole guarantee that a document is what it purports to be. No one could prove a will which was not lawfully signed and sealed. This deposition of the Sacraments of the Gospel from Bishop Ryle's their rightful place is a grievous error, degradation of endorsed by Bishop Ryle who said, "We the Sacraments. refuse to admit that (the Sacraments) are the grand media between Christ and the soul, *above faith, above preaching, and above prayer."* (*Knots Untied*, p. 13.)

The only logical outcome of such teaching as this is the Quaker's denial of Sacraments *in toto.* Virtual It is necessary to notice here a book called "Quakerism." *The Catholic Faith : a Manual of Instruction for members of the Church of England,* by Dr. Griffith Dr. Griffith Thomas, which was published in 1904 Thomas on when the author was Principal of Wycliffe the "Catholic Hall, Oxford. The tone of the book reflects Faith." the scholarship and culture of the author, but he unhappily identifies himself with error by his recommendation of a list of books, which includes

Bishop Ryle's " Knots Untied " as well as " English Church Teaching." To recommend a book to students is to incur a definite responsibility for its teaching, especially when the man who so recommends it is the Principal of a Theological College. We are not surprised to find that Dr. Griffith Thomas is himself infected with Lutheran and Calvinistic errors. He is not so crude

His erroneous view of Original Sin.

in his own statements on the subject of " Original Sin " as the authors are whom he recommends, but his expressions, "*Sin changed man's nature into evil*"; "*Man lost God's image*," have a Lutheran taint, and in the teeth of the assertion in Gen. ix. 6, which Archbishop Trench rightly interprets as meaning that the " Image of God " (even if it be as on a coin defaced) is still to be attributed to fallen man, the absolute statement that " Man lost God's image " must be condemned as contrary to the Catholic Faith. Upon the question of

He teaches the Lutheran doctrine of Justification.

" Justification by Faith " Dr. Griffith Thomas is frankly Lutheran. His definition of Faith is that it is " personal *trust* in a person " (p. 30), which is Luther's *fiducia*. He gives an unscholarly and distorted meaning to Heb. xi. 6, which he only partially quotes. He says, " Not without real force then is the word, *he that cometh to God must believe*. Trust is the correlative of Truth "

He misinterprets, Hebrews xi. 6.

(p. 31). But the omission of the words " *that He is*," is fatal to a use of this passage as implying merely *fiducia*. Bishop Westcott gives us the sound interpretation that the text means, " belief (a) that God *is*, and (b) that He is morally active," in other words it is a Faith in the existence and in the moral government of God. (*Westcott on Hebrews*, p. 356.)

He avoids one Lutheran error by quoting Hooker's words : " God doth justify the believing man, not for the worthiness of his belief, but for His worthiness Who is believed." He says : " All that believe are justified. *Trust* implies our dependence on someone else, and the consequent cessation of dependence on ourselves. Faith is the correlative to promise. Trust responds to Truth " (p. 87).

These words imply that we are justified by the Lutheran " fiducia." " *Fides justificans—est fiducialis apprehensio Christi*," said Gerhard, one of Luther's ablest followers. (De Justif, 120.)

Dr. Griffith Thomas subsequently says : " The next distinctive principle of the Reformation was *the true spiritual access of the soul to God*, as indicated by the phrase ' Justification by Faith ' " (p. 344). Putting aside the unwelcome inference that the author may mean that there was no " *true spiritual access of the soul to God* " until Luther discovered it, and the consequent theory of Bishop Ryle and others that Christianity went to sleep at the death of the Apostles, and did not wake up till Luther roused it, we find that Dr. Griffith Thomas states categorically that " the Reformation position on Justification must also be maintained at all costs. Nothing is so potent in opposition to all sacerdotal claims as the insistence upon the direct access of the soul to God, based upon the acceptance of the righteousness which is of God by faith " (p. 356). The Catholic Church has never, at any period of her history, denied " *the direct access of the soul to God*." She is the visible Corporation which is called the Kingdom, the City, and the Body of Christ. It is a common controversial device to set up a fallacy which no thoughtful Christian would for one moment admit, and then proceed to demolish it with a great flourish of trumpets.

The Catholic Church is meant to bring souls into *direct access* to God. That is the meaning of the " Sacerdotium " of our Blessed Lord, as expressed in the Apostolic Ministry which He appointed, and which also finds its expression in " the Priesthood of the Laity."

His error on the " Access of the soul to God."

To fling empty phrases about, such as "the so-called Anglo-Catholic conception of the Church," and call it "a narrow and ignoble conception of the Body of Christ" (p. 366) ; to state fearlessly that "there is no function or office of the Christian priesthood that cannot be exercised by any and every individual believer in Christ of either sex, wherever and whatever they be," does not lead impartial critics to view Dr. Griffith Thomas as a Catholic theologian, or to regard his book as having any true claim to be called an exposition of the "Catholic Faith."

We may note here a distinct piece of evidence that the Edwardian Reformers were, for the most part, averse to the extreme view of the Lutheran heresy on Justification. They saw clearly that it had led to the Antinomian excesses of Luther's "left wing." The Anabaptists and their heresies were detested in England. An Apologist for Henry VIII. (quoted in *Dixon's History of the Church of England*, vol. ii. p. 161) State of religion says of the state of religion in England, in the reign of after the King had broken with the Papacy, Henry VIII. "How can any sane man call Englishmen heretics, or schismatics, or infidels ? Englishmen believe in the Creeds and in the Holy Scriptures. *They detest the Anabaptists and all other Sacramentarians.* His persecution They reverently solemnise the Holy of the Sacraments and all the laudable ceremonies. Anabaptists. They have daily Masses." In 1538 Philip of Hesse wrote to Henry VIII. asking him to persecute the Anabaptists as dangerous to the State. Henry was glad to show his "orthodoxy," and issued a Commission to that effect to Archbishop Cranmer and some of the Bishops, which resulted in two Anabaptists being burnt at Smithfield.

The word "Sacramentarians" was used to designate all who held and taught the "Real Absence" Sacrament- instead of the "Real Presence" in the arians. Holy Eucharist. The Edwardian Forty-two

Articles of 1553 condemn the Anabaptists by name, and the Thirty-nine Articles of 1571 condemn their doctrines. The Second Prayer Book of 1552, which touched the "high water" mark of "foreign Protestant" influence upon the English formularies, gives no countenance to the Antinomianism of such logical upholders of Luther's teaching on Justification as the Anabaptists, and his more immediate follower John Agricola. In addition to the Catholic teaching of the ancient Collects, the Reformers of 1552 put the significant text Ezekiel xviii. 27, as the first of the selected passages of Scripture which they for the first time introduced as prefatory to Matins and Evensong. The words, "*When the wicked man turneth away from his wickedness, which he hath committed, and doeth that which is lawful and right, he shall save his soul alive,*" would be as abhorrent to Luther as the Epistle of S. James. The "Evangelical" clergy of the nineteenth century for the most part made a point of omitting this text when they began Matins or Evensong. The writer very well remembers this omission being defended to him by an "Evangelical" Vicar, on the ground that to read it might mislead the congregation and cause them to disbelieve in "Justification by Faith only."

Second Prayer Book of 1552.

Text against Antinomians inserted.

Objection to Ezek. xviii. 17 by Evangelicals.

It is not necessary to examine the Calvinist "Confessions" in detail upon "Justification by Faith." Calvin's doctrine of "Irresistible Grace" and "Absolute Predestination" naturally obscured the crudeness of the Lutheran heresy on Justification. The "elect" only had saving faith, which, as the "Westminster Confession" says "*is no dead faith, but worketh by love.*" (Chap. xi.) But when the "Westminster Confession" says "that God did, from all eternity, decree to justify all the

Calvin's doctrine of Justification coloured by his theory of Predestination.

View of the Westminster Confession.

elect," and, further, that the elect " can never fall from the state of justification," we are in a different region of heresy from Luther's, although his assertion of the " slavery of the human will " was the origin of Calvinism, as Professor Mozley remarks. The Edwardian Reformers asserted the freedom of the will in their Ninth Article, and the title of our present Tenth Article is " De *libero* Arbitrio," a sharp contrast to Luther's Treatise " De *servo* Arbitrio." The " Necessary Doctrine," which represented the doctrinal standpoint of the English Church in 1543, and has never since been formally repudiated, teaches that " the power of man's free will hath need of a physician to heal it and an help to repair it," which is practically in accord with Article X.

The Edwardian Reformers assert Free Will.

They do not vary from the " Necessary Doctrine " of 1543.

It is unnecessary here to quote from the Calvinistic writings of the early Evangelicals or their successors. It is enough to state that Scott, the commentator, their chief scholar and divine, expressed his entire agreement with the Calvinistic " Articles of the Synod of Dort." (*Life*, p. 267.) But it must be remembered that a minority of the Evangelicals were, like Wesley, Arminians. The " Cumminsite " Eighteenth Article, "Of Election, Predestination and Free Will " is distinctly Arminian, and can be construed in a Catholic sense.

Calvinism of Scott and the early Evangelicals.

" Cumminsite " 18th Article Arminian.

It remains for us to examine the Lutheran theory of " Private Judgment." Luther founded his " new teaching " on Justification upon his own private judgment, apart from the two-fold witness of the Bible and the Church. He paid no respect to the teaching of the Undivided and Primitive Church, and, as has already been stated, he rejected the Epistle of S. James because he could not fit it in with his novel theory of " Solifidianism."

Lutheran theory of Private Judgment.

Professor Mozley ends his " Essay " on Luther with these significant words on Luther's heresy on Justification. " The Lutheran dogma, however, can only stand by the suppression of a large part of Scripture, and it seems reasonable to expect that any part of Scripture which is violently overborne must vindicate itself at last." (*Essays*, vol. i. p. 438.)

Professor Mozley on Luther's suppression of Scripture.

The Protestant doctrine of the " Right of Private Judgment " is the apotheosis of a wayward individualism.

The Catholic doctrine of Private Judgment involves the exercise of the reason and conscience, guided by the Spirit of God, to whom we pray that He may give us " *a right judgment in all things*," so that we may learn *whatsoever* our Lord *hath commanded* His Apostles and their successors, as the organs of the Teaching Body (which is His Church, Catholic and Visible) to set forth to the world as the authoritative Message of the One Faith of the One Gospel.

Catholic and Protestant doctrines of Private Judgment contrasted.

The Lutheran and Calvinistic assertions upon the unqualified " Right of Private Judgment " were based upon the individual conviction of both Luther and Calvin that they were *directly* commissioned by God to teach a new form of Christianity. In Luther's well-known " Letter to the Elector Frederic," he said that " *he had received his Gospel, not from men, but from Heaven alone—from Jesus Christ.*" Luther had been ordained Priest, although subsequently his ordination was supplanted in his mind by his extraordinary assertion of his individual Divine Mission. Calvin, who was never ordained at all, speaks of " *his ministerial office, which he doubts not was founded and sanctified by the vocation of God.*" (Calvin, *Opusc.*, p. 105.)

Luther and Calvin believed themselves directly commissioned from God.

There was, therefore, no room in the doctrinal system of these Reformers for the authority of the Church in interpreting the Holy Scriptures, and teaching the world " whatsoever our Lord has commanded."

This view abolished Church authority.

In 1541 the Conference at Ratisbon between Catholics
and Lutherans agreed on the statement that
"to the Church alone belongeth the interpret-
ation of Scripture." Luther could agree to
no such statement, but so accurate a writer
as Hallam believed that he did not carry his followers
to the extremes of his own teaching. "It
is often said that the essential principle
of Protestantism, and that for which the
struggle was made, was a perpetual freedom
from all authority in religious belief, or what goes by
the name of the right of *private judgment.* But to
look more nearly at what actually occurred, this per-
manent independence was not much asserted and still
less acted upon." (Hallam, *Literature of Europe*, p. 521.)

The Ratisbon Conference vindicated Church Authority.

Hallam believes that Lutherans did not reject Church author- ity as Luther did.

Whatever may be thought of Hallam's accuracy with
regard to the Continental Reformation there is no doubt
that his words are true with regard to the position of
the Anglican Articles on this subject. Article XX., "Of
the Authority of the Church" is most
explicit in its teaching. Bishop Gibson
divides its statements as follows (p. 524):—

Article XX. on Church Authority.

The Legislative Power.   *The Judicial Authority.*

The Church hath

i. *Power to decree Rites or Ceremonies,*	ii. *Authority in controver- sies of faith.*

And yet it is not lawful for the Church

i (a) to ordain anything contrary to God's word written.	ii (a) neither may it so ex- pound one place of Scripture that it be repugnant to another.

Wherefore, although the Church be a Witness
and a Keeper of Holy Writ

yet as

i (b) it ought not to decree anything against the same	so, besides the same ought it not to enforce anything to be believed for necessity of salvation.

This teaching is that of Archbishop Bramhall, who
said : " I do implicitly and in the preparation
Archbishop   of my mind, submit myself to the true
Bramhall's view
Catholic Church, the Spouse of Christ, the
Mother of the Saints, the Pillar of Truth. And seeing my
adherence is firmer to the Infallible Rule of Faith—
that is the Holy Scriptures interpreted by the Catholic
Church—than to mine own *private judgment* or opinions,
although I should unwittingly fall into an error, yet
this cordial submission is an implicit retractation
thereof, and I am confident will be so accepted by the
Father of Mercies, both from me and all others who
seriously and sincerely do seek after peace and truth."
(Bramhall : *Works*, p. 141.)

The Anglican Article distinctly affirms that the Church
Catholic has authority, not merely *weight* or
Church author-   *influence*, but *authority*, in Archbishop
ity not merely
weight or   Bramhall's sense, in controversies of faith.
influence.
But this authority is conditioned in its
sphere and exercise by the parallel authority of the
Holy Scriptures. Whilst still in communion
Dr. Döllinger's with Rome, Dr. Döllinger wrote as follows
view.
on this subject : " We must maintain in
accordance with the frequently repeated testimony of
the Fathers and other writers of the Ancient Church,
that there is no point of Christian doctrine which is not
attested and laid down in the Apostolic Writings. The
Church cannot and dare not receive any teaching which
does not find its justification in the Bible, and is not
contained somewhere in the New Testament in a more
or less developed form, or at least indicated and implied
in premises of which it is the logical sequel, and thus
shown to fit into the harmony and organic whole of
Christian doctrine." (Döllinger, *First Age of the
Church*, ii. chap. i. p. 152.)

The Church has interpreted the Bible (a) by her
Creeds, (b) by her Liturgies, whereby her *Lex
orandi* shows forth her *Norma credendi* ; and (c) by

her yearly round of Festival and Fast—the balanced
teaching of the "Christian year"—and by
the decisions of her "*Œcumenical*" (not
"General") Councils which have won the
after-recognition of Christendom, as formu-
lating Scriptural doctrine. These decisions
constitute the formal expression of the
Judgment of the Catholic Church, and, in the words
of Sir W. Palmer, "such a judgment is irrevocable,
irreformable, never to be altered." (*Treatise on the
Church*, vol. ii. p. 114.)

The irreform-able judgment of the Catholic Church.

Sir W. Palmer on Church Authority.

The assertion that every individual Christian "has a
right to judge *for himself,* by the word of
God, whether that which is put before him
as religious truth, is God's Truth or not"
(Bishop Ryle, *Knots Untied*, p. 54) virtually makes
every individual Christian into a private and personal
"Œcumenical Council," whose decisions affect himself
only, and cannot affect others. Where every individual
Christian becomes in this fashion his own *Judex
ordinarius* in controversies of faith, the obvious result
is religious chaos and anarchy. *Quot homines tot
sententiæ.* Bishop Ryle had thec andour to admit this
consequence of his unbalanced assertion of the "*right
of private judgment.*" "Grant for a moment," he said,
"that private judgment has led to divisions,
and brought about varieties. Give me Protestant divisions, certainly, rather than
Popish Unity." (*Knots Untied*, p. 63.)

Bishop Ryle denies Church Authority.

He owned that Private Judg-ment causes divisions.

We pass by this illogical and impossible antithesis
with the remark that, granting the Bishop's premises,
two *wrongs* do not make a *right.*

The Bishop curiously misapplied S. Paul's "Prove
all things" (I. Thess. v. 21). This cannot,
from the context, be applied to the individualism of private judgment in *proving*
and *judging* the central truths which our Lord commanded His Church to *teach with authority.* Its true

He misapplied S. Paul's "Prove all things."

parallel is S. John's direction to test or *prove* the teaching of those who claimed to be "spiritual" teachers by the test of the central truth of the Incarnation (I. S. John, iv). We must use our private judgment to examine whether the teachers are teaching in accordance with the "faith once delivered to the Saints," but neither passage authorises an individual Christian to oppose his private judgment to the Catholic Faith, as taught by our Lord to the Catholic Church. Bishop Ryle deliberately denied all this, and quoted S. Paul's words as prescribing unlimited private judgment. "S. Paul says 'Prove all things.' He does not say, *Whatsoever the Universal Church pronounces true, that you are to hold*. No! he says, 'Prove all things'" . . . Will our erring in company with the Church remove our responsibility for our own souls? Surely it is a thousand times better for a man to stand alone and be saved, than err in company with the Church and be lost." (*Knots Untied*, pp. 55-58.)

And denied the Authority of the Universal Church.

These assertions of the late Bishop of Liverpool are in direct conflict with the doctrine of Article XX. and of Article XXXIV., which directly forbids the abuse of "Private Judgment." But they are in direct accord with the "Cumminsite" Article XXIII., "*Of the authority of General Councils*," in which the words occur, "No law or authority can override individual responsibility, and therefore *the right of private judgment*. For the individual Christian . . . is to be judged by the Word." Dr. Griffith Thomas has made himself responsible for Bishop Ryle's teaching. But his own is practically the same, although he avoids crudities of diction. He says that "the Church *has power to decree rites or ceremonies*. In controversies of Faith, however, it is to be noticed that the Church has not this full legal right, but *authority* (*auctoritas*), which means moral

Bishop Ryle in accord with "Cumminsite" Article XXIII.

Dr. Griffith Thomas holds the same view.

authority, arising out of the testimony of the Church as a whole, throughout the ages. *The ultimate* Court of Appeal must of necessity be the spiritually enlightened judgment of the individual Christian, with regard to any and every matter of truth and conscience." *(The Catholic Faith*, p. 319.)

The "individual Christian," according to Dr. Griffith Thomas, is the judge of "any and every matter of truth and conscience." He must not believe in the Incarnation and the Trinity, or the other facts of our Lord's teaching as revealed in the Creeds without exercising his "private judgment" upon them. Dr. Griffith Thomas raises a futile logomachy in his distinction between *jus* and *auctoritas* The verbal distinction exists, but it will not carry with any unprejudiced scholar the undue weight he puts upon it. And he ignores the fact that the Catholic Church is "the Body of Christ," as the "*cœtus fidelium*"; and that therefore the "teaching authority" of the Church is, in fact, the "teaching authority" of our Lord Himself, Who is with His Church "all the days," that she may continue to teach *whatsoever He has commanded* her to teach.

He raises a futile distinction between jus and auctoritas.

The teaching Authority of the Church is the Authority of our Lord.

Bishop Drury (in *English Church Teaching*, p. 163) says: "We uphold most fully the right or rather the duty of *private judgment*, i.e. that every man must believe and do what his conscience ultimately tells him is right and true."

Bishop Drury not in accordance with Article XX.

But the Bishop says nothing about the necessity of the guidance of the individual conscience by authority. He hints at it when he says that "the Church, as a visible body, declared that there were certain lines on either side of which lay not *truth*, but *heresy*." His statements are less objectionable than those of Dr. Griffith Thomas and the late Bishop Ryle, but they are not in accordance with Article XX., and curiously

7

resemble the tone of the " Cumminsite " Article XXIII.

It is impossible to avoid the conclusion that the writers whose utterances we have been criticising are in accord with " foreign Protestant " error upon the subject of *Private Judgment,* and that their erroneous views on this important matter have influenced the faction of militant and disloyal Protestants in the Anglican Communion. Certain of these writers are in open or covert sympathy with that strange un-

The Evangelical Alliance based on foreign Protestant errors.

denominational union, which was formed in 1846 under the title of the "Evangelical Alliance." It put forth Nine Articles of Doctrine as its basis. The first asserts the " Inspiration, Authority, and Sufficiency, of the Holy Scriptures."

The second Article is purely Lutheran, and asserts, without any qualification, "*the right and duty of Private Judgment* in the interpretation of the Holy Scriptures." The fourth Article is also Lutheran and Calvinist in its assertion of "*the utter depravity of human nature* in consequence of the Fall." The sixth Article is a bare assertion of Lutheran " Solifidianism," and maintains absolutely "the Justification of the sinner by Faith alone." Bishop Moule was at one time a member of this " Evangelical Alliance." Quite apart from its impracticable basis of unity, it is absolutely in accord with the main errors of " foreign Protestantism," and no loyal Anglican who accepts the plain teaching of the Prayer Book and Articles, could join such a society as this without forfeiting his claim to be considered logical and consistent in his Churchmanship.

CHAPTER III.

THE DOCTRINAL ERRORS OF FOREIGN PROTESTANTISM ON
THE SACRAMENTS, CONSIDERED WITH REFERENCE TO
THE TRUE TEACHING OF THE ENGLISH CHURCH
UPON THE SACRAMENTS IN GENERAL, AND HOLY
BAPTISM IN PARTICULAR.

WE have already seen that the Conference at

Luther, Zwingli and Calvin equally in error on the Sacraments.

Marburg in 1539 resulted in mutual recriminations between Luther and Zwingli, and a final "parting of the ways" between the Lutherans and the Swiss Reformers. At the outset it is necessary to observe that Luther's doctrine of "Consubstantiation" is, in its practical issues, as heretical as Zwingli's "Real Absence," and it is impossible to consider Calvin's figment of a "Virtual Presence" as being any nearer to the true teaching of the Catholic Church than Zwingli's "Real Absence." The Lutheran and Swiss Reformers were also at variance upon the doctrine of the Sacraments

The Catholic doctrine of the Sacraments.

in general, which must now be considered in its Catholic aspect. The Sacraments are objective channels of grace, and "certificated points of contact" with the Incarnate Life of Jesus Christ our Lord, whereby, through the operation of the Holy Spirit, we are made living branches of the True Vine, and sanctified, that the life, then given, may abide in us. This is the Sacramental teaching of the Prayer Book and Articles of the Church

Article XXV. denies the heresy of Zwingli.

of England. Article XXV. begins by stating, in opposition to Zwinglianism, that "Sacraments ordained" of Christ be not only badges or tokens of Christian men's profession *(non tantum sunt notæ professionis Christianæ).* This is a direct contradiction of Zwingli's words : " *Sacraments therefore are badges or ceremonies, with which a man proves himself to the Church that he is either a candidate, or a soldier of Christ.*" *(De vera false relig..* ii. 198.)

The view of so moderate an Anglican as the late Bishop Harold Browne upon Zwinglianism is worth recording. He says : "Zwinglius rejected sacramental grace entirely. He held Sacraments to be *bare signs,* outward tokens of Christian profession, but in no sense means of grace. He defined a Sacrament to be *an external symbol, by which we testify what we are, and what is our duty, just as one who bears a national badge testifies that he belongs to a particular nation. (Sacramentum ergo . . . symbolum externum, quo quales simus et quodnam sit officium testamur, significat,* etc.—Zwingli, *De Baptismo,* Op. i. 60.)

And again : " A Sacrament is the sign of a sacred thing ; when therefore I speak of the Sacrament of Christ's Body, I mean no more than that bread which is the figure and type of Christ's Body (dead for us). *(Cum ergo Sacramentum Corporis Christi nomino, non quicquam aliud, quam panem, qui Corporis Christi pro nobis mortui figura et typus est, intelligo.*" (Zwingli *De Cæna Domini.* Tom. i., 274). (Bishop Harold Browne on the *Articles,* p. 594.)

Here we have, in all its un-Scriptural crudity of assertion, the Zwinglian doctrine of the " Real Absence" which Archbishop Temple declared to be inadmissible in the Church of England. As to the Sacraments in general, Zwingli says : " I believe, yea, I *know,* that all Sacraments are *so far from conferring* grace that they *bring* nothing with them and *dispense* nothing." (Zwingli, in

Niemayer's *Collectio Confessionum*, p. 24.) Article
XXV. further calls the Sacraments " *certain*
sure witnesses and effectual signs of grace
and God's good will towards us."

Article XXV. on
"effectual signs."

Dr. Griffith Thomas says that " they are *effectual as
signs*. The Sacraments are thus effectual or efficacious
pledges or seals of grace, for the idea of a sign
(signum) is not that of a channel or pipe. Baptism
and the Lord's Supper are *pictures of grace.*" *(The
Catholic Faith*, pp. 590-591.) This is the view of
Calvin, who says : "Baptism testifies that we *have
been* cleansed and washed ; the Eucharistic Supper that
we *have been* redeemed " *(Inst.* iv. xiv. 22). And
Dr. Griffith Thomas makes Calvin's error
his own by the words " the Sacraments *are
the signs and seals of a transaction already
accomplished* " (Ib. p. 155). It is manifestly
impossible to harmonise such teaching as this with
the Anglican formularies.

Dr. Griffith
Thomas agrees
with Calvin on
the Sacraments.

Bishop Moule agrees with Dr. Griffith Thomas in
his view that the Sacraments are mere
" seals." He says that "the original source
of the possessions is *not* in the seals.
They are, to the spiritual promises of the Gospel,
what the Great Seal is to the royal will, expressed in
a royal patent." *(English Church Teaching*, p. 90.)
It is not easy to reconcile Bishop Moule
with himself. He proceeds : " We may say
that the Holy Sacraments have, as their
work, *not the pouring in of Divine Life, as if they were
pipes*, but the confirming the covenant promise and
our possession of it as seals." (Ib. p. 96.)

Bishop Moule
holds them to
be mere "seals."

And denies
that they convey
grace.

According to Bishop Moule the Sacraments do not
convey or *impart* grace. Under no circumstances are
they the "channels of grace." They do not pour into
us Divine Life. They are *not*, what the
Article calls them, "effectual signs of
grace." This phrase of the Article was

Luther denied
that they were
efficacia signa

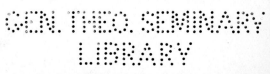

intended to contradict Luther's denial that the Sacraments were *signa efficacia gratiæ* (cf. *Gibson on Articles* p. 591). It was also intended to contradict Melanchthon's words: "Circumcision is nothing; so is baptism nothing; the communion of the Lord's Supper is nothing; they are rather testimonies and *seals* of the Divine Will." (Vide Möehler's *Symbolik*, p. 208.)

So did Melanchthon.

Bishop Ryle stated the same doctrine as Bishop Moule in more forcible terms: "Men sometimes say it makes no difference whether we think all baptised persons are regenerate or not. I see fresh reason for dreading the doctrine that all baptised persons are regenerate. I see it ultimately producing in some minds a mere *Sacramental Christianity*—a Christianity in which there is much said about union with Christ, but it is a union begun only in baptism, and kept up only by the Lord's Supper, a Christianity in which Christ has not His rightful office, and faith has not its rightful place." *(Knots Untied*, pp. 186-187.)

Bishop Ryle held the same error.

How this teaching can be reconciled with Bible truth is a question beyond the capacity of any Christian who reads S. Paul's Epistles, and believes them to be of doctrinal authority. Bishop Ryle evidently held, with Dr. Griffith Thomas, that the Sacraments are "seals of a *transaction already accomplished*." Behind all this teaching lies Calvinism, as well as Zwinglianism. The "transaction already accomplished," apart from the Sacraments, is the election of certain persons to accept Christ by a justifying faith in Luther's sense. Grace, full and direct, is given to these persons *because* they believe, and this grace is *irresistible* and *indefectible*. Its consequence is the *final perseverance* of the believer unto life eternal. There is no room in this system for Sacraments as *effectual signs of grace*. The salvation of the believer

This error flows from the Calvinistic doctrine of Election and Indefectible Grace.

is a *transaction already accomplished*, and there is no need of Sacraments to convey grace to a person already furnished with *grace indefectible*.

Foreign Protestant theology was compelled, *malgré lui*, to find some subordinate position in its system for the Sacraments, because Sacraments have Scriptural authority, and, as Chillingworth said, " The Bible, and the Bible only, is the religion of Protestants." But the position of Sacraments must necessarily be so subordinate that it is practically a nullity. A recent writer on German " reduced Christianity "(the outcome of the creedlessness begotten of the German school of Biblical criticism) says : " When Luther broke away from the Church instead of reforming it, he founded a body with no Orders and no Apostolic authority. In a body with no Orders, Sacraments lose their meaning. When Sacraments lose their meaning, the Incarnation stands isolated. A purely human Church, with merely commemorative institutions, logically predisposes men to see only a purely human Christ. And that is all the leading Lutheran theologians are able to see."

[margin: Subordinate position of the Sacraments in the foreign Protestant system.]

Bishop Ryle showed his true position when he said : " I take occasion to say that I view with strong dislike the modern practice of substituting the Lord's Supper for a sermon at Episcopal and Archidiaconal Visitations. The thing has a very suspicious and unsatisfactory appearance. Preaching the Word, in my judgment, is a far more important ordinance than the Lord's Supper. The subject is one about which Evangelical Churchmen should be on their guard. This studied attempt to thrust in the Lord's Supper on all occasions has a most unfortunate tendency to make men remember the Popish Mass." *(Knots Untied*, p. 215.)

[margin: Bishop Ryle sets preaching before the Holy Eucharist as being more important.]

It is difficult to characterise such language as this without descending to its peculiar polemical level.

The Holy Eucharist in the Roman, the Eastern, and the Anglican Church is the " Lord's own Service," the central act of worship which is the one Service of obligation, not only for priests and laity meeting on special occasions, but for all Christian people. The attempt to exalt " preaching" as " a more important ordinance " than the Holy Eucharist is an impossible position for any loyal Anglican to take up who reads his Bible and desires to abide by our Prayer Book and Articles.

Bishop Ryle said : " The grace, faith, and holiness of many Quakers are beyond all question. . . .

Bishop Ryle on Quakers.

Would God that many baptised Christians were like them ! I can only suppose that God allows the Quakers to be a perpetual testimony against Romish views of *water-baptism*, and a standing witness to the Churches that God can, in some cases, give grace without the use of any sacraments at all ! " (*Knots Untied*, p. 108.)

The Holy Catholic Church, in its accredited teaching, is a sure witness to the truth that *Deus non alligatur Mediis*, for, if this were not so, we should be compelled to deny grace to the separated communities of Christians who have no valid Orders, for, with the exception of the lay-baptism which they validly administer, they are in the same position as the Quakers. But the Church has never denied the freedom of God's grace in its overflow beyond and outside of its certified Sacramental channels, and Bishop Ryle is asserting a truism of Catholic theology unconsciously, whilst he is assuming that Quakerism has a divine mission to preserve us from attaching their true Scriptural value to the Sacraments—a value which he does not accept.

Bishop Moule has raised a curious point with regard to the Catechism definition of a Sacrament.

Bishop Moule on " grace given unto us " in the words of the Catechism.

On p. 93 of *English Church Teaching* he gravely informs us that the " comma " inserted in the " Book Annexed " after the word "grace," changes the usual and obvious meaning of the definition. The words in the " Book annexed to the Act of Uniformity " in 1662 run thus : "*An outward and visible sign of an inward and spiritual grace, given unto us, ordained by Christ Himself*," etc.

According to Bishop Moule the " comma " after " grace " shows that the " sign " is given unto us, but *not* the "grace." The "comma" is made to bear a very heavy burden. It carries Zwinglianism on its back. But unfortunately for Bishop Moule, Canon Bright's letters on the " comma " in the *Guardian*, in September, 1891, show conclusively that " no certain conclusion can be drawn from the punctuation of that date, and the early translations of the Catechism support the view which is here expressed. It is the ' grace ' which is ' given,' and the ' sign ' which is ordained." (Robinson on the *Church Catechism*, p. 139.)

The burden of a " comma."

Dr. Bright's common-sense view of this " comma."

Dr. Griffith Thomas here agrees with Dr. A. W. Robinson in omitting the " comma," as all modern editions of the Prayer Book do, and founding his argument that " grace " is not " given unto us " through the " sign " upon other premises. He uses the ambiguous phrase " the conditional efficacy " of the Sacraments (p. 356) by which, apparently, he does not mean that the *matter* and *form* alone, and in certain Sacraments, the *minister*, must be valid, but that " they are beautifully simple, as *emblems* and *pledges* of the Love of God in Christ " (p. 161). How an " *emblem* " or " *pledge* " can give " conditional blessings " is a curious exercise in metaphysics. He uses the illustration of the " Brazen Serpent " (p. 158) for his " Emblem " theory of the Sacraments. But there was no " conditional " blessing in that history, unless to *look* was a condition, which would bring Dr. Griffith Thomas within a measurable distance

Dr. Griffith Thomas calls the Sacraments " emblems.'

His mistaken analogy of the "brazen serpent."

of Eucharistic Adoration. The blessing conveyed by
the sight of the " Brazen Serpent " was positive and
instantaneous. The " emblem " was the channel of
healing grace.

We have already noticed the fact that the Calvinistic
theory of Election, with its accompanying
heresies on the subject of " Irresistible
Grace " and " Final Perseverance," must
necessarily involve the rejection of the
Catholic Doctrine of the Sacraments.

*Calvinistic
heresy of "Inde-
fectible Grace"
incompatible
with the Catholic
Doctrine of the
Sacraments.*

The *objective* character of Sacramental grace cannot
be made to fit in with a theory that confines the grace
of the Sacraments to those who are predestined to
" final perseverance." To persons thus *absolutely*
saved beyond the possibility of falling, Sacraments are
useless. They do not need them, and they only tolerate
them as graceful pieces of symbolism.

Article XXV. contradicts this " foreign Protestant "
theology. The Elizabethan Reformers
were very seriously tainted with it. But
they were Englishmen, and therefore
illogical. Half the nation clung to the
ancient Faith, and the Articles were drafted so as not
to offend them unnecessarily.

*Article XXV.
denies the
Calvinistic view
of Sacraments*

This Article gives us the Catholic Faith in the
phraseology of the Reformation. It does
not deny the title " Sacrament " to the
" Lesser Sacraments," and the Homilies
directly call Marriage " a Sacrament," and
of Holy Orders, they use the remarkable phrase
" neither *it*, nor any *other* Sacrament else be such
Sacraments as Baptism and Communion are," which
is of course what all Catholics believe. (Forbes on
Articles, p. 451.) There is a wide difference between
Calvin's rejection of the " Five *falsely named* "
Sacraments (*Inst.* iv. n. 19), and our Article's
judicious phrase, " Those five *commonly called*

*It admits the
Five " com-
monly called "
Sacraments.*

Sacraments." It is an apt illustration of the inherent

desire of the English Reformers to stand by the ancient definitions in contrast to Calvin's fierce repudiation of them. It may be noted here that Dr. Griffith Thomas says : " The other five ceremonies or rites mentioned in the Article, are *not* to be called Sacraments." (*The Catholic Faith*, p. 159.) *English Church Teaching* (p. 261) has the phrase " the five *so-called* Sacraments." Both these statements are in line with Calvin's " falsely named " Sacraments, and are virtual denials of our Article's careful phrase "commonly called " Sacraments.

There is no space to deal fully with Calvinist and Lutheran errors on the " Lesser Sacraments." We have already mentioned the Lutheran denial of the Sacrament of Marriage, and we shall have to touch upon foreign Protestant heresies on Confirmation and Ordination. Behind every form of these errors lies the denial that the Sacraments are channels of grace *per se*. This truth was expressed by the phrase that the Sacraments convey a special grace to us from our Lord "*ex opere operato*," or in other words *objectively*,

as a direct consequence of their being administered and received, *according to Christ's Will and Ordinance*. Luther and Calvin, for reasons before mentioned, attacked the Catholic doctrine of the " *opus operatum* " with a fierce vehemence. As usual they invented a parody of the Catholic doctrine which they readily demolished. They said that the Catholic doctrine meant that the Sacraments worked mechanically, like a *charm*, quite apart from the dispositions of the recipients. And having invented this parody, the Augsburg Confession (Article XIII.) solemnly proceeds to demolish it by stating that *faith*

is required in the use of Sacraments, and condemning those who teach that sacraments justify *ex opere operato*, or *objectively*.

Bellarmine well says of the Sacraments that "Good Will, Faith, and Repentance, are necessarily required of an adult recipient." (*De Sacram*, iii. p. 108.)

All that Catholic theology says is that the Sacraments confer grace on those who do not put a *bar* in the way of its reception by their own lack of Repentance and Faith.   Here is the warrant for the spiritual regeneration of infants in Holy Baptism in *every case*.   They cannot, in their morally unconscious state, put a bar (*ponere obiicem*) in the way of the Gift of the Holy Ghost whereby they are born again, as members of Christ.

Infants cannot put a bar in the way of baptismal grace.

The original Edwardian Article of 1553 contained this Lutheran denunciation of the "*opus operatum*," in the words "*and yet that* (grace of Sacraments), not of the work wrought (*ex opere operato*) as some men speak," etc.   This very phrase re-appears in the "Cumminsite" Article XXV.   "And in such only as worthily receive Baptism and the Lord's Supper are they of Spiritual benefit, *and yet not that of the work wrought* (*ex opere operato*), as some men speak."   This re-insertion by Bishop Cummins of the phrase, discarded by the Elizabethan Reformers, is in itself significant testimony of his separation from the teaching of Article XXV. in its present form.   The Elizabethan Reformers, in pursuance of their policy of comprehension, deliberately struck out of Article XXV. the words which condemned the phrase "*opus operatum*," as describing the *objective* grace of the Sacraments.   No loyal Anglican at the present day can condemn the phrase that the Sacraments convey grace *ex opere operato*.   But Bishop Ryle, who set the Articles above the Prayer Book, condemned the phrase over and over again, because of his rejection of the fact that the Sacraments *convey* grace.   Bishop Moule says that the view that "infants are

Condemnation of *opus operatum* in original form of Article XXV. subsequently struck out.

Denial of Baptismal Regeneration by Bishop Ryle and Bishop Moule.

baptised, because they cannot resist the grace of God"
is "a theory of human thought," and that a child,
"baptismally regenerated," needs to be "*actually*
regenerated." "The infant," he says, "who in sacramental title *is* born again, still *needs* to be born
again." (*English Church Teaching*, pp. 103, 104.)

On p. 106, the Bishop's subjective view of Sacra-
Bishop Moule denies Rubric asserting the Salvation of baptised infants. ments leads him to say that the salvation
of *baptised* infants who die in infancy is
uncertain. He cannot accept the Rubric
which says "it is *certain* by God's Word
that children which are baptised, dying before they
commit actual sin, are undoubtedly saved." This
clear declaration of the "work wrought" (*opus
operatum*) in Baptism cannot be reconciled with Protestant Theology. Bishop Moule evades the plain
meaning of the Rubric, and Dr. Griffith Thomas, who
cannot fit it in with his theory that the Sacraments
Dr. Griffith Thomas makes a wrong statement on the original form of this Rubric. do not convey grace, makes the extraordi-
narily inaccurate statement "that the
original form of words had this significant
addition *and if otherwise not.* This clearly
shows that the mere administration of the
Ordinance is not to be regarded as a guarantee of grace."
(*Catholic Faith*, p. 286.) "As Head of a Theological
College, Dr. Griffith Thomas ought not to have made
such a blunder as to state that the "original form of
the words" in our Rubric contained the words "and
if otherwise not." The Rubric of 1549 says: "It is
certain by God's word that children being baptised (if
they depart out of this life in their infancy) are
undoubtedly saved." The words "*and if otherwise
not*," are not to be found in any Anglican formulary,
and Dr. Thomas ought to have known this. It is true
that a denial of the salvation of unbaptised infants
appeared in the "Ten Articles" of 1536, but this
denial never appeared in the Prayer Book, and even if

it had, the futility of founding an argument upon
it that the Sacrament of Baptism "is
not to be regarded as a guarantee of grace"
is self-evident. It is interesting to compare
Bishop Ryle's denial of the "grace given" in Baptism
with the language of the "Confession" of the Quakers,
published in 1675, which is still the official representa-
tion of their opinions. The twelfth Article of this
Quaker document says: "As there is one
Lord, and one Faith, so there is one
Baptism, which is not the putting away of
the filth of the flesh, but the answer of a
good conscience before God . . . And this
baptism is a pure and spiritual thing . . . of which
the baptism of John was a figure, which was commanded for a time, and not to continue for ever."
And on this basis the Quakers reject "water baptism."
Bishop Ryle accepts it, but evacuates it of any real
sacramental efficacy. He says: "Above all I find
S. Peter telling us expressly that the baptism which
saves and whereby we are buried with Christ . . . is
not *water baptism* only, whether infant or adult. It is
not the putting away the filth of the flesh, but the
answer of a good conscience. *(Knots Untied*, p. 160.)

Marginal notes:
And founds a false argument upon it against Baptismal grace.

Bishop Ryle's view of water baptism compared with Article XII. of the Quaker Confession of Faith.

Again the Bishop said: "We must beware of
making an idol of baptism. Many in the
present day exalt baptism to a position
which nothing in Scripture can possibly
justify. If they hold infant baptism they
will tell you that the grace of the Holy Ghost
invariably accompanies the administration of the
ordinance—that in every case a seed of Divine Life is
implanted in the heart to which all subsequent religious
movement must be traced—and that all baptised
children are, as a matter of course, born again and
made partakers of the Holy Ghost!" (Ib., p. 126).

Marginal note:
Bishop Ryle on making "an Idol of Baptism."

The Bishop said that "*nothing in Scripture could
possibly justify*" this simple statement of fact. This

is the deliberate language of a Bishop of the Church of England who had undertaken personally to uphold the teaching of the Prayer Book and Articles of the Church of England, and to require the same adhesion from those whom he ordained to her ministry. The Quaker denial of "water baptism" is more consistent and logical than Bishop Ryle's illogical retention of the otiose ceremony of a "water baptism" incapable of conveying grace to all who do not put a bar in the way of its reception. There is nothing to choose between his denial of baptismal grace and Dr. Colenso's assertion that there is no *inherent* spiritual difference between a baptised and an unbaptised person. In his "Commentary on the Romans" (p. 114) Dr. Colenso said:

Quakerism more logical than Bishop Ryle's view.

Bishop Ryle, Bishop Moule, and Dr. Griffith Thomas repeat Dr. Colenso's heresy on Baptism.

"We have already died unto sin and risen again unto righteousness *in our very birth hour* by that mysterious union with Christ *which we all enjoy as members of the great human family.*" Dr. Griffith Thomas teaches this same error (*The Catholic Faith*, p. 296). Dr. Colenso's premises may have differed from those of Dr. Thomas and Bishop Ryle, but the result at which they all arrived is the same, namely, that Baptism, as a Sacrament, does not necessarily convey grace to every one who does not "put a bar" in the way of its reception. This heresy of Dr. Colenso was condemned *eo nomine* by Bishop Gray's judgment. Charge iii. against him was "that Dr. Colenso denied that the Sacraments of Baptism and the Holy Communion *conveyed any special grace,* and that he also denied that they were generally necessary to salvation." The judgment condemned him on this charge (that the Sacraments do not *convey grace*) and said that he contradicted the express teaching of the "Church Catechism, the Offices for Baptism and Confirmation, and Articles XXV., XXVI.,

Dr. Colenso's heresy on Baptism formally condemned in the Colenso Judgment.

XXVII. and XXVIII." This judgment is binding upon
the South African Church, and was also accepted by
the Convocation of Canterbury, the American Church,
and the Colonial Churches. It is the *canonical* and
legal condemnation of Zwinglianism, just as Archbishop Temple's " Charge" was the official condemnation of the same heresy on the personal responsibility
of the Primate of All England.

Bishop Moule's language is more cautious than
Bishop Ryle's. But he teaches the same
doctrine. We have already seen and noted
his " Zwinglian comma." He says of Holy
Baptism *"that its place in the New
Testament is not primary."* He also

Bishop Moule
denies the
primary place
of Baptism in
the New
Testament.

denies that the blessing of Holy Baptism is "the
infusion of a Divine Humanity," and he denies that
Scripture teaches that Baptism *applies to us* the
Incarnation. He explains away the words, "As many
of you as have been baptised into Christ have put on
Christ " (Gal. iii. 27). He says : " Christ is savingly
applied to man in the inmost reality, *not by any rite*,
but by the inward working of the Holy Ghost." He
says (of Titus iii. 5) that " Christian Baptism is *called
the Bath of Regeneration* ; not necessarily the Bath
which *causes* Regeneration, but the Bath which signifies
and *seals* it." *(English Church Teaching*, pp. 98-100.)

Bishop Moule here teaches a curious mixture of
Quakerism and the " obsignatory view" of the Sacraments. His words " not by any rite " would be accepted
by Quakers, and cannot be forced into agreement with
the Catechism answer: " In my Baptism, wherein
I was made a member of Christ, a child of God, and
an inheritor of the Kingdom of Heaven."
Dr. Griffith Thomas says that the Reformers " did not hesitate to speak of
the baptised as *sacramentally* regenerate,
without expressing any opinion as to their

Dr. Griffith
Thomas declares
that the Regen-
eration of
Infants is
" hypothetical."

being *really* regenerate." *(The Catholic Faith*, p. 287.)

He holds, with Bishop Ryle, that the language of the Baptismal Office is not to be taken literally but *hypothetically*, so that when the declaration is made that " *this child is regenerate*," the real meaning is that it is *possibly or probably* regenerate. This *hypothetical* or *conditional* interpretation of the Baptismal Office is sheer Calvinism. Bishop Ryle calls it "the great principle upon which the whole Prayer Book is drawn up" (Ib., p. 164). And then his Calvinism has free play. He says that the Church's "ministers cannot see *the book of God's Election*. They cannot read the hearts of parents and sponsors. They can never say of any individual child, *This child is certainly receiving baptism unworthily*. And this being the case the Church assumes hopefully of each child that it receives baptism worthily, and uses language accordingly" (Ib., p. 166). Dr. Griffith Thomas agrees with Bishop Ryle. He makes much of the fact that Bucer did not object in 1552 to the words "Seeing now that this child is regenerate," and quotes Canon Barnes Lawrence's statement that the Church after the Reformation was Calvinistic, and that the Calvinistic view of the Baptismal Office was "dominant and authoritative, and it was the *hypothetical* interpretation." Bucer's share in the bigamy of Philip of Hesse, which has been mentioned in a previous chapter, does not conduce to a high estimate of his judgment on any matter concerning religion, and the strength of the Calvinistic party, before Archbishop Bancroft disabled it at the beginning of the seventeenth century, is considerably overstated. But this speciously dishonest *hypothetical* view shall be confuted by the words of Canon H. Melvill, who is claimed as a genuine Evangelical leader in Balleine's " *History of the Evangelical Party* " (p. 197). He is there called "the Evangelical Chrysostom," and

Bishop Ryle asserts the Calvinistic view of the Baptismal office.

Dr. Griffith Thomas asserts the same view.

Canon Melvill the "Evangelical Chrysostom" denies the "hypothetical view" as dishonest.

he wrote in the early " forties," just when the controversy on Baptismal Regeneration was at its height
after the publication of Dr. Pusey's great Tract on
Baptism.   The " Evangelical Chrysostom " was loyal
to the plain teaching of the Prayer Book and Articles,
and he said : " That the Church of England *does* hold,
and *does* teach Baptismal Regeneration would never,
we venture to think, have been disputed, *had not men
been anxious to remain in her communion, and yet to
make her formularies square with their own private
notions.*"   (This self-evident truth, coming from one
who was a loyal Evangelical, hits the " left wing" of
the militant Protestants, and the erroneous theology
of Bishop Ryle and their other leaders much harder
than any criticisms contained in this book.)   Canon
Melvill proceeds : " The words put into the mouth of the
officiating minister immediately after every baptism,
*Seeing now, dearly beloved brethren, that this child is
regenerate,* seem too distinct to be explained away,
and too general for any of those limitations by which
some would restrict them.   You may tell me that the
Church speaks in the judgment of charity, on the
supposition that there has been genuine faith in
those who have brought the infant to the font.   We
cannot however admit that the language is only the
language of that *charity which hopeth all things.*   Had
the Church not designed to go further than this, she
might have said, *Seeing that we may charitably believe,*
or, *Seeing that we may charitably hope that this child
is regenerate;* she could never have ventured on the
broad unqualified declaration—a declaration to be
made whensoever the Sacrament of Baptism has been
administered, *Seeing that this child IS regenerate;* and
then have gone on to require of the congregation to
express their gratitude in such words as these, *We
yield Thee hearty thanks . . that it hath pleased Thee
to regenerate this infant with Thy Holy Spirit.*   We
really think that no fair, no straightforward dealing

can get rid of the conclusion that the Church holds what is called Baptismal Regeneration . . . I do not see how I can be commonly honest and yet deny that every baptised person is, on that account, *regenerate*." (Canon H. Mevill. See *Pereira on Baptism*, p. 318.)

These strong words from a recognised Evangelical leader are more convincing for the purpose of this book than quotations from Anglo-Catholic divines such as Keble, Pusey, and Liddon. One point in the Prayer Book is absolutely conclusive against this *hypothetical* theory. The Office for Private Baptism The office for substitutes for the words (in the Public Private Baptism Office) "Seeing now, *that this child IS* declares the child " by *regenerate*"; the significant alteration Baptism regen- "Seeing now . . that this child is *by* erate " without sponsors. *Baptism* regenerate." The child, *privately* baptised, is brought to Church and the Priest is ordered to say that it is "by Baptism regenerate," *quite apart from the faith of sponsors*, who have *no place* in a *private Baptism*. Baptism is thus declared to be the instrument of regeneration *ex opere operato*.

It is well known that the Evangelical Archbishop Sumner's early work on "Apostolic Preaching" was the means of converting Cardinal Newman from the Calvinistic view of Holy Baptism to the Catholic doctrine of Baptismal Regeneration. (*Apologia*, p. 67.)

The chief leader of the Evangelicals in the early Simeon upheld nineteenth century was the pious and the orthodox devout Charles Simeon of King's College, view of Baptism. Cambridge. But, although some of his theology was gravely defective, he was loyal to the teaching of the Prayer Book on Holy Baptism. He would not have endorsed the teaching of Bishop Moule and Dr. Griffith Thomas. He took the teaching of the Prayer Book as he found it, just as Canon Melvill did. Bishop Ryle looked to him as a great leader, but he led the "loyal" or "right wing" of the Evangelical party, and his teaching is diametrically opposed to

Bishop Ryle's denial of the truth "that in every case a seed of Divine life is planted in the heart," etc. (*vide supra*). Simeon, on the contrary, said : " It appears that in the opinion of the Reformers, regeneration and remission of sins *did* accompany Baptism. But in what sense did they hold this sentiment ? Did they mention that *there was no need for the seed* then sown in the heart of the *baptised person to grow up, and to bring forth fruit?* " [Sermon on *Baptismal Service* (note).] Simeon's baptismal doctrine was thus diametrically opposed to the un-Scriptural teaching of Bishop Ryle. It is pleasant to find two eminent Evangelicals like Simeon and Melvill, who were loyally owned as leaders by the best type of Evangelicals, taking their stand upon the true teaching of the Prayer Book and Articles, and proclaiming the doctrine of Baptismal Regeneration with no uncertain voice. Would that their modern followers, who profess to hold their memories in honour, would abide by their teaching on this point instead of following the "sacramentarian" heresy of Dr. Colenso, and of the formularies of the " Cumminsite " sect ! Besides their Reformed " Articles of Religion," the " Cumminsites " put forth "a Declaration of Principles," which

The " Cumminsite " denial of Baptismal Regeneration. " condemns and rejects the *erroneous and strange doctrine that Regeneration is inseparably connected with Baptism*." This gravely erroneous statement finds its fitting parallel in Dr. Griffith Thomas' question, " How can the spiritual reside in the material ? " Regeneration means God's own life. How can *that* reside in *water ?* (*Catholic Faith*, p. 420.)

Bishop Ryle was also in agreement with this " Cumminsite " Declaration of Principles when he had the hardihood to say: "I cannot find the slightest ground in the Articles for the notion that all baptised persons are necessarily regenerate " (*Knots Untied*,

p. 179). " I am going to say and to prove that the Articles, and not the Prayer Book, are the first, foremost, and principal test of a true Churchman " (*Ib.*, p. 82). It is waste of time to disprove this curiously inaccurate statement. Bishop Ryle appealed to the Articles. By them, then, shall his statements be judged. The Latin and English Versions are of equal Synodical authority. Article IX. states that Baptism takes away the guilt of Original Sin, and states that "there is

no condemnation to them that believe, and *are baptised* " (Latin form of Article *renatis et credentibus*). The use of *renatis* in the Latin Article as an equivalent for the word "baptised" in the English Version shows that the framers of the Articles considered that all the baptised were *renati*, or "regenerated." This one phrase puts Bishop Ryle, Bishop Moule, Dr. Griffith Thomas, and all who deny that regeneration *invariably* accompanies Baptism, into a position of direct conflict with the teaching of the Articles. Then Article XXVII. states that Baptism is " a sign " of regenera-

tion or new birth whereby, as by an instrument, " they that receive Baptism *rightly* (*recte* in the Latin Version) are grafted into the Church." The word "sign" here lends no countenance to the " obsignatory " theory of the Sacraments. It means (as Bishop Gibson well says *ad loc.*) " an effectual sign " whereby the blessings of regeneration are *conveyed* to all those who receive a valid Baptism with *water*, in the Name of the Father, the Son and the Holy Ghost. Dr. Griffith Thomas makes an astonishing confusion between " right " (or *valid*) reception and " worthy reception." The two Latin adverbs *recte* and *digne* which are used in the Latin Version of the

Articles, and are rendered respectively in the English
Difference
between
digne and
recte. Version by "rightly," and "worthily," mean
two very different things.   *Recte* means
"rightly," or "properly," in accordance
with Christ's ordinance.   *Recte* is used *objectively* of
the right and valid use of the water and the Baptismal
formula, or in other words the due use of the *matter*
and *form* of the Sacrament as ordained by Christ.

Digne is used *subjectively* of the spiritual efficacy
of the Sacraments generally, when wrought out in our
lives, as the " extension of the Incarnation " within
the " covenanted sphere " of grace.   And yet we find
Dr. Griffith Thomas giving a purely *subjective* interpretation of *recte*.   He says :   " *They that receive
Baptism rightly*.   The Church evidently implies that
it is possible to receive Baptism *wrongly*, thus
bringing to view the distinction between right
reception and use, and that which is unworthy and
wrong." (*Catholic Faith*, p. 166.)

Bishop Ryle made precisely the same blunder in
commenting upon this Article.   He said :
Bishop Ryle
confused
digne with
recte. " *Worthy reception* is essential to the full
efficacy of the Sacrament.   There is not a
word said about a great inward and
spiritual blessing invariably and necessarily attending
the baptism of an infant " (Op. cit. p. 177).   Coup-
ling these words with his previously quoted statement
about the possibility of an " elect " infant receiving
baptismal regeneration, we are compelled to say that
the Calvinistic snake lies hidden under the fair foliage
of this righteous jealousy that Sacraments shall be
worthily received.   Every Christian desires that the
Sacraments, as channels of grace, should convey into
our being their gifts of the Spirit in fullest measure,
and that no sin or hardness of heart on our part
should put a barrier to hinder the Grace of God thus
" given to us."   But this desire need not find its fulfilment in subjective heresies which " overthrow the

nature of a Sacrament" and reduce it to an empty symbol, or (as Dr. Thomas says) " a picture of grace."

Bishop Ryle quotes Water-land as an authority. Bishop Ryle made a great point of quoting Waterland as supporting his Zwinglian view of the Holy Eucharist, though Waterland condemned Zwinglianism in strong terms *(Works*, vol. vii. p. 194). But he carefully avoids quoting Waterland on Baptismal Regeneration. Waterland says: " It is very *improper* language at least to call upon those who have once been *regenerated* in their infancy, who have had their *new birth* already at the font, to be *now* regenerated ; or to bid them expect a *new birth.* Such But Waterland affirms Baptis-mal Regenera-tion. applications might properly be directed to Jews, Turks, or Pagans, or to such *nominal* Christians as have thrown off Water baptism, for such really want to be regenerated, or born again, being still in their natural state . . . There is no instance, no example in Scripture, of any exhortation made to Christians to become *regenerated* or *born anew*, but to be reformed only, or renewed in the *inner man*, which is a very different notion from the other. Even Simon Magus, who had been baptised in iniquity, was not exhorted to be regenerated after-wards, or *born again*, but to *repent.* Having shown how improper the language is when Christians are called upon to be *regenerated*, I may next observe how *mischievous* it is in many ways. The telling of the common people that they ought *now* to be re-generated, instead of telling them plainly that they ought, with the help of God's grace, speedily to *repent* and *amend*, is giving them only a dark lesson instead of a clear one. If, instead of reminding them to *preserve* and *repair that* regeneration which they received in their baptism, they are called upon to receive a *second*, they may thereby be led off from looking back to their baptismal vows." *(Works*, vol. vi. pp. 363-366.)

Dr. Waterland in the eighteenth century was here reproducing the teaching of Hooker at the close of the sixteenth century. Hooker's balanced judgment got the better of his Calvinistic bias when he said: "Predestination bringeth not to life without the grace of external vocation wherein our Baptism is implied. For as we are not naturally *men* without *birth*, so neither are we *Christian* men in the eye of the Church of God, but by *new birth;* nor according to the manifest ordinary course of Divine dispensation *new born*, but by that Baptism which both declareth and maketh us Christians." (*Eccl. Pol.* v. c. 60).

So does Hooker.

These statements of Waterland and Hooker are *in accord* with the whole consensus of Catholic teaching from the Apostles' days to the Reformation. It seems an abnormal aberration of religious thought, and an unusually flagrant corruption of the teaching of the New Testament to confuse, as some of the Reformers did, *Regeneration* with *Conversion*. *Regeneration* is an act *once effected* for good, or for evil. *Conversion* is a life-long process of "turning to God" which springs from the grace of our Baptismal Regeneration or New Birth. The fact that too many baptised and regenerate people are not converted to God and lead evil lives is *nihil ad rem*, as an argument against the truth that *all* who, "by Baptism regenerate," *are* thereby grafted into the True Vine. They may become withered and fruitless branches, only meet to be cast into the fire of God's wrath. But none the less have they been *made* in baptism members of Christ, children of God, and heirs of His Kingdom. The condition of a *regenerate* and yet *unconverted* person is full of spiritual peril. Yet when the penitent turns to God in conversion his first step is to realise his previous "Baptismal Regeneration." By virtue of it he still claims the dormant gift

Confusion of Regeneration with Conversion in Protestant theology.

of the Holy Ghost, which is the baptismal " grace given
unto him," whereby he is grafted into the Incarnate
Life of Christ, and as thus sharing His manhood, he
has a special and personal claim upon the Fatherhood
of God. This is the direct teaching of our Lord in the
Parable of the Prodigal Son. The *regenerated* son,
Its fatal effect. although he has forgotten all about his
regeneration, is still a *son*, and can say,
in the process of his *conversion*, " I will arise and
go to my Father." I am still His son by virtue " of
my regeneration." All this sound and Scriptural teaching, with eighteen centuries of continuous Church
authority behind it, is utterly rejected by the Calvinists
and the modern Protestant writers who deny Baptismal
Regeneration. Bishop Ryle made a curious blunder
in arguing against the teaching of the Prayer Book
and Articles of Baptismal Regeneration. He said : " I
cannot suppose that the Articles and
Bishop Ryle's
strange blunder Liturgy were meant to be contrary to each
concerning the other." (N.B.—It is self-evident, of course,
framers of the
Elizabethan that they are *not* contrary.) And then he
Articles. went on to argue that " the men who drew
up the Thirty-nine Articles in 1562 were the men who
compiled the Prayer Book in 1549 " (*Knots Untied*,
p. 179). His argument apparently is that the
Edwardian Reformers who, as he wrongly supposes,
denied Baptismal Regeneration in the Prayer Book of
1549, were the *same* men who drew up the Elizabethan
Articles of 1562! His history is as faulty as his
argument. The Book of 1549 was Cranmer's work in
the main. It was doctrinally in accord with the " Ten
Articles " of 1536, which taught Baptismal Regeneration in explicit terms. How Bishop Ryle could have
been guilty of the slip of stating that *Cranmer* and
his colleagues of 1549 were the *same men* who drew
up the Elizabethan Articles can only be explained by
the old tag, *Aliquando bonus dormitat Homerus.*
With a strange perversion of Scripture, Bishop Ryle

said : "I believe that, *according to Scripture,* Regeneration is that great change of heart and character which is absolutely needful to man's salvation. Sometimes it is called *Conversion*" (Ib., p. 158). Could confusion further go? Imagine our calling the Festival of the *Conversion* of S. Paul, the Festival of the *Regeneration* of S. Paul! In his case the *Conversion* of the Damascus road was followed by his Regeneration by Baptism, and the grace of that *Regeneration* supplied the motive power to complete and continue his *Conversion* until the day when, on the eve of his martyrdom, he could say : *I have fought a good fight, I have finished my course, I have kept the faith.* Bishop Ryle actually spoke of the *Regeneration,* or "new birth" of S. Paul as "a sudden and violent change attended with much distress of mind" (Ib., p. 137). Again he said that the minister "may baptise with water in the Name of the Trinity ; but *unless* the Holy Ghost accompanies and blesses the ordinance there is no death unto sin and new birth unto righteousness" (Ib., p. 139). The word "unless" destroys the whole idea of covenant grace, and denies the Bible truth that the baptised *have* "put on Christ" and *are* "temples of the Holy Ghost." Bishop Ryle substituted with unconscious irreverence a fitful and capricious action of the Holy Spirit (so that Baptism may regenerate its recipient in one case and not in another) for the definite certainty of regeneration in every Baptism where no bar is put in the way of the Divine gift thereby conveyed.

Bishop Moule also identifies Regeneration with Conversion. He admits that *recte* means "under right conditions," which may be supposed to imply the use of the right "Matter" and "Form" of Holy Baptism.

His identification of Regeneration with Conversion.

He called S. Paul's "Conversion" his "Regeneration."

And denies the certainty of Baptismal grace.

Bishop Moule also identifies Regeneration with Conversion.

He says that " *Regeneration* does not merely mean *a seed of life*, which may or may not grow up ; it means actual holiness in which *all things are become new*" *(English Church Teaching*, p. 106). But this surely involves the life-long process of *Conversion*, which is the result of Regeneration, whereby the " seed of life " is planted in the hearts of the baptised, and the seed grows up by the daily renewal of the Spirit of God. All this erroneous teaching on Baptismal Regeneration which has been reviewed in this chapter is more directly traceable to the writings of the Swiss Reformers rather than to the detailed statements of their " Confessions of Faith." Those docu-

The writings of foreign Protestant Reformers err more definitely than their formularies.

ments were drawn up to conciliate opponents and to minimise differences. The Augsburg Confession and the Lutheran " Formula of Concord " contain definitions of the grace of Baptism which are capable of being harmonised with the Catholic Faith. The " Sixty-seven Articles of Zwingli," published in 1523, contained no mention of the Sacrament of Baptism.

The *first* and *second* Helvetic Confessions are Zwinglian and Calvinistic.

The first " Helvetic Confession " of 1536 is Calvinist. It calls Baptism the " laver of regeneration " for the " elect " only. The second " Helvetic Confession " of 1566 was drawn up by Bullinger, who wrote the " Decades," a series of doctrinal sermons which were recom-

Bishop Moule commends Bullinger's " Decades."

mended for the study of the English Clergy in Elizabeth's reign when the Convocations had been temporarily captured by Calvinism. Bishop Moule actually refers with approval to this Calvinistic work as endorsing his own view of the Sacraments. *(English Church Teaching*, p. 96.) The Bishop is, of course, in agreement with the Second Helvetic Confession on Baptism (cap. xx). In this document Bullinger frankly sets forth the

His doctrine identical with Bullinger's.

" obsignatory " view of Baptism. It is " a perpetual seal of our adoption " *(perpetua obsignatio adoptionis nostræ)* whereby

Original Sin is removed, and we are brought into covenant with God. All these things are sealed to us in baptism *(obsignantur hæc omnia in baptismo)*. Bullinger omits all mention of baptismal grace, as *conveyed* to us by the *channel* of Holy Baptism. Baptism to him is the " sign of the covenant " *(signum foederis Dei)*, and nothing else. Bishop Moule's teaching on Holy Baptism is derived almost verbally from this " Second Helvetic Confession," and

Dr. Griffith Thomas compares the doctrine of the Articles with the Westminster Confession.

it cannot be harmonised with our Prayer Book and Articles. Dr. Griffith Thomas appeals to the similarity of doctrine shown by a comparison of our Articles with the Westminster Confession *(Catholic Faith,* p. 412). We have already noted the fundamental change which the Westminster Confession made in

Fundamental difference between Article IX. and the Westminster Confession.

the phrase it borrowed from our Article IX. on " Original Sin " in order to express the heresy of the " Total Corruption " of human nature. So much for the alleged similarity of doctrine upon a crucial question of Faith. The Westminster Confession also permits re-marriage after a divorce granted for *desertion* only (chap. xxiv.) wherein it is in flat contradiction to the Catholic doctrine of the indissolubility of marriage, which is the undisputed law of the Church of England *(vide Blackstone's Commentary)*. And on Baptism the Westminster Confession says plainly that " although it be a great sin to contemn or

The Westminster Confession denies Baptismal Regeneration.

neglect this ordinance, yet grace and salvation are not so inseparably annexed unto it, as that no person can be regenerated or saved without it, *or that all the baptised are undoubtedly regenerated.* This is the selfsame " hypothetical " baptismal doctrine of Bishop Ryle, Bishop Moule, and Dr. Griffith Thomas.

It has now been sufficiently proved that these leaders of the " left wing " of the Evangelicals not only contradict the teaching of such of their own leaders as Charles Simeon, Henry Melvill, and Archbishop Sumner, but that their teaching is derived from foreign Protestant error, and as Melvill says (of its disloyalty to the formularies of our Church) it expresses only the views of men *"anxious to remain in her communion, and yet to make her formularies square with their own private notions."*

In the next chapter we shall see that the ancient Court of Arches, whilst it still retained its spiritual character as a Church Court, boldly and openly vindicated the Catholic doctrine of the Holy Eucharist in the Bennett case.

The Gorham Judgment and the Court of Arches.

And this chapter may be fitly closed with the vindication of the Catholic doctrine of Baptismal Regeneration by the Court of Arches in the Gorham case. Because the Privy Council reversed the righteous and Catholic decision of the Court of Arches in the Gorham case it has been too little noticed. The Privy Council, a purely secular Court, acquired jurisdiction as a Court of Appeal from the Court of Arches, through a blunder in the year 1832, which was subsequently admitted by Lord Brougham. The Church of England never accepted this usurped jurisdiction of the Privy Council in her Convocations, and the Bishops, as a corporate body protested against it in the House of Lords. Therefore the decisions of the Arches Court on the Two Great Sacraments of the Gospel still bind the Church of England. "The intrusion of secular judges into spiritual matters is an impious heretical trick," said Jeremy Taylor, and Catholic Churchmen do not care one jot for the reversal of the Court of Arches judgment (affirming Baptismal Regeneration) by the Privy Council or for the acceptance by the Privy Council of the Court of Arches judgment affirming the Catholic doctrine of the Real Presence.

The Gorham case, in brief, was as follows :

Bishop Philpotts of Exeter refused to institute Mr. Gorham to the benefice of Brampford Speke, because he denied the doctrine of Baptismal Regeneration. He held the views of Bishop Ryle, Bishop Moule, and Dr. Griffith Thomas, with certain subtleties of method which were original. He applied to the Court of Arches to compel the Bishop to institute him. In 1849 Sir H. J. Fust, the Dean of Arches, decided the case in the Bishop's favour. This ought to have settled the matter for all loyal and well-instructed Churchmen. But Mr. Gorham appealed to the Privy Council, and the judgment of the Court of Arches was reversed. People imagined wrongly that a " secular " Court could override a " spiritual " Court, and that the Church of England was committed to heresy by the Privy Council judgment. The Privy Council judgment was null and void from a spiritual point of view, and even if it was *not* Sir R. Phillimore says that it does not legalise the ordinary Protestant view of Baptism. " This case," he says, " will be found on examination *not* to support the view sometimes, *but erroneously*, entertained of it, as deciding that it is competent for a clergyman of the Church of England to hold, nakedly and without qualification, that infant children are not regenerated by virtue of the Sacrament of Baptism." Sir R. Phillimore gives but cold comfort to the militant Protestants who regard the Privy Council as the palladium of their heresies.

CHAPTER IV.

The Doctrinal Errors of Foreign Protestantism upon
the Holy Eucharist considered with reference
to the True Teaching of the English Church.

The Lutheran doctrine of Consubstantiation is a
The Lutheran perverted parody of the Catholic doctrine
doctrine of Con- of the Real Objective Presence of the Body
substantiation. and Blood of Christ in the Holy Eucharist.
It denies the Eucharistic Sacrifice, and it is linked
with Luther's heresy which asserted the Ubiquity of
the Glorified Manhood of our Lord. Archbishop
Temple, by some process of mental confusion, thought
that it was practically the same doctrine as was taught
by Dr. Pusey and Mr. Bennett, and that it had been
pronounced tenable in the Church of England by the
judgment of the Privy Council in the Bennett case.
(*Charge*, p. 12.) As the chief error of the Zwinglian
and Calvinist Reformers lies in their teaching " the
Real Absence," in some form or other, instead of " the
Real Presence," which the Lutherans taught in a
corrupted form, it will not be necessary to deal further
with the Lutheran doctrine of Consubstantiation.

We have already seen that the Zwinglian heresy
The Zwinglian of the " Real Absence " is contrary to our
heresy. Article XXV., and that it contradicts the
teaching of our Prayer Book. It is
now necessary to examine Calvin's modification of
The Calvinist Zwinglianism, in which he used language
adaptation of that had an orthodox sound to express
Zwinglianism. unorthodox doctrine. Calvin held a

"virtual Presence, in the heart of the communicant."
This "virtual Presence," according to Calvin, is the
result of the *faith* of the recipient, and, as Canon
Newbolt has well remarked, is "an act of equal pretension with that of consecration by an authorised
and ordained priesthood" *(The Sacrament of the*

The Virtual
Presence
involves a
miracle which
overthrows the
nature of a
Sacrament. *Altar*, p. 60). The theory that the communicant can, by his own act of faith,
create for *himself*, apart from the blessing
of the Holy Spirit upon the words and acts
of the consecrating Priest, a "virtual
Presence" of our Lord, demands an individual miracle
in the case of each separate "faithful recipient" which
is founded on no warrant of Scripture, and a miracle
more perplexing than that purely physical theory of
Transubstantiation disallowed by the Council of Trent,
to which the term "Transaccidentation" or "Trans-
elementation" would more properly belong. So gentle

Mr. Keble called
it "Real
Absence." a controversialist as Mr. Keble felt con-
strained to say that, "Virtual Presence is
Real Absence." It involves the "Real
Absence" of the Body and Blood of Christ "under the

Mr. Dimock
holds the "Real
Absence." form" of Bread and Wine—the Real
Absence of our Lord (as Mr. Dimock puts
it) "in or under the form of the consecrated elements considered in themselves." *(The
Doctrine of the Lord's Supper*, p. 23.)

   Mr. Dimock speaks of "the great chasm of cleavage,
deep and broad" between the doctrine of the "Real
Absence" and the Catholic doctrine of the Real Presence. He says: "We maintain that the *thing signified
and really given* is not really *in* the sign . . . Giving
and receiving require (of necessity) no Real Presence
at all." And he quotes the Zwinglian Œcolampadius
with approval, and expresses agreement with his
dictum, *Per fidem absentissimum Corpus Christi,
animo præstantissimum est* (Ib., pp. 39-41.) And

then Mr. Dimock uses Catholic phraseology and tells
His theory
equally with
Transacciden-
tion overthrows
the nature of a
Sacrament. us of the *Unio Sacramentalis* and the
Res Sacramenti when he has " over-
thrown the nature of a Sacrament " by his
heresy of a Real Absence. There is no
more room for the *Res Sacramenti* in a
sacred rite which is a figure of a thing absent than
there is for the " accidents " of the outward elements
in the theory of Transaccidentation.   Both theories
deny the Catholic doctrine of the Eucharist, and
equally overthrow the nature of a Sacrament, which
conveys invisible grace through the direct channel of
its visible and outward part, as has already been
noted in the previous chapter.

   Mr. Dimock is a candid and courteous controversialist.   The reader of his books is in a very
Mr. Dimock,
Bishop Moule,
and Bishop
Ryle have
asserted that the
Church of
England teaches
" Real Absence." different atmosphere from that of the "red
hot Gospeller" polemics of the late Bishop
of Liverpool.   Mr. Dimock rightly says, of
the fundamental theological difference
between those who uphold the novel
doctrine of the " Real Absence," and
those who hold the primitive and Catholic doctrine of
the " Real Presence," that "there is no consistent
standing place between the two sides of this chasm.
From the point of view of either side the teaching of
the other side must be seen as a thing strongly to be
opposed." He then says: " The history of our English
Book of Common Prayer makes it unmistakably clear
that the Reformed Church of England takes its stand
on *this* side [the " Real Absence" side] of this broad
doctrinal chasm.   The teaching on the other side
must assuredly be included among the erroneous and
strange doctrines contrary to God's Word, which this
Church of England requires us and binds us by our
solemn ordination vows to be ready with all faithful
diligence to banish and drive away." *(The Doctrine of
the Lord's Supper*, pp. 24-25.)

Bishop Moule's official commendation of Mr. Dimock's book, which is prefixed to the 1910 edition, commits him personally to Mr. Dimock's words, as quoted above. Bishop Ryle said the same thing in "Knots Untied." Dr. Griffith Thomas says the same *Dr. Griffith* thing, when he asserts that "it is certain *Thomas holds* that the doctrine of the Church of England *the same view.* on the Lord's Supper is *that of Calvin,* and those who thought with him."

He defines the doctrine of the "Real Presence" correctly as "a Real Objective Presence of Christ's glorified Body in, or under the elements after consecration, apart from any presence in the faithful recipient," and he says "*the Church of England nowhere teaches this.*" (*The Catholic Faith*, pp. 412-415.)

Here is a fair and square issue, which will be plainly *The Zwinglians* and effectually controverted in this chapter. *and Calvinists* The first point to be considered is one of *abolished kneeling at reception* ceremonial and outward observance. We *to emphasise the* have already noted in Chapter I. that *"Real Absence."* Zwingli carefully avoided any approximation to the consecration of the elements in the Holy Eucharist of the Catholic Church in the Zurich form for the "Lord's Supper." His rite was a new invention which studiously omitted every detail of the Divine Liturgy, and, whereas kneeling to receive the Holy Eucharist had become the universal custom of the Western Church, this outward act of reverence was abolished, as a matter of principle, by Zwingli and Calvin. They were logical enough in this abolition of kneeling. The Western Church intended kneeling reception to be an outward sign of reverence to the Real Objective Presence of our Blessed Lord in the Sacrament of the Altar. There is no reason for kneeling in a vaguely commemorative rite that *The doctrinal* involves the "Real Absence" of our Lord. *chasm between* The Zwinglians and Calvinists, who teach *kneeling and* the doctrine of the "Real Absence," are *non-kneeling reception.* logically conformed to their own teaching by the outward symbolism of refusing to kneel and preferring to sit at a commemorative meal invented by their leaders. And so we arrive at a Western and primitive ceremonial observance which is a distinctive mark on each side of Mr. Dimock's "broad chasm." To *kneel* at the reception of the Holy Eucharist is the mark of those who believe in the "Real Presence." *Not* to kneel is the mark of those who believe in the "Real Absence." The English Prayer Book, as a Western Liturgy, expressly directs "kneeling reception."

The words of our Rubric "*all meekly kneeling*" have a strong controversial history behind them, and mark by their presence in the Book of 1662 the deliberate and final act of the *Ecclesia Anglicana* as standing on the "Real Presence" side of the doctrinal chasm. And this Rubric first took shape in the full tide of the Edwardian Revolution, when foreign Protestant influences dominated the Parliamentary revision of the Prayer Book in 1552, and when Cranmer, and other leaders, were tainted with Calvinist and Zwinglian error upon the subject of the Holy Eucharist.

The Prayer Book of 1552 orders kneeling reception.

The history of this Rubric is interesting, and, as Mr. Keble says, "This question of the receiver's posture at Holy Communion supplied *an outward and visible symbol* of the deep doctrinal differences which were really at issue." (*Eucharistic Adoration*, p. 136.)

Mr. Keble on this Rubric

Archbishop Cranmer's own doctrine on the Eucharist was unsound and defective. Practically he was, although he would not have admitted it, on the side of the "Real Absence" of the Swiss Reformers. But he hated violent innovations, and he was a Conservative in his desire to retain Episcopacy, and to preserve with it as much of the older forms and customs of reverence and order in the services as were compatible with his Protestant ideals.

Cranmer's position on this question.

He disliked Hooper and committed him to prison
for refusing to wear the customary vesture of the
Episcopate. He disliked Hooper's "Non-conformity
within the Church," which differed *toto cœlo* from the
Non-conformity of a subsequent period, which resulted
in "Separatism." He was opposed to Hooper's per-
sistent efforts to transform the Church of England into
a Zwinglian sect. Hooper was logical. His
belief in the "Real Absence" led him to
inveigh bitterly against kneeling reception
of the Eucharist in a sermon preached
before King Edward VI. in 1550. He was considerably
incited on this point by Laski, a Polish
Zwinglian, whose fanaticism as a Reformer
in East Friesland had made Germany too
hot to hold him. He settled in London as Superinten-
dent of a congregation of Zwinglian foreigners, and
abused Cranmer's tolerance by bitterly
attacking the Prayer Book of 1549. John
Knox, who was ministering under the
authority of Edward's Council at Berwick-on-Tweed,
took upon himself to use a form of his own instead of
the Book of 1549. "I thought it good," he said, "to
avoid all other gestures than Christ used, and to use
sitting at the Lord's Table." (Lorimer's *Life of Knox*,
p. 31.)

The "Communion Book" of 1548 ordered kneeling
at the Eucharist, but the Prayer Book of
1549, although it retained the ancient and
familiar word "Mass" for the Eucharistic
Office did not prescribe kneeling, apparently
because no one thought of adopting any other posture.

But when the foreign Protestant influence was at its
zenith, the Book of 1552 definitely prescribed kneeling,
in spite of the denunciations of Laski, Hooper, and
Knox. Cranmer knew that the mass of the English
people were still Catholic at heart, and he dared not
give way too much to the foreigners. Besides which

Hooper's sermon against kneeling reception.

Laski incited Hooper.

Knox attacks kneeling reception.

Kneeling reception ordered in 1548, omitted in 1549, re-enacted in 1552.

his own liturgical instincts were stronger than his theology, and so he insisted upon kneeling at the Eucharist. Here is the curious story of what Mr. Dixon, in his great "History of the Reformation" (p. 488) calls the "First Kneeling War."

The First kneeling War.

The Book of 1552 was already printed, but not issued, on September 26th, and the Council stopped its issue, because Knox, a few days

Knox preaches against kneeling.

before, had preached a violent sermon against kneeling at the Eucharist before the King. The Council then called on Cranmer to consult with the foreigner Peter Martyr and Ridley with a view to withdrawing the Rubric which ordered kneeling. Cranmer replied on October 7th,

Cranmer defends it.

that the Rubric had been well weighed by a great many Bishops and well learned men, and proceeded to ask the Council, "Is it wisdom to alter without Parliament what has been concluded by Parliament, as the bidding of glorious and unquiet spirits who would still find fault if the Book were altered every year? They say that kneeling is not commanded in Scripture : and what is not commanded in Scripture is unlawful. There is the root of the errors of the sects ! If kneeling be not expressly enjoined in Holy Scripture, neither is standing or sitting."

We may note here that the Book of 1552 had not been authorised by Convocation. It was purely Erastian in its inception and completion and was set forth by the sole authority of Parliament. It never came into general use, and was only intended by the Council to pave the way for a more drastic liturgical

Knox protested against the defence of kneeling in Cranmer's draft of the Article.

revolution, which never took place. On the 21st of October, the Royal Chaplains were ordered to examine Cranmer's first Draft of XLV. Articles of Religion which subsequently took shape as the XLII.

Articles of 1553.   Knox, as one of their number, pro-
tested in writing to the Council against Article
XXVIII., because it affirmed that kneeling at the
The Council
add the " Black
Rubric." Eucharist was right and proper.   On October
27th the Council ordered the Black Rubric
in its original form, which denied the
" Real and Essential" Presence of our Lord in the
Eucharist to be printed as a fly-leaf, and added to the
Its utter lack of
authority. Prayer Book, as a concession to Knox and
Hooper.   But this Declaration had no
authority from Convocation or Parliament,
and was abolished in 1559.   It emanated from the
Council under the sole authority of the signature of
the King, who was a minor.   The Church of England
was never committed to it, and the usage of kneeling
remained as a witness against its false doctrine.

The serious rebellions, which ensued after the issue
of the Prayer Book of 1549, were put down with
merciless severity, but the joy with which the nation
The mass of the
clergy and
people were
against the
Zwinglianism of
Edward's
Council. welcomed the accession of Mary was testimony enough to the fact that the mass of
the clergy and people were averse to the
official Zwinglianism of Edward's Council.
The bulk of the people were too illiterate to
follow the meaning of the concessions to Zwinglianism
in the Book of 1552, even if it had been brought into
general use, which it never was.   They saw with their
eyes that *kneeling* was ordered, and the bulk of the
clergy followed the accustomed ceremonies of the Mass
in using the Prayer Book.   The majority of the people
had no sympathy with the foreign Reformers, or with
Omission of the
Manual Acts in
1552 had no
practical effect. the Protestant heresies favoured by
Edward's Council.   Even the omission of
the direction to use the Manual Acts in the
Consecration Prayer in 1552 meant nothing
to the Church as a whole.   The intention of this
omission was purely Zwinglian, but the mass of the
clergy paid no attention to it.   This omission continued

till the final Revision of 1662, but the Manual Acts of the Mass were sedulously continued. There is an interesting case to prove the continuance of unwritten law in the reign of Elizabeth. In 1573 one Johnson, Chaplain to the Lord Keeper Bacon, was accused before the High Commissioners of omitting the repetition of the "Words of Institution," required to consecrate more wine, when that which had already been consecrated had been consumed. Johnson relied upon the absence of any direction to repeat the "Words of Institution" in the Elizabethan Prayer Book. The Dean of Westminster, as one of the Judges, remarked : Saint Augustine saith, *accedat verbum ad elementum et fit sacramentum.* Now you lacked the word, therefore it was no sacrament." The Bishop of London (Sandys) said : " But what is the meaning of the Book ?" Johnson replied : " Men may make what meaning they list, but I refer myself to the Book whether it be so appointed or no." But the fact that the Prayer Book contained no specific direction to consecrate afresh in case of necessity did not save Johnson from imprisonment. He was condemned for violating a law of the Catholic Church, although it was unwritten in the Book of Common Prayer as it then was. "Omission" is not "prohibition." Otherwise the Rubrics could not logically be carried out. Here is a fitting place to notice a blunder of Dr. Griffith Thomas, which is strange indeed to be made by a man who is responsible for the training of Ordination candidates. He says : "*After consecration,* we pray that we, *receiving these Thy creatures of Bread and Wine, may be partakers* of the spiritual blessing." (*The Catholic Faith*, p. 253.) The words he quotes occur *before* the consecration, as everyone who reads the Prayer of Consecration knows. Whatever view may be taken in the Eastern Church of the recital of the " Words of Institution," there is no manner of

Continuance of unwritten law of the Church proved in Johnson's case.

Curious blunder of Dr. Griffith Thomas concerning the Prayer of Consecration.

doubt that our Prayer Book teaches that the Consecration of the elements is effected by the recital of the " Words of Institution." We need not go back to Johnson's trial to prove this, for the direction for a fresh Consecration in our present Book of 1662 orders the repetition of the " Words of Institution," beginning, in the case of the Bread, " Our Lord Jesus Christ after that He was betrayed," etc.; and in the case of the Cup, " Likewise after Supper He took the Cup," etc. Dr. Griffith Thomas might have remembered that the words " these Thy creatures of Bread and Wine " do not *follow* the Act of Consecration, but *precede* it. And to found an argument in favour of the " Receptionist " doctrine of Calvin upon such a palpable blunder is surely the sign of a very weak case.

To return to the Second Prayer Book, it may well be noted that the Zwinglianism of Edward VI. and his Council never committed the Church of England to the doctrine of the " Real Absence." Somerset and Northumberland cared nothing for religion. All they desired was to find a convenient excuse for plundering the Church under the *ægis* of foreign Protestantism. They exercised a tyranny in the name of the King which the Church and nation never accepted. Their Zwinglian foreign allies had no more title to be considered true members of the Church of England than Hooper and Knox.

The Book of 1552 did not commit the Church to Zwinglianism.

Irreligion of Somerset and Northumberland.

And those in the present day who teach within the Church of England the Zwinglianism of Hooper and the Calvinism of Knox, have no more a true place in the historic *Ecclesia Anglicana* than those Reformers had. The Church of England, by its Synods, and by the vast majority of its clergy and people, was never committed to the Puritan Revolution of 1552. The " left wing " of the Evangelicals point to this date as the historic justification of their present

Their foreign Protestant allies and their modern successors cannot claim to be true Churchmen.

position. It is no historic justification at all, and they could far more logically claim to be the legal heirs of Cromwell's Revolution, which cast out the true Church of England, silenced her Service Book, and proscribed her clergy. For the militant Protestant party to claim that it is the duty of the clergy to "banish and drive away," as erroneous and strange doctrines, the Catholic teaching upon Baptismal Regeneration and the Real Objective Presence which is taught by our Anglican formularies is a delusion so strange that it overpasses the bounds of all reasonable and sober controversy. Upon the subject of the Holy Eucharist the Protestant party

Sir R. Phillimore's judgment in the Bennett case.

appealed to the Courts. The case of Mr. Bennett, Vicar of Frome, was decided in the Arches Court by Sir Robert Phillimore, who was a lawfully appointed Spiritual Judge, which his so-called successors, appointed under the Public Worship Regulation Act of 1874, are not. Mr. Bennett was charged, by his Protestant Prosecutor, with teaching the doctrine of the Real Objective Presence which Mr. Dimock, Bishop Moule, and other Protestant leaders have categorically denied. Judgment in this case was given on July 23rd, 1870. The substance of the decision is contained in the following

He lays it down that the Real Objective Presence is the doctrine of our formularies.

words : "Upon the whole it will appear, I think, from all examination of the formularies, that they were intended to set forth, and do set forth, the doctrine of a Real Spiritual Presence in the Holy Eucharist. It may be said with truth that in some formularies this doctrine is more doubtfully or more faintly expressed than in others, but the result which I have stated is not only the legal inference from the construction of all the formularies, but also especially from those which are in their nature the most important and, as a matter of history, the latest in date. I say that the Objective, Actual, and Real Presence, or the Spiritual Real

Presence, *a Presence external to the act of the Communicant*, appears to me to be the doctrine which the formularies of our Church, duly considered and construed so as to be harmonious, are intended to maintain " (Phillimore, *Report of Judgment*, p. 117). Sir R. Phillimore's careful definition of the Anglican doctrine of the Real Objective Presence has never been superseded. It is the language of a theologian, as well as of a judge. He is careful in the same judgment to state that the " Receptionist " view of Hooper and Waterland is not so contrariant to the formularies as to be inadmissible, but he is quite clear on the point that it is not the teaching of the formularies. The tolerance of the *Ecclesia Anglicana* can allow for a view that expresses *less* than the full truth, but it does not permit a flat *denial* of the truth such as Zwingli and Calvin affirmed. A distinction can be drawn between the " Receptionist " doctrine, and the view of a " Virtual " Presence, involving a " Real Absence," which Waterland condemned in specific terms as Calvinist error. (*Works*, iv. p. 608.) The judgment condemns in open and unmistakable terms the Zwinglianism of Bishop Ryle, who said : " Christ as Man is in Heaven, and *not* on the Communion Table at the celebration of the Lord's Supper. He is *not* present under the form of bread and wine. The consecrated bread is *not* the Body of Christ, and the consecrated wine is *not* the Blood of Christ. Those sacred elements are the emblem of something *absent*, and not of something *present* " *Untied*, p. 295.)

His view of the " Receptionist " doctrine.

His judgment condemns the " Real Absence " taught by Protestants.

This is sheer Zwinglianism, in sharp contrast to Waterland's statement that the outward elements after consecration " are no bare signs, no *untrue* figures of a thing *absent* " (*Works*, vi. p. 42). Waterland's words, if short of the full truth, do not *deny* it. Bishop Ryle's

Bishop Ryle's Zwinglianism contrasted with Waterland.

words positively *deny* the truth which Sir R. Phillimore
lays down, and decides to be the teaching of our
formularies. Bishop Moule's teaching is
practically the same. He quotes the "Black
Rubric" thus: "The natural (i.e. *non-figurative*) Body and Blood of our Saviour
Christ are in Heaven and not *here*." To interpret
"natural" as the equivalent to "non-figurative" is a
transparent perversion of terms. "Natural" is opposed
to "spiritual" by S. Paul in I. Cor. xv., and Bishop
Moule might have remembered this. And the Council
of Trent denies that our Lord's "natural" body is
present in the Eucharist. Bishop Ryle
admitted this much when he quoted Jewel's
opponent Harding as defining Transubstantiation to be a Presence of Christ "not after
a corporal or carnal, or *natural* wise, but supernaturally,
spiritually, divinely, and in a manner by Him known."
And this "Spiritual Presence," after Consecration,
Bishop Ryle categorically denied in more logical terms
than Bishop Moule, who also denies that the Sacraments
of the Gospel are (in Bishop Jeremy Taylor's
words) "the extension of the Incarnation."
(*Worthy Communicant*, i. 2). This denial
is endorsed by other Protestant writers, and
it cuts at the root of S. Paul's teaching that
our Lord is the Second Adam in Whom we all are
"made alive." It is inconceivable that any student of
the New Testament can deny that our sacramental
union with our Lord, as the Second Adam, and the
Head of redeemed humanity, is the source of our
justification and sanctification. How Bishop
Moule could bring himself to write that the
blessing of Baptism is not "the infusion of
a Divine Humanity," and that the view that
"the communicant takes into his being the
glorified Humanity of our Lord," is *not* "that of the
Church of England nor of Holy Scripture" (*English*

Margin notes:

Bishop Moule's Confusion of " Natural will " non-figurative.

Transubstantiation involves a Spiritual Presence.

Bishop Moule denies that the Sacraments are an " extension of the Incarnation."

He also denies that the Sacraments infuse into us the Divine Humanity.

Church Teaching, pp. 100-118), passes the comprehension of ordinary and simple minds, who are face to face with the declaration of our Catechism that by Baptism we are " made members of Christ " and that "the Body and Blood of Christ are verily and indeed taken and received " in the Holy Eucharist.   We may note that the phrase " members of Christ " must refer to our Lord's Glorified Manhood, just as the phrase " Body and Blood " point to His Human Nature, glorified and eternal by virtue of the union of the Godhead and Manhood in the Person of God the Son, "the Word made Flesh." To deny our sacramental union with the Glorified Manhood of our Lord is a form of misbelief perilously near to that virtual effacement of our Lord's true Manhood which constituted the heresy of Eutyches. Bishop Moule also denies the doctrine of the Eucharistic Sacrifice.   He says : "The Holy Supper

Bishop Moule's denial of the Eucharistic Sacrifice.

of the Lord is an occasion for our sacrifice of praise and our sacrifice of self.   But it is not a Sacrifice ; it is a Sacrament " (*English Church Teaching*, p. 127).   This is Zwingli's doctrine.   His Eighteenth Article denies the Eucharistic   Sacrifice   in   the   words '*missam   non   esse sacrificium.*'   This curious antithesis of " Sacrifice " and "Sacrament" is utterly foreign to   the   whole tenor of   the   continuous   teaching   of   the   Church Catholic.   The   idea   conveyed   by   it   is   utterly misleading.   To say that a "Sacrament" cannot be at   the   same   time   a   " Sacrifice "   is   in   flat   contradiction to S. Paul's Eucharistic teaching in I. Cor. xi. 25-26.   Bishop Ryle said, "Let us often

Bishop Ryle denied the Eucharistic Sacrifice.

remind our people that there is *no sacrifice* in the Lord's Supper—no Real Presence of Christ's Body and Blood in the bread and wine."   (*Knots Untied*, p. 221.)

Dr. Griffith Thomas repeats Bishop Moule's statement "that the Lord's Supper is not a Sacrifice but a Sacrament." He quotes Canon Mason's *Faith of the Gospel* (p. 330); "He allows us at the Altar to do with Him what He Himself does in Heaven. In this sense we may say that the Eucharist is a propitiatory sacrifice." He proceeds to state that "the Prayer Book will be searched in vain for any such doctrine of a Eucharistic Sacrifice . . . If the words Eucharistic Sacrifice mean some sacrifice which is offered only at and in the Lord's Supper, then we assert that no such idea occurs in Bible and Prayer Book." (*The Catholic Faith*, pp. 418-420.)

[sidenote: Dr. Griffith Thomas says that the Eucharistic Sacrifice is not to be found in the Bible or Prayer Book.]

A person who has made two such obvious blunders as we have previously noticed does not improve his chance of being accepted as an authority by the bare crudity -and emphasis of his negations. And it is necessary here to note another of his blunders. He confidently asserts that the Revision of 1662 did not mean the offering of the "Bread and Wine" by the word "Oblations," but only gifts "in kind" as opposed to "alms" which were gifts "in money." Mr. Dimock, although in doctrinal agreement with him, was too widely read a scholar to fall into any such error. He quotes Baxter as explaining "Oblations" as "the creatures of Bread and Wine offered or presented before God." (*History of Our Prayer Book*, p. 61.)

[sidenote: He also denies that the word "Oblations" refers to the offering of Bread and Wine.]

"English Church Teaching" has a curious Zwinglian statement on the subject of the celebrant of the Holy Eucharist. Zwingli of course denies that there is a Christian Priesthood. He said "*Ordo sacer, humanum figmentum est.*" And the book, for whose presentment of "English Church Teaching" Bishop Moule

[sidenote: "English Church Teaching" is unable to explain why a layman may not celebrate the Eucharist.]

and Bishop Drury are responsible, says of lay folk being permitted to baptise in case of necessity: "Why laymen should be allowed to minister *one* sacrament, and yet should be *precluded* from administering the *other*, *it is not easy to explain*" (p. 253). Here is the true essence of foreign Protestant error clearly expressed. How these Bishops can reconcile their statement with the Preface to the Ordinal, and how they can include such a statement in a book which they call " English Church Teaching " defies explanation. Such leaders of the Evangelicals as Simeon, Melvill, and Archbishop Sumner would have repudiated it utterly. Their statement is on a par with the declaration of a beneficed Evangelical clergyman who said, " I should have no hesitation whatever in asking my churchwarden to celebrate for me next Sunday if it were only legal for him to do so." (See Cobb's *Sequel to Kiss of Peace*, p. 121.)

To return to the question of the Eucharistic Sacrifice which is categorically denied by Bishop Moule and the other writers of his school, What warrant have they for saying that the formularies of the Church of England deny the doctrine of the Eucharistic Sacrifice?

Sir R. Phillimore holds that the Eucharistic Sacrifice is lawfully in accordance with our formularies.

They have no warrant at all for such a statement. Mr. Bennett, of Frome, was accused of depraving the formularies by his teaching on the subject of the Eucharistic Sacrifice. Sir Robert Phillimore's judgment vindicated his language on this point, and said that it was lawful to hold "the Eucharistic Sacrifice " and to speak of the " Sacrifice offered by the Priest," and also to speak of the " sacrificial character of the Holy Table." One result of Sir R. Phillimore's judgment was the secession of the Rev. Capel Molyneux, Vicar of S. Paul's, Onslow Square. The confirmation of this judgment by the Privy Council meant nothing to sound Churchmen, who did not acknowledge the authority of a secular

Secession of the Rev. Capel Molyneux.

Court in matters spiritual. But it meant much to clergy who taught Zwinglianism, and Mr. Molyneux seceded from the Church in 1872, and published a pamphlet calling upon all Evangelicals to follow his example. His appeal fell flat, because the Zwinglian party knew that the dubious honesty of their position would not be seriously attacked by loyal Churchmen who were content to leave them face to face with their own inconsistencies. The Zwinglians were loth to sever themselves from the official prestige of the Anglican Establishment, as Mr. Molyneux had bravely and honestly done. They clung to their untenable position within the Church of England, and did not emulate the boldness of the American Protestants who followed Bishop Cummins.

The Zwinglians did not follow his example.

Their own theological position was the same as that of the "Cumminsites," for the Seventeenth Article of the Reformed Episcopal Church teaches the "memorial symbolism" of the "Real Absence." It says that "the Supper of the Lord is a symbol of the soul's feeding upon Christ," and further states that "we feed on Him, whether at our private devotions or in our meditations, or on any occasion of public worship, *or in the memorial symbolism of the Lord's Supper.*"

Their position the same as that of the "Cumminsites."

This is the doctrine of Mr. Dimock, Bishop Moule, Bishop Ryle and Dr. Griffith Thomas when brought down to its logical reality, and divested of its pious verbiage. And this doctrine was officially condemned as heretical in the Colenso judgment. Dr. Colenso was condemned under Charge iii. in the case of his Presenters, for denying that "the Holy Communion conveyed any special grace." In his published sermon on the Holy Communion, Dr. Colenso said : "It is the result of man's theorising, and not derived from God's Revelation, to attempt to make a distinction *in kind* between our Lord's Presence in the

Their doctrine on the Eucharist was condemned by the Colenso judgment.

Dr. Colenso's heretical teaching on the Eucharist.

Holy Eucharist, and that which He vouchsafes
to us when we kneel in our own retirement, or
meet in our ordinary assemblies of prayer or praise."
Again he said of persons living away from the ordinary
ministrations of the Church : " We can, under such
circumstances, eat the Sacred Body and drink the
Precious Blood of Christ by devout meditation and
prayer—at home, in our retirement, without the use of
Bread and Wine, with no table on which to spread
the elements, with no minister at hand to bless them."

Dr. Colenso was not speaking of what Catholics know
as an act of "spiritual communion."   He was asserting
his belief, which he elsewhere expressed,

His denial of
Maurice's
Eucharistic
teaching.

that there was no " special grace " in the
Eucharist.   He wrote strongly to his friend
F. D. Maurice in 1858, denying the view
that Maurice had expressed of a " special grace " and
"special Presence of our Lord in the Holy Eucharist."
He dismissed Dean Green from the office of Examining
Chaplain, because he refused to endorse his Bishop's
view that there was no difference in *kind* between our
Lord's Eucharistic and Sacramental Presence and His
Presence " where two or three are gathered together "
in His Name.   Dr. Colenso's heresy on the Eucharist
is exactly expressed by the seventeenth "Cumminsite "
Article.

The Colenso judgment condemned this doctrine of
the " Real Absence " just as Sir R. Phillimore's judgment asserted the doctrine of the Real Presence of the
Eucharistic Sacrifice.

We may briefly note the formal Eucharistic teaching

The "foreign
Protestant"
formularies on
the Holy
Eucharist.

of the foreign Protestant Confessions of
Faith.   The Confession of Augsburg was
intended to conciliate Catholic opinion.   Its
tenth Article says that " the True Body and

Blood of Christ are truly present under the form of Bread and Wine, and are there communi- *The Augsburg Confession.* cated and received by those who partake of the Lord's Supper." This statement as well as the parallel statement in the Lutheran " Formula of Concord " (which also rejects Zwingli- *Zwingli's Eighteenth Article.* anism) can be considered capable of a Catholic interpretation. The Eighteenth Article, put forth in 1523 by Zwingli, denies the Eucharistic Sacrifice, and says that the Eucharist is *The First Helvetic Confession.* merely *sigillum redemptionis.* The First Helvetic Confession of 1536 in Article XXII. teaches Zwinglianism. It states that " the Body and Blood of the Lord are not united to the Bread and Wine, but that they are symbols."

The " Second Helvetic Confession " contains the very *The Second Helvetic Confession.* error for which Dr. Colenso was condemned. " This eating the Flesh and drinking the Blood of the Lord takes place *apart from* the Lord's Supper, as *often*, and *whenever*, a man shall have believed in Christ " (cap. 7.)

The " Westminster Confession " takes the " Symbolic " *The West- minster Confes- sion.* view of the Lord's Supper in Article V. which says that "the outward elements are sometimes called by the names of the things they *represent*, to wit, the Body and Blood of Christ." Article II. denies the reality of the Eucharistic Sacrifice. The " Westminster Confession " must be reckoned with " foreign Protestant " formularies because it reflects their teaching. and because it is the official " Con- fession " of Scottish Presbyterianism, which is a form of foreign Protestantism introduced into Scotland from Geneva. The teaching of the foreign Protestant formu- laries (except the Lutheran) may be generally summed up in the words used by Canon Liddon to describe the *Canon Liddon on Zwing- lianism.* teaching of Zwinglians within the Church of England, that, in celebrating the Holy Communion, " they did not suppose

themselves to be doing anything more serious than
taking a little bread and wine in public in memory of an
absent Christ." *Letter on the Purchas Judgment*, p. 25.)

Dr. Griffith Thomas teaches the " Real Absence " by
stating that " the minister cannot possibly
give the Body and Blood of Christ "
(The Catholic Faith, p. 174). But Article
XXVIII. says *Corpus Christi datur,* etc.
The mediæval theological term *Corpus Christi* is
deliberately adopted by the Elizabethan divines, and,
with equal deliberation, they say that It is *given* in
the Holy Eucharist to the faithful. It is a curious
instance of theological confusion of thought that Dr.
Griffith Thomas quotes these words, on the very next
page of his book, in apparent oblivion of the fact that
he had just flatly contradicted them. He
also makes use of the Rubric on " Spiritual
Communion " in the Communion of the
Sick, just as Dr. Colenso did, to emphasise
his denial of the Real Objective Presence. Bishop
Ryle made the same use of this Rubric,
as showing " the views of those who
drew up our Prayer Book." *(Knots Untied,* p. 210).
" The importance of this Rubric," says Dr. Griffith
Thomas, " as giving us the mind of our Church on
the real relation between the outward sign and the
inward grace can hardly be exaggerated." *(Catholic
Faith,* p. 280.)

The Rubric says that, if a person is prevented by
the Act of God from reception, he can yet
make an act of " spiritual communion,"
although " *he do not receive the Sacrament with his
mouth.*" From this Dr. Griffith Thomas argues (i) that
the Rubric conveys a new doctrine expressing the
mind of the Reformers, and (ii) that this new
doctrine embodies an identification of " spiritual "
and " sacramental " communion which denies any
Objective Presence of our Lord in the Sacrament,

Marginal notes:
Dr. Griffith Thomas denies the Real Presence.

His misuse of the Rubric on " Spiritual Communion."

Bishop Ryle also misused it.

Futility of their argument.

prior to, and *apart* from, the act of reception. The futility of both points of this argument is self-evident.

S. Augustine's *Tantum crede et manducasti.*

S. Augustine believed firmly in the Real Objective Presence. But the whole Western Church followed him in saying *Tantum crede, et manducasti,* of the case where a person is *physically* debarred from " sacramental " communion. His words passed into a theological maxim. In the

Quoted in the Sarum Rubric on " Spiritual Communion."

Sarum Manual for the Visitation of the Sick the priest is directed to say to a sick person, thus physically debarred, " *Frater, in hoc casum sufficit tibi vera fides et bona voluntas. Tantum crede, et manducasti.*" The Reformers did not express any new doctrine in their Rubric, which is only an expansion of the Sarum

Its teaching was repeated by the Reformers in our Rubric.

Rubric : " Brother, in this case true faith and good-will sufficeth for thee. Only believe and thou hast partaken." To make an argument against the Real Presence out of the Reformers' repetition of the teaching of the Sarum Rubric is the outcome of an ignorance which, in a student of Liturgiology, almost seems wilful. The Reformers, whatever their own views may have been, were only repeating in this Rubric the universal doctrine of the Catholic Church on the question

The same teaching set forth by Archbishop Egbert of York.

of " Spiritual Communion." Archbishop Egbert of York (eighth century) speaks thus of the case of a man dying without being able to receive the Blessed Sacrament : *Si homini alicui Eucharistia denegata est, et ipse interea moriatur, de his rebus nihil aliud coniicere possumus nisi quod ad iudicium Dei pertineat, quoniam in Dei potestate erat quod absque Eucharistia obierit.* The Rubric, which Dr. Griffith Thomas glorifies as a new doctrinal departure, practically repeats Archbishop Egbert's teaching that the case of a man dying without the Eucharist is to be left to the care of God's overruling mercy and providence.

CHAPTER V.

THE DOCTRINAL ERRORS OF FOREIGN PROTESTANTISM UPON THE VISIBLE CHURCH, THE APOSTOLIC MINISTRY AND THE LESSER SACRAMENTS, CONSIDERED IN REFERENCE TO THE TRUE TEACHING OF THE ENGLISH CHURCH.

LUTHER, Calvin, and Zwingli deliberately rejected the divinely revealed truth that the Holy Catholic Church, as a visible society, is the Kingdom of Heaven on earth, and further, that it possesses a threefold Apostolic Ministry, derived by succession from the Apostles, as the organs of the Body of Christ, and the stewards of His sacramental channels of grace.

Luther, Calvin and Zwingli denied the true doctrine of the Visible Church.

These Reformers established a series of human societies of Christians which tended to increase and multiply, owing to the fissiparous tendency of unbridled private judgment. At first these "human societies," named as they mostly were after their human founders, retained a certain portion of the creed of Christendom. But the inevitable tendency of the "human society" is to produce the Unitarian conception of a "human Christ." It has been so, even in that Mecca of Calvinists, In the middle of the nineteenth century Calvin's own city had so far departed from his teaching as to expel Calvinist ministers who still retained their belief in the Godhead of our Lord.

And supplanted it by human societies.

The human "Church" produces a "human" Christ.

Geneva.

The Genevan Calvinists of to-day reject the Incarnation.

The modern descendants of the Huguenots in France have followed their Genevan co-religionists in
So do the modern French Protestants. becoming practical Unitarians. Lutheran Germany of to-day has also practically become Unitarian, and the Lutherans, a few years ago, were only prevented from abolish-
So do the modern Lutherans. ing the Apostles' Creed by the personal intervention of their *summus episcopus*, the Kaiser. A very large proportion of the Nonconformists, who were ejected in 1662
So did the bulk of the Noncon-formists of the eighteenth century. for their refusal to accept the Book of Common Prayer, became Unitarians during the early part of the eighteenth century.

The fact that a large number of Presbyterians,
The orthodoxy of many Separa-tists does not affect the main argument. Wesleyans, and members of other religious bodies still hold fast to the Nicene Faith, is a matter for devout thankfulness. But it does not affect the plain verdict of history in general, which is that a man-made Church tends ultimately to produce a man-made con-ception of Christ, instead of the Divinely revealed definitions of the Three Creeds of the Holy Catholic Church.

In Chapter I. we have already quoted Professor Mozley's trenchant words on Luther's man-
Professor Mozley on the Lutheran "Church." made "Church." "The new Lutheran Church," he said, "rose up because the Lutheran doctrine wanted it, and appealed to no other sanction or right." So it was with the man-made "Churches" of Calvin and Zwingli, the "Brownists," or Independents, the Anabaptists, the Quakers, and, in later days, the Wesleyans, and num-erous other religious sects. But these man-made "Churches" possess certain common features. They agree in rejecting the Apostolic Succession of the

Christian ministry, conveyed through the Episcopate, which Bishop Lightfoot truly called the "historic backbone" of the Church. All the Protestant writers whom we have been quoting are accustomed to state that Luther, Calvin, Bullinger, Beza, and others, would have retained Episcopacy if it had been practicable for them to do so. In Chapter I. we have effectually disproved this baseless theory, on the testimony of Luther's own words and actions, and by the acute comments upon them which appear in Bishop Creighton's "History of the Papacy." They unanimously reject the *Sacerdotium* of the ministerial Priesthood of the Catholic Church, and with it they reject Sacramental Confession, and its corollary, the gift of Absolution, as conveyed through the Christian Priesthood, as the certified channel of God's Pardon for sins committed after Baptism. They reject Confirmation, as the Sacrament of sevenfold grace, given unto us by the Laying-on of the hand of the Bishop, as the Successor of the Apostles. They deny the sacramental character of Holy Matrimony as an indissoluble union. All these common features are characteristic of "foreign Protestantism," and are distinctly contrary to the teaching of the Church of England.

The " human " Churches deny the Apostolic Succession and the Sacerdotium as well as the grace of the " Lesser Sacraments."

But Bishop Drury asserts " that it is nowhere stated that Episcopal Ordination is essential either to the Sacraments, or to the Covenant which they seal, or to the grace which they convey. Nothing but the express command of Christ could lead us to assert that the absence of Episcopal orders, however desirable and useful they are, constitutes an actual rent from the Church " (*English Church Teaching*, pp. 186-187). Dr. Griffith Thomas commits the same error when he says : " There is no trace in Scripture of any covenanted connection between grace and Episcopacy " (p. 354). It is therefore

Bishop Drury's denial of the necessity of Episcopacy.

Dr. Griffith Thomas takes the same line.

necessary to call attention to one position which has been urged as a necessary test of Catholicity—namely, what is termed Apostolic Succession, but which really means to those who use the phrase, Episcopal Succession. The Church of England has never committed herself to this untenable position, either in her formularies or in the writings of her best and most representative men. Unbroken *episcopal*, or indeed any other ministerial succession, is no necessary guarantee of Catholicity. We can see this in the entire absence of any reference to Episcopacy in the Articles—a silence which is significantly admitted by Dr. Gibson in his important work on the Thirty-nine Articles." (*The Catholic Faith*, pp. 352-3.)

It is perfectly true that the Elizabethan Reformers, as Keble says (*Preface to Hooker*, p. 59), did not do more than say that Episcopacy was ancient and allowable. They were infected with "foreign Protestantism," but their successors, such as Archbishop Bancroft, taught the necessity of Episcopacy as Andrewes and Laud did. But the reference to Bishop Gibson's words is a curious instance of controversial special pleading.

His reference to Bishop Gibson is mere special pleading.

It is true that he speaks of the silence of the Articles, as caused by the hesitating attitude of the Elizabethan Reformers. But in the *very next* sentence he says : " for the *deliberate judgment* of the Church of England *we must look elsewhere.*" And on the very same page (*Articles*, p. 745) he quotes Bishop Hall (whom the Protestant party claim as their own) as saying that " Episcopacy is not only an *holy* and *useful* but a *Divine Institution*, and therefore cannot be abdicated without a manifest violation of God's Ordinance " [*Episcopacy by Divine Right* (A.D. 1639), *Works*, vol. ix. p. 160]. Bishop Gibson proceeds: "The Church of England, as judged by her formal documents,

Bishop Gibson's real judgment on Episcopacy.

He quotes Bishop Hall's words on the Divine Institution of Episcopacy.

recognises *none* but *Episcopal Orders*. She feels
compelled to insist upon Episcopal Ordination
in every case, and can recognise no other " (*Ib.* p. 746).
Dr. Griffith Thomas perverts Bishop Gibson's plain
meaning, and boldly states that Presbyterian ministers
were allowed to accept benefices in the Church of
England between 1552 and 1662. The well-known

Dean
Whittingham's
case proves that
Presbyterians
could not
officiate in the
Church of
England.
case of Dean Whittingham of Durham, who
was prosecuted by Archbishop Sandys of
York in 1578 for being in Presbyterian
orders, and who would have been deprived,
if he had not died whilst his case was
pending, shows that Dr. Griffith Thomas
makes statements incapable of proof. An evil legacy
from mediæval times permitted laymen to hold
Church benefices, but they were not expected to
exercise any ministry. Whittingham admitted that
" he was neither deacon nor minister according to the
laws of this realm," and his appointment was a
political sop to the Puritans. These irregularities
speedily ceased, and it cannot be proved that Presbyterian ministers were allowed to exercise their

John Knox was
a validly
ordained Priest.
ministry, even in times of transition.
John Knox, when officiating as Chaplain
to Edward VI., had been validly ordained
priest before he turned Reformer.

We may here remark that if the Church of England
did not consider Episcopacy to be of the *esse*, and not
merely the *bene esse*, of the Church, her attitude of
exclusiveness and non-recognition of any but Episcopal

If Episcopacy is
not essential,
the Church of
England sins
against unity.
Orders would be a grievous crime against
Christian charity, and an open offence
against Christian unity. Unless Apostolic
Episcopacy is of Divine Right, and neces-
sary to the conveyance of the grace of valid Sacraments,
it is a breach of charity to insist upon it as the
Ordinal undoubtedly does. It is either a vital necessity or a thing indifferent. If it is a thing indifferent,

as Bishop Drury and Dr. Griffith Thomas infer, there is no excuse for their continuing to adhere to the Church in which they hold office, since its teaching is diametrically opposed to theirs. Bishop Ryle, of course, took the same line as they do in more forcible language. Quoting the Preface to the Ordinal, he said, "The Church of England calmly asserts that its own ministers are scripturally ordained. . . . But it nowhere says that none but Bishops have power to call. . . . Never anywhere does Scripture say, from Matthew down to Revelation, *Except a man belong to a Church governed by Bishops he cannot be saved*. . . . I can never take up the ground that some men do in this day, who say that the Episcopal Church is the only true Church in Great Britain" (*Knots Untied*, pp. 278, 279, 280). "We protest against the idea of unity based on a common Episcopacy" (*Ib.* p. 16). "Let us be satisfied that our own Communion is Scriptural, but let us never pretend to unchurch all communions except our own. I loathe the idea of handing over the communions to which such men as Matthew Henry and Doddridge and Robert Hall and McCheyne and Chalmers belonged, to the uncovenanted mercies of God, or saying that such men as these were not *really* and *truly* ordained. People dare to talk of their not belonging to the *Catholic Church*, and of their being guilty of schism! People may shut them out from what they call the *Catholic Church*, but I am firmly persuaded they will not shut them out from the Kingdom of God " (*Ib.* p. 281).

Here is an amazing ignorance of elementary theology! What Catholic theologian has ever said that Episcopacy was so necessary to salvation that non-Episcopalians were, *ipso facto*, shut out of the Kingdom of God? Bishop Ryle apparently forgot that all Catholics hold that all

Bishop Ryle's denial of the Divine Right of Episcopacy.

His ignorance of Catholic Theology.

baptised people are members of Christ, and therefore
members of the Catholic Church. But
this elementary fact does not render valid
the ordinations or sacraments (other than
Baptism) of a man-made society of baptised
persons who have organised themselves
apart from the visible polity of the Catholic Church,
and invented a ministry of their own, apart from the
Threefold Apostolic Ministry ordained by Christ. The
adherents of these man-made societies, who accept
the central truths of the Creeds, will be
judged in accordance with the measure of
their adherence to those truths. To their
own Master, and ours, they stand or fall.
We do not judge them uncharitably. We believe that
the words, "according to your faith, so be it unto
you," apply to them in their measure and degree. A
Zwinglian who eats some bread and drinks some wine
in remembrance of the Atonement, may have spiritual
profit from his action, just as it is profitable for us to
meditate upon our Lord's Cross and Passion. But he
does not believe that there is such a thing as the Holy
Eucharist, as Catholics believe in it. A believer in
the "Real Absence" cannot expect to receive the
gift of the "Real Presence." Those who deny
Sacramental grace do not expect to receive it.
They are content with invalid ministrations, and
therefore receive nothing which they do not expect
to receive. But that does not exclude them
from the reception of a *lower measure* of grace,
if, by inherited prejudices or invincible ignorance,
they sever themselves from the certificated channels
of grace which are guaranteed through the Divinely
appointed Apostolic Ministry. The Protestant writers
we have been quoting practically assert (i) that those

The true position of religious bodies organised apart from the Catholic Church.

Their adherents are judged according to the measure of their faith.

who adhere to these man-made ministries and
The assertions of Protestant writers on the Apostolic Ministry are baseless. organisations lose no grace at all, and possess the same spiritual privileges as those who adhere to the Ministry and Sacraments of the Catholic Church. They also assert (ii) that Catholic theologians practically affirm that none can receive grace outside the " certified channels " of Sacramental grace and Apostolic ministry. Both assertions are equally baseless and false. What Catholic theologians affirm is that Christ and His Apostles bequeathed to the Catholic Church, as the visible Body of Christ, a Threefold Apostolic Ministry, which is the guarantee, by its orderly and unbroken succession, of valid Sacraments, ministered according to Christ's ordinance, as the certified channels of grace. We also affirm that to depart from this ministry, and to set up in its place a
A " human Church " produces an Arian or " Human Christ." man-made ministry, as Luther and Calvin did, is to substitute an unreality for a reality, to say the very least, and we repeat that a man-made ministry, and a human " Church," has been proved in the long run, by the present heresies of the Lutherans, the Calvinists of Geneva, and the French Protestants, to produce the fatal conception of an Arian or Humanitarian Christ. If this evil tendency is not fully manifested amongst the more orthodox and conservative bodies who reject
The " down-grade " tendency of modern Non-conformity. Episcopacy, it is because of their adherence to the Creeds upon the subject of the Trinity and the Incarnation. But the " down-grade " tendency, which the late Mr. Spurgeon lamented amongst English Nonconformists, has found its development in the " New Theology " of Mr. Campbell, which is a modern mixture of Gnosticism and Unitarianism, in flat denial of the Catholic Faith concerning the Blessed Trinity and the Incarnation of our Lord.

Mr. Dimock's denial of the Apostolic Ministry took the form of a learned treatise on the doctrine of the Christian Priesthood, or *Sacerdotium*, in which he made the following assertions: I. There is no Christian Priesthood in the New Testament.   He denied categorically Bishop Gore's words that "the English Church had a serious mind to *continue* the old orders in the Reformed Church" (*R. C. Claims*, p. 158).   He said that the changes made in the Reformed Ordinal were meant to abolish the *Sacerdotium*, and to create a new order of "Ministers of the Gospel," and he agreed with the denial of Anglican Orders by Pope Leo XIII. on this very ground.   His words are: "If such an intention (i.e. the conferring of the *sacerdotium*) is necessary to the validity of orders, then there certainly has been no validly ordained Priest in the Church of England for more than three hundred years" (Dimock, *Sacerdotium*, p. 38).   He gloried in this allegation, and proceeds: "Have we no true *Sacerdotium?*   From Rome's point of view, Pope Leo says true when he declares that we have none. In all sincerity and kindness of heart, we doubt not that he has said it.   In truth and in charity we are persuaded that he could have said nothing else" (*Ib.* p. 42).

Mr. Dimock's chastened rejoicing over the Papal condemnation of Anglican Orders is fitly paralleled by the late Archdeacon Taylor's letter to the Press in 1896 when the Pope's Bull appeared.   His joy was unrestrained, and from the militant Protestant standpoint, he told the Catholic Clergy that Pope Leo had served the Protestant cause in denying the validity of the Anglican Priesthood, which he and his Orange Protestant friends had also always denied.   With regard

Mr. Dimock's denial of the Christian Priesthood.

He denied the continuity of the Anglican Priesthood.

And states that no valid Priest has been ordained in the Church of England for 300 years.

He agrees with the Papal Condemnation of Anglican Orders.

to Pope Leo's action in condemning Anglican
Orders in 1896 it may be observed
that he was well aware that the clergy
of the Evangelical "left wing" denied
their own Orders in rejecting the Apostolical Succession and its direct consequences, the
Sacerdotium of the Christian priesthood. It was
natural for the Pope to argue : How can I admit the
Priesthood of these Anglicans when a considerable
body of clergy within their own communion vehemently repudiate the validity
of their own Priesthood? A reference to
the Introduction of this book will show
how the Eastern Church regarded "the Calvinian
current" in the Anglican Church as a barrier to reunion. The action of the Pope in condemning
Anglican Orders in 1896 is mainly attributable to the
same cause. We have already seen that
Dr. Griffith Thomas asserts that "there is
no function or office of the Christian
Priesthood which cannot be exercised by
any and every individual believer in Christ
of either sex." This strange assertion was
practically carried into effect by the daughter of Dr.
Colenso in Natal in her effort to perpetuate her
father's schism after his death. In her
evidence before the Natal Parliament in
1909 Miss Colenso admitted that she had
personally "administered Communion,"
with the Prayer Book service, in a native
mission chapel, rather than allow the natives to join
the "sacerdotal" South African Church, which had
deprived her father of his Bishopric. This instance
of perverted filial piety would be quite justified by the
language of Dr. Griffith Thomas.

II. Mr. Dimock denied that the words in the
Preface to the Ordinal "to the intent that
these Orders may be continued," have any
reference to the historical continuity of the

Side notes:
Leo XIII. knew that the Protestant party denied their own Orders.

Hence his Condemnation of Anglican Orders.

Dr. Griffith Thomas denies all Priesthood save that which is common to all Christian men and women.

His language would justify Miss Colenso's exercising priestly functions in Natal.

Mr. Dimock denied the Continuity of Anglican Orders.

Priesthood at all. He said that the compilers of the Ordinal never meant to continue the Threefold Apostolic Ministry with its historic *Sacerdotium* derived from our Lord's commission to the Apostles. He explained away the words, " Whose sins thou dost forgive," etc., in the formula of Ordination, and says " The Ordinal tells its own tale. Is it not a new Ordinal ? " (*Ib.*, p. 73). But flat denials of this character only prove the mental perversity of those who made them. Neither Mr. Dimock, nor the other writers who hold similar views, can evade the consequence of the crucial fact that, in accordance with the Preface of the Ordinal, and the law of the English Church a Roman Catholic Priest, or a Priest of the Eastern Church, can join the English Church and exercise the full rights of his Priesthood without re-ordination ; whereas a Lutheran, Presbyterian, or Wesleyan minister, or any other minister of a non-episcopal body, must be regularly re-ordained Deacon and Priest before he can minister the Word and Sacraments in the *Ecclesia Anglicana*.

No one can evade the fact that Roman and Eastern Priests can minister in the Church of England without re-ordination.

And the further fact that all non-episcopal Ministers must, under like circumstances, be re-ordained.

There is no escape for Mr. Dimock and his Protestant friends from the consequences of this fact. It is useless to quote Cranmer's private opinions. We have to do with the Ordinal, *as it is*, with the amendments of 1662. Before those amendments it was a valid Ordinal, and that it is intended to convey the *Sacerdotium*, and *does* so convey it, is a fact untouched by the contrary opinion of Pope Leo XIII. on the one hand, and the agreement with that opinion expressed by his Protestant allies on the other hand.

The Ordinal conveys the Sacerdotium.

Mr. Dimock naturally objected to the *Responsio* of the Archbishops to the Papal condemnation of

Anglican Orders. So did Cardinal Vaughan, and the Protestant attempt to discredit the theology of the Archbishops is as futile as the Roman Catholic attempt. Mr. Dimock said: "It contains some expressions which seem to warrant a *distinct disclaimer* of its being a declaration of the doctrines of the Anglican Church" (*Ib.*, p. 59). Most persons who read it will recognise its value as a most moderate and cautious statement of Anglican Theology. But because it teaches the doctrine of our Prayer Book and Articles upon the true *Sacerdotium* of the Anglican Priesthood it met with a "distinct disclaimer" from Mr. Dimock. On the one side we have two representative men of moderate views, namely the late Archbishops Temple and Maclagan. On the other side we have Mr. Dimock, and the "foreign Protestant" element, which survives as an excrescence upon the surface of the English Church.

Mr. Dimock's objection to the Responsio of the English Archbishops.

The Responsio teaches the true doctrine of our formularies.

There is no possible comparison between them. The Archbishops in their *Responsio* frankly and fairly interpreted our formularies. The "foreign Protestant" School is driven to non-natural interpretations of plain facts and plain words. The unconscious special pleading of Mr. Dimock is more pleasant reading than the illogical polemic of the late Bishop Ryle. But its agreement with "foreign Protestant" and "Cumminsite" formularies is just as manifest in the one case as in the other. The portions of the *Responsio* which declare Anglican doctrine and are objected to by Mr. Dimock are as follows: "We truly teach the doctrine of the Eucharistic Sacrifice, and do not believe it to be a 'nude commemoration' (*nuda commemoratio*) of the Sacrifice of the Cross." But Mr. Dimock says that the Anglican doctrine of the Eucharistic Sacrifice *is* a *nuda commemoratio*. His words are: "We must acknowledge the charge they bring against

Mr. Dimock denies the teaching of the Responsio on the Eucharistic Sacrifice.

And wrongly affirms that our doctrine is a nuda commemoratio.

us. Our doctrine of the Eucharistic Sacrifice is just
what they mean by a *nuda commemoratio*, and
from the standpoint of Rome's doctrine it ought to be
condemned as heresy. (*Ib.*, p. 28.)

On pages 16 and 17 of his book, Mr. Dimock
He also denies strongly deprecates the words of the
the teaching of Responsio of the English Archbishops
the Responsio
upon the con- which declare the union between our
nection between Lord's *Sacerdotium* in heaven and the
our Lord's
Priesthood and Sacerdotium of His Priests on earth,
priesthood of
the Catholic who minister the Eucharistic Sacrifice in
Church. the Church Militant. They say that that
reverence precludes "too precise definitions of the
manner of the Sacrifice, or of the relation which unites
the sacrifice of the Eternal Priest and the Sacrifice of
the Church, which in some way are certainly one."
The English Primates speak positively of the
Sacerdotium of the Anglican Priesthood, and maintain
that we teach the Sacrificial aspect of the Eucharist,
and its union with the Heavenly Sacrifice offered by
our Eternal High Priest. Addressing themselves to
the Pope and to the Catholic Bishops of the whole
Church, Eastern and Western, the Archbishops were
The Responsio is careful enough not to overstate Catholic
a very valuable doctrine as taught in the Anglican formu-
antidote to
Protestant laries. But their very moderate statement
errors on the of our Doctrine of Sacraments and Holy
Sacraments.
Orders is poles asunder from the Protestant
definitions of Mr. Dimock, Bishop Moule, Bishop Ryle
and Bishop Drury. This *Responsio* is a most
valuable antidote to the errors of "foreign Protestant"
theology, as taught by the "left wing" of the
Evangelicals. It is a touchstone of loyalty to the
Catholic heritage of the *Ecclesia Anglicana*, and
deserves careful study on the part of all loyal
Anglicans. Its careful defence of the Catholic
character of our Ordinal, and of its intention to continue the Threefold Apostolic Ministry of the Catholic

Church, is most logical and conclusive against the baseless assumptions of Mr. Dimock and others, that

The "Cumminsite" denial of the Catholic character of Holy Orders. the Reformed Ordinal was intended to abolish "Priests," and substitute for them "Ministers of the Gospel." The Protestant denial that Anglican Orders are "Catholic" Orders finds its fulfilment in the "Cumminsite" formularies. Article XXIV. (*Of Ministering in the Congregation*) says : "That doctrine of *Apostolic Succession* by which it is taught that the ministry of the Christian Church must be derived through a series of uninterrupted ordinations, whether by tactual succession or otherwise, and that without the same there can be no valid ministry, no Christian Church . . . is wholly rejected as unscriptural and productive of great mischief." Here we have plain speaking in plain terms. The honesty of Dr. Cummins and his body of "Reformed Episcopalians" is most commendable. They seceded from the American Church, because they declined to put a forced and unnatural construction upon its formularies. The "left wing"

Agreement of Bishop Ryle and others with the doctrine of the Cumminsites. of the Evangelicals agrees with this Twenty-fourth Article of the "Cumminsites" rather than with the Preface to the Ordinal and the teaching of our formularies on the Apostolic Ministry. The quotations in this chapter from Bishop Ryle, Bishop Drury, and Dr. Griffith Thomas clearly prove that their true theological standpoint is that of the "Reformed Episcopal Church," and *not* that of the Church of England. Bishop Cummins was well acquainted with "foreign Protestant" teaching. His denial of the Apostolical

The Second Helvetic Confession, the French Confession, and the Belgic Confession take the same line. Succession is fitly paralleled by Zwingli's views, as cited in a previous chapter. The "Second Helvetic Confession," which was drawn up by Bullinger, denies the Three-fold Apostolic Ministry by asserting "the parity of all ministers" in cap. xviii. sec. 16.

In sec. 8 it is laid down that ministers are *elected* by the people and *ordained* by the elders. In sec. 10 the *sacerdotium* of the Priesthood is denied. The French Confession of 1559 teaches the same errors in chapters xxx-xxxiv. So does the Belgic Confession of 1551 in Articles XXX. and XXXI. So does the Scotch " Confession of Faith " of 1560 in Article XXII.

Bishop Drury holds that the Holy Eucharist can be validly administered without a lawfully ordained Priest, and he tries to pervert the plain words of the Lambeth Conference of 1888 to support this error. He says that the Lambeth Conference stated that the sole essentials of a valid Eucharist are : " The use of Christ's Words of Institution and of the elements ordained by Him." In other words " the form and the matter are the only essentials named." (*English Church Teaching*, p. 170.)

Bishop Drury's denial that a Priest is necessary for the Consecration of the Holy Eucharist.

But the words he quotes form part of the famous Lambeth " Quadrilateral," or fourfold conditions of Christian Unity, and the very next condition insists on a valid priesthood by laying down the necessity of the " Historic Episcopate" as a *sine quâ non*. Controversial statements of this character are liable to incur the charge of a *suppressio veri*, even if we acquit the writer of a conscious *suggestio falsi*. The denial of Apostolic Orders involves a denial that Ordination conveys grace and power. So we expect to find the statement that appears in p. 258 of *English Church Teaching*, that " Ordination simply means authoritative appointment, but it does not confer *grace* or *power*." This Manual which calls itself " *English Church Teaching*," and is mainly written by two Bishops of the Church of England, thus flatly denies that the words of our Ordinal : " Receive the Holy Ghost for the office and work of a Priest in the Church of God,"

His misinterpretation of the Lambeth " Quadrilateral."

" English Church Teaching" denies the grace and power of Ordination.

convey any *grace*, and that the further words : "Whose sins thou dost forgive," etc., convey any *power*.

It is impossible to avoid the conclusion that the "foreign Protestant" theology of both these Bishops has driven them into a position of open contradiction of the plain words and teaching of the Ordinal they have both solemnly pledged themselves to use. The denial of the Apostolic Ministry, and of the *sacerdotium* which it involves, carries with it a denial of the Visible Church, as one Body. If non-episcopal Ordinations are valid, as these writers assert, there is no Visible Church, but only a collection of visible societies of equal standing, such as Episcopalians, Presbyterians, Wesleyans, and others, including the Quakers, who deny the existence of a visible Ministry and Sacraments.

The foreign Protestants abolished the Sacrament of Confirmation. *English Church Teaching*, (p. 255) allows it, but says *it is by no means identical* with the rite administered by the Apostles in Acts viii. Dr. Griffith Thomas says : "We retain the exact form of the Apostolic action (i.e. Laying-on of hands) *but with a different* purpose" (*The Catholic Faith*, p. 181). And this *purpose*, according to Dr. Griffith Thomas, is *not* the reception of the inward and spiritual grace of the Sevenfold Gifts of the Spirit, through the visible sign of the Apostolic Laying-on of Hands, which is named in Hebrews vi., v. 2, amongst the "Six First Principles" of the Doctrine of Christ. To turn from this erroneous view of Confirmation to Sacramental Confession and Absolution, we find Dr. Griffith Thomas says that the Prayer Book phrase, "the benefit of Absolution," means only "the application of Scripture to the special need" (p. 390). He ignores the Absolution in the

Marginal notes: Abolition of Confirmation by the Foreign Protestants. Dr. Griffith Thomas and others deny its Sacramental character. His further errors on Sacramental Confession and Absolution.

Visitation of the Sick, and contents himself with saying that "no Auricular Confession and Absolution can be found in the Prayer Book or formularies of the Church of England" (p. 392). He does not tell us how he explains Canon 113 of 1604 which not only admits and pre-supposes Auricular Confession, but re-enacts, in the "Reformed Church of England," the ancient canonical penalty of "Irregularity," to be inflicted on any Priest who should divulge the secrets of the Confessional. The punishment of "Irregularity" is the heaviest censure upon a Priest. It renders him incapable of administering the Sacraments, or officiating at any public service of the Church (*vide* Lyndwood, lib. i. tit. 4).

Canon 113 of 1603 asserts Auricular Confession.

Bishop Drury dismisses the whole question of the personal "Absolution" in the "Visitation of the Sick" by the ingenious subterfuge of saying that he interprets Canon 67 of 1604 as giving permission to every clergyman "licensed to preach," to use the Service for the Visitation of the Sick, or not, as he pleases. On this convenient theory the Absolution vanishes, and the whole service is relegated to absolute disuse by every Priest "licensed to preach." (*English Church Teaching*, p. 176.)

Bishop Drury's erroneous view of Canon 67.

If Bishop Drury knew anything of the Canon Law, such an interpretation of Canon 67 would be impossible to him. The liberty permitted by the Canon does not touch the authority, or the doctrinal witness of our Office for the Visitation of the Sick, nor does it touch its position, as combining our *lex orandi* with our *lex credendi*. All it does is to give the same reasonable permission to our Anglican Priests, which a Roman Catholic, or Eastern Priest has : namely, that he shall not be tied solely to the prayers and exhortations of an authoritative formulary, but that he has the power of using his own discretion in supplementing

The Canon does not touch the doctrinal witness of the Prayer Book form of Private Absolution.

or abbreviating the form appointed. The fact that Canon 113 deals with Auricular Confession and Private Absolution is proof enough that Canon 67 was not intended to abolish it by a side-wind, as Bishop Drury thinks. The outspoken dislike of Bishop Ryle to the witness of "the Visitation of the Sick" to Auricular Confession and Private Absolution is more honest than the subterfuges of Dr. Griffith Thomas and Bishop Moule. After attempting the explanation that the Absolution "only declares a person absolved *who is already absolved by God*"; and that, "*I absolve thee,*" *can only mean* "I *declare* thee absolved,*" Bishop Ryle said (of Auricular Confession and Private Absolution) "I deeply regret that the formularies of the Church contain any expressions which are capable of being twisted into an argument in defence of the doctrine, *and I should rejoice to see them removed.*" (*Knots Untied*, p. 326.)

Bishop Ryle desired to expunge all Prayer Book expressions which teach Private Confession and Absolution.

But he did not in the least understand the doctrine which he condemned. He imagined that confession before the Priest was the *substitution* of confession to a *man* for confession to *God*. (See pp. 327-328.) Whereas every instructed Catholic knows that we confess to God in the presence of His Priest, who is the channel of God's pardon and absolution, and who acts, ministerially, as the ambassador and representative of our Eternal High Priest, Who is the sole Absolver of penitents, and in Whose Name His Priests convey to sinners His Pardoning Grace and Forgiveness.

His ignorance of the true doctrine involved.

With regard to the Sacrament of Marriage we find Dr. Griffith Thomas denying its *sacramental* character (*Catholic Faith*, p. 159), apparently oblivious of the fact that Marriage is directly called "a Sacrament" in the Seventh Homily of the First Book of the Homilies. Protestant writers eagerly fly to the

Denial of the Sacrament of Marriage by Dr. Griffith Thomas.

Homilies for controversial extracts to suit their purposes. They must not complain of this reference to Marriage as " a Sacrament," although the Homilies possess no real doctrinal significance. Anglicans do not reckon Marriage as " a Sacrament" because the Homily calls it " a Sacrament," but because the Catholic Church has always taught that it *is* a "Sacrament." We need not recur to Luther's evil onslaught upon the Sacrament of Marriage. The Swiss Reformers were less indecent than Luther, but they destroyed the "sacramental character" of Marriage. Mr. Dimock

The *Reformatio Legum* on Marriage.

and other Protestant writers are fond of referring to that abortive attempt to foist a Protestant code of Canon Law upon the Church in the reign of Edward VI., which was known as the *Reformatio Legum.*

In this Code, which was the work of Cranmer and Peter Martyr, we see how the " foreign Protestant " leaven was working upon the Church of

Its un-Catholic laxity.

England. Cap. 5 allows the " so-called " innocent party in a divorce for adultery to re-marry. Cap. 8 allows " desertion " as an adequate cause for divorce *a vinculo.* Cap. 9 allows divorce and re-marriage if one of the parties to a marriage is absent for " two or three years." Cruelty and enmity were also grounds for divorce and re-marriage. The personal influence of Queen Elizabeth caused this

The Westminster Confession's lax view of Marriage.

Reformatio Legum to be shelved when an attempt was made to give it the force of law in her reign. Broadly speaking, it gives us the Protestant view of marriage and divorce. The Westminster Confession (cap. xxiv. sec. 5) gives permission for divorce for adultery or

The First Helvetic Confession equally lax.

wilful desertion. Hence the lax view of marriage and the strange marriage laws of Scotland. The Twenty-eighth Chapter of the First Helvetic Confession allows divorce *a vinculo,* and consequent re-marriage.

Bullinger had a chief hand in this document. It is the root of the present Swiss laxity and freedom of divorce in the Protestant Cantons, just as the lax views on marriage of the New England Puritans are

Milton's advocacy of Divorce.

at the bottom of the abominable divorce laws which are prevalent in America. Milton, who is regarded as a Puritan hero, carried the " foreign Protestant " laxity on divorce further than Zwingli or Bucer. In his work on the " Doctrine and Discipline of Divorce " he allowed divorce by mutual consent, or even by the desire for divorce of either party to the marriage. The Evangelicals have not gone so far as Milton. But Dr. Griffith Thomas can

Bishops voted for the Divorce Act of 1857.

compare the Westminster Confession with our Articles, without a word of reprobation for its evil teaching on divorce. And we cannot forget that the Evangelical Bishops, Bickersteth of Ripon, Pepys of Worcester, and Campbell of Bangor, joined with Bishop Tait of London in voting for the Divorce Act of 1857, which has proved so

Bishop Bickersteth of Ripon voted for marriage with a deceased wife's sister.

disastrous to the morals of the people of England. Bishop Bickersteth also voted for marriage with a deceased wife's sister in the House of Lords, thereby proving that, as a leader of the Evangelicals, he was more in sympathy with " foreign Protestant " laxity than with the Catholic law of marriage as declared in our Table of " Kindred and Affinity."

Protestant omission of Unction of the Sick.

One of the most evil effects of the " foreign Protestant " influences, which dominated the revision of the Prayer Book in 1552 was the omission of the sacramental rite of Unction of the Sick. It was retained in the First Prayer Book of 1549, and, writing in 1867, Bishop Forbes called it " the lost Pleiad of the Anglican Firmament " (*Articles*, p. 465).

Its Scriptural character, evidenced by the Epistle of

S. James, has caused its sure and gradual restoration
Bishop Forbes on Unction. in the Anglican Communion, since Bishop
Forbes wrote some forty years ago.
His words that " there is nothing to hinder the
revival of the Apostolic and Scriptural custom of
anointing the sick, whensoever any devout person
may desire it " (*Ib.* p. 474) have been practically
Its restoration in America and in the Colonies. endorsed by the Lambeth Conference of
1908. Its use is so common in our sister
Church of America that it has ceased to be
a party question. It is in use in the Scottish and
South African Churches and in many colonial dioceses.
It is within the *ius liturgicum* of any Bishop to consecrate the Oil for the Sick, and to authorise an Office
for its use. Such an Office is authoritatively in use
in most of the South African dioceses. Strange to
Curious revival of Unction by extreme Protestants. say, an unauthorised use of anointing the
sick has been adopted by certain Pro-
testants. In a book called *What hath
God wrought*, published by mission
preachers of the Keswick Convention, we find that this
unauthorised use of unction is mentioned. This is
referred to on p. 400 of Strong's *Manual of Theology*.
It is possible to hope that Protestants may pass from
this unauthorised use to a true conception of the
Sacrament prescribed by the Apostle S. James. For
the First Book of 1549, which enjoined Unction, was
called " a very godly order " by the very men who
established the Book of 1552, which omitted Unction,
and which, we may be again reminded, never came into
practical use in England.

CHAPTER VI.

A BRIEF SKETCH OF THE HISTORY OF " FOREIGN PRO-
TESTANT " INFLUENCE WITHIN THE CHURCH OF
ENGLAND UP TO THE CLOSE OF THE EIGHTEENTH
CENTURY.

THE Reformation of Henry VIII. was a political
movement, forced upon Church and people
by the despotic will of the King. Henry
VIII. used Parliament and Convocation as
the tools of his despotism, but he was most careful to
veil his tyranny under the existing forms of law.
Parliament and Convocation were threatened and
coerced into obedience to his will.

Character of the
Reformation of
Henry VIII.

The Wars of the Roses had destroyed the power of
the feudal nobility. The middle classes
had not risen into power. The Tudor
despotism was an absolute Monarchy, in
which the despotic will of the monarch was carried
out by a subservient Parliament. The public opinion
of the nation was non-existent, and individuals who opposed the King promptly
became the victims of judicial murder.
The savage executions of the Carthusians, and of men
of European reputation, like Sir Thomas More and
Bishop Fisher of Rochester, terrorised the people of
England. The Suppression of the Monasteries is a
terrible story of foul slanders and royal greed. The
clever stroke of policy, whereby the King
bribed his servile nobles to be yet more
servile, by giving them the spoils of the

The Tudor
despotism.

The judicial
murders.

Sacrilegious
suppression of
the Monasteries.

monasteries, aided his policy, whilst it involved them and their descendants in the curse of sacrilege, which the King had already incurred in his own person.

The ecclesiastical history of the reign of Henry VIII. cannot be dealt with in this volume. It must be studied in Dixon's great " History of the Church of England," and in Dr. James Gairdner's admirable volumes on " Lollardy and the Reformation." Some words of Dr. Gairdner's are worth quoting.

Dr. Gairdner on the effects of the Reformation.

" Looking back we ought to be aware that the great shipwreck of the old system really did produce disastrous and demoralising results; that it set men afloat on tempestuous seas on rafts made of broken timbers of what had once been S. Peter's Ship, that the attempt to preserve the unity and independence of a National Church only led to cruelty and oppression ; and that at last we have found peace —if we have found it even now—in what might almost be called the principle of an Agnostic State, trying to hold the balance even between contending denominations." (*Lollardy and the Reformation*, vol. ii. p. 229.)

The title of this book deals with the story of " an alien Theology " which obtained a footing within the Church of England. In using the term " alien Theology " the author does not mean to ignore the fact that Wyckliffe, an English Priest, founded Lollardy in England, and that his doctrines were disseminated on the Continent by his followers Hus, and Jerome of Prague. Wyckliffe's heresy caused the religious war in Bohemia with its appalling bloodshed and disastrous consequences. We have already seen that the infection of Wyckliffe's Communism and Socialism spread from Bohemia to Germany to bear fruit in the horrors of the Peasant War, whilst his heresies paved the way for the blasphemies and excesses of the Anabaptists.

Wyckliffe and Lollardy.

His evil influence on the Continent.

But the main point to be remembered is that, although the heresies of Wyckliffe prepared the ground,

His social Anarchy.

after his death in 1384, through his followers who were condemned by the Council of Constance in 1414, the new teaching of Luther, Zwingli and Calvin was in great measure original, and not copied from Wyckliffe. Luther was the friend of Princes, and his conduct in denouncing the Peasants showed his hatred of Wyckliffe's social anarchy. So that it is true to say that the " foreign Protestant " theology which dominated the Church of England in 1552 was " alien," and not merely Wyckliffe's heresies, re-entering England in a new garb, fashioned on the Continent. Dr. Gairdner makes it quite plain that Lollardy had little influence at the beginning of the reign of Henry VIII. The following summary of Wyckliffe's teaching is

A summary of Wyckliffe's teaching.

condensed from Dr. Gairdner's book. (i) The socialistic view that *all men's goods should be in common*, which thus anticipated the French anarchist's view that " all property is robbery." (ii) " *Dominion is founded on grace*," by which Wyckliffe meant that if a King, or Ruler, were not " a man of God," and did not govern according to a literal interpretation of Scripture, he was not to be obeyed. (iii) All Church endowments were to be abolished, and the laity were to withdraw payment of tithes from any priest whom they considered unworthy. (iv) No one was a true member of the Church unless he was predestined to be saved.

Dr. Gairdner very rightly discriminates between

Wyckliffe was not the forerunner of Lutheranism as such.

these anarchical doctrines of Wyckliffe, and the subsequent views of the foreign Protestant Reformers. Wyckliffe did not assert any doctrine of Justification resembling Luther's, although in some sense he was the forerunner of Luther and Calvin in his assertion of Predestination. He attacked the ecclesiastical polity of the

Church rather than its doctrines, and why he should be called " the Morning Star of the Reformation " by modern Protestants, is just as amazing as the curious fact that a number of law-abiding Evangelicals, who were certainly neither Communists, Socialists, or Anarchists, should have founded a theological seminary at Oxford in the nineteenth century for the purpose of training Protestants for Holy Orders, and given it the name of " Wyckliffe Hall." Dr. Griffith Thomas, who was Head of this Institution, may be able to explain this strange historical anomaly. There is something to be said for calling the kindred institution at Cambridge " Ridley Hall "; but the name " Wyckliffe Hall " is a standing monument of illogical incongruity.

Curious anomaly in making Wyckliffe a forerunner of Protestantism.

The first person to inculcate " foreign Protestant " ideas in England was William Tyndale. His translation of the Bible into English was marred by bitter and virulent marginal notes, which expressed the leading heresies of the Continental Reformers. His polemical bias led him into virtual mistranslations of the original text. He agreed with Luther's relaxations of the law of marriage, and anticipated their development in modern Germany by advocating the marriages of uncles and nieces, and of a man with his deceased wife's sister and a woman with her deceased husband's brother. He went further and actually advocated in certain cases the marriage of brothers and sisters. (*Lollardy and the Reformation*, vol. i. p. 379.)

William Tyndale the first English Protestant Reformer.

His strange views on Marriage.

Dr. Gairdner has told the truth about Tyndale, as it appears to the impartial view of the historian. He also disposes of the false idea that the Mediæval Church forbade the use of the Bible in the vernacular to the laity. Sir Thomas More truly said in his

Sir Thomas More denies that Tyndale's was the first English translation of the Bible.

Dialogue that there were English versions of the Bible before Wyckliffe's and Tyndale's translations. "The whole Bible," says Sir Thomas More, "was, long before his days, by virtuous and well learned men translated into the English tongue, and by good and godly people with devotion and soberness well and reverently read." What the Church objected to was unauthorised translations, by private individuals, especially such a translation as Tyndale's with its heretical notes and glosses. If the Church is "a witness and keeper of Holy Writ" (as our Twentieth Article declares) it is the bounden duty of the Church to authorise all translations of the Scriptures, lest false and inaccurate versions should be circulated to the damage of souls.

Its unauthorised character and its heretical glosses.

Tyndale went abroad in 1524 and conferred with Luther at Wittemberg, where he printed his English translation of the Gospels of S. Matthew and S. Mark on Luther's model. In 1526 his entire New Testament in English was smuggled into the country, and vehemently denounced by the moderate and gentle Bishop Tunstall, who preached against it, and declared he had found no fewer than three thousand errors in it. The book was condemned, and the Bishop bought up the whole edition from Tyndale and destroyed it. The shrewd Reformer did not mind the burning of his books, for he said he could use the Bishop's money for printing a new edition, which he promptly did. The Convocation of Canterbury condemned Tyndale's version, and set about a version of their own, for which Bishop Gairdner translated two of the Gospels. Coverdale's Bible was authorised by Thomas Cromwell before his fall, but "Matthew's" Bible was set up in the Churches by authority in 1539.

His translation denounced by Bishop Tunstall.

And condemned by the Convocation of Canterbury.

Dr. Gairdner says of Tyndale's "Old Testament" that "it had numerous marginal annotations of a biting and sarcastic

Dr. Gairdner on Tyndale's translation.

character." He had not proceeded quite to these lengths in defiling the New Testament with partisan glosses, but his general intent, even there, was obvious enough to his contemporaries. (*Ib.*, vol. ii. p. 244.)

If William Tyndale was the first leader of those who corrupted the Church of England with "foreign Protestant" theology, his place and influence were afterwards more than filled by John Hooper, the "father of English Nonconformity." Hooper was no "Separatist." His desire was to turn the Church of England into a Zwinglian sect. He did not conceal it. Canon Dixon has written the best and most impartial History of the Reformation which has yet been published. Here is his character sketch of Hooper. "He was a man of strong body and perfect health, of strong but unimaginative mind, by no means incapable of humility, but extremely self-sufficient, learned, of tireless patience, absolute sincerity, and considerable benevolence ; but so sour and forbidding that those who came to consult him had been known to go away without opening their purpose, repelled by his gloomy looks. (Dixon, vol. iii. p. 181.)

John Hooper.

Canon Dixon on Hooper's character.

He had been a monk, like Luther, and hated monasticism with a hatred like Luther's. Luther had a certain joviality of manner, and could unbend with genial companions, as his "Table-talk" shows. Hooper's gloomy and forbidding manners made him the forerunner of the Puritans of Cromwell's day. He fled the kingdom when Henry VIII. passed the Law of the Six Articles, and lived at Zurich, where he saw the triumph of Zwinglianism. He came back when Edward VI. had been two years on the throne to convert England to Zwinglianism. Cranmer and Ridley looked on him with the disfavour with which men regard one who has overpassed their

His career.

own boundaries in the direction of change and innova-
tion. He preached a course of violent sermons
His violent Sermons. before the King, which anticipated the
attacks of the Elizabethan and Cromwellian
Puritans upon Church order. He violently attacked
the English Ordinal and the use of the
A specimen quotation. vestments, including the surplice. "It is
ordered," he said, "that he that will be
admitted to the Ministry must come in white vestments. That is not in God's Word, nor in the primitive
and best Church." The Communion, he said, "should
be received standing or sitting rather than kneeling."
"Priests who chanted the Mass," he said, "deserved
eternal damnation." "The minister of Christ is to be
known from the minister of the Devil by his preaching
tongue, not by cap and vesture." "As concerning the
Ministers of the Church, I believe that the Church is
bound to no sort of people, *or any ordinary succession*
of Bishops . . . and none of them should be believed
but when they speak the Word of God." Hooper also
desired to take away the chancels of churches, so that
the Puritan ideal of a rectangular "preaching house"
should supersede the dignity and seemly order of the
mediæval chancels. But the Prayer Book ordered that
"the Chancels shall remain as in times past," and so
they were preserved from the iconoclastic fury of
Hooper's refusal Hooper and his followers. Ridley was
to wear the Sur- content to destroy the "Altars of the Lord"
plice and Cope. in the diocese of London without any legal
authority. But, like Cranmer, he objected to Hooper's
desire to destroy the Chancels. Cranmer and Ridley
eventually put Hooper in prison for refusing to wear
the usual vestments of a Bishop when he was
nominated to the See of Gloucester. He said, when
nominated, "I cannot put on me a surplice and a cope."
He was called before the Council and was asked to
His open subscribe certain Articles, one of which
Zwinglianism. stated that the Sacraments *convey* grace.

Here was the touchstone of Zwinglianism. Hooper promptly replied (almost in the words of Dr. Griffith Thomas, Bishop Moule and Bishop Ryle), " They *seal*, they *testify* grace, but do not confer it." Cranmer appealed to the foreigners Bucer and Martyr, who, Protestants as they were, advised Hooper to conform.   Martyr added some wholesome criticism on Hooper's sermons.   " Take advice," he said,

Peter Martyr rebukes Hooper's violence.

" cease those unseasonable and bitter sermons which are a hindrance to your usefulness."   Hooper replied by a virulent pamphlet in which he desired that sermons should be preached *every day*, for the Sunday sermons were not frequent enough.   Hooper is here the forerunner of that strange Puritan exaltation of preaching, which made Bishop Ryle say, as has already been noted, that *preaching* is of more importance than the Holy Eucharist.   Laski, the Pole, vehemently espoused Hooper's cause against Cranmer and Ridley.   The controversy continued for nearly a year.   In 1551 he was committed to the

Hooper's opposition to Vestments as a sign of his historical continuity.

custody of Cranmer to be admonished and punished.   He flouted Cranmer's admonitions, and was committed to the Fleet Prison.   Then he gave way, and was consecrated in the abhorred vestments, which he was allowed to discard except on special occasions, or when preaching before the King.   Thus began the opposition of the " foreign Protestant " party and their allies to the historical continuity of the Church, which the vestments of her clergy symbolise.   The "alien influence" of Geneva and Zurich has caused a controversy from Hooper's days to the Twentieth Century, and the end is not yet.   Although Bucer and Martyr

His yielding a source of grief to his friends.

advised Hooper to temporise, their followers, such as Utenhovius, called Hooper's yielding " a great grief and stumbling block to all good men," a sentence which combines the arrogance of these foreign Protestants with their determination to turn the Church of England into a Zwinglian sect. [All the quotations and references in Hooper's matter are from chap. xvii. and p. 255 of *Dixon's History*, vol. iii. The whole chapter should be carefully studied.] Fuller's *Church History* is a book to be read, although Laud's biographer, Heylin, criticised his leniency to the Puritan faction. His quaint words on the rise and progress of Nonconformity, or, in other words, the growth of the alien " foreign Protestant" element within the Church of England are worth quoting.

"Alas ! that men should have less wisdom than locusts, which, when sent on God's errand, did not thrust one another, whereas here such shoving and shouldering, and hoising, and heaving and jostling, and thronging between clergymen of the highest parts and places. For now Nonconformity in the days of King Edward was conceived, which afterward, in the days of Queen Mary (but beyond the seas at Frankfort) was born ; which in the days of Queen Elizabeth was nursed and weaned, which under King James grew up a young youth or tall stripling ; but towards the end of King Charles' reign shot up to the full strength and stature of a man, able not only to cope with, but to conquer the Hierarchy its adversary." (*Fuller's Church History*, p. 401.)

Fuller on Nonconformity.

Fuller's graphic picture of the rise and progress of "foreign Protestantism " within the Church of England is true enough. The quarrels at Frankfort between the Marian exiles who desired to use the Edwardian Prayer Book, and the thoroughgoing men, who were convinced Zwinglians and Calvinists, can be studied in Dixon's *History*, vol. iv. p. 690. John Knox inveighed against the use of the Prayer Book, and Whittingham (afterwards the Presbyterian " Dean " of Durham), supported him against Dr. Cox of Oxford, who desired

The Frankfort troubles.

the Edwardian service.   But after the Marian re-
action, the exiles brought their quarrels back to
England with them.   The extreme party,
The Foreign Protestant party in the reign of Elizabeth. led by Travers, determined to force the full
Genevan discipline upon the Church of
England, just as Knox was enforcing it in
Scotland.   In Elizabeth's reign the " foreign Pro-
testant " party worked skilfully underground.   Under
the outward shadow of devotional meetings, called
" Prophesyings," was an inner secret league, which
Its dishonest efforts to intro- duce the Geneva dicipline secretly. actually set up the Presbyterian system in
Northamptonshire and in other places.   The
Presbyterian " classis " with its lay elders
was surreptitiously established.   A man,
lawfully ordained Priest by a Bishop, was secretly re-
ordained after the Genevan fashion, on being " called "
to a parish by the " classis."   The ordination by the
Bishop was called his " civil " or " legal " ordination, so
that he could get possession of the temporalities of his
benefice.   But the *real* ordination, in the minds of these
disloyal members of the Church of England, was the
Presbyterian " function " secretly conducted by the
" Classis."   Archbishop Whitgift, although partially
Archbishop Whitgift's resistance. inclined to Calvinism, set his face resolutely
against this dishonest attempt to change the
constitution of the Church of England by a
propaganda of covert disloyalty.   He believed in the
Divine Right of Episcopacy, as a matter of *principle.*
His predecessor Grindal only believed in it as a matter
of expediency, and if Queen Elizabeth had not suspended his jurisdiction, for his refusal to put down the
" Prophesyings," the "foreign Protestant" policy might
have obtained a complete victory.   As things were, as
Dr. Frere tells us, " the Puritan Clergy had been
Dr. Frere on the Elizabethan Puritans. managing their parishes according to the
provisions of the *Book of Discipline* to
which many of them had bound themselves
by a formal subscription, and in defiance of the

discipline of the Church of which they were ministers. They had been taking their commission from the Presbyterian bodies, and not from the Bishops, except as a matter of legal form, and their directions from the *classes* and rival synods, and not from Convocation. They had used only such parts of the rites of the Church as they pleased, worn what they pleased, preached as they pleased, done what they pleased and depraved everything with which they were displeased, and yet they continued to occupy the rooms and take the revenues of the Church, whilst they pledged themselves to seek to pervert its government. The Puritan conscience was somehow able to justify what the conscience of the loyal Churchmen and the Sectary alike condemned." And Dr. Frere very justly says that the Puritan, or "foreign Protestant," party, took up " *a position which in itself was inherently dishonest.*" (*History of the English Church in the Reigns of Elizabeth and James I.*, p. 281.)

Dr. Frere is right in saying that these Puritans, who remained within the communion of the Church, whilst they disbelieved its doctrines and tried to overthrow its polity, were dishonest. The Separatists, who made a small beginning during Hooper's time in the reign of Edward VI., and who increased in strength under Elizabeth, had the merit of *honesty*, as Dr. Cummins and his Reformed Episcopal followers had in their separation from the American Church in 1873. And it is an open question whether the adherents of "foreign Protestantism" under Elizabeth, who remained within the Church, whilst they openly attacked Episcopacy and the Prayer Book, were any more dishonest than the " Militant Protestants " of to-day who, as we have traced in the preceding chapters, profess to accept Episcopacy and the Prayer Book, whilst they deny the necessity of the one and the plain teaching of the other. The severity of Elizabeth's

government against the Separatists had some justification.   In 1592 they formed a plot to
assassinate the Queen in order to bring
the nation under the Genevan " Discipline."
This action on their part seriously annoyed the Puritan
leaders within the Church, because it compromised
their position.   The quarrel was embittered
by the fact that the Puritans *within* the
Church held the same Genevan doctrines as
the Sectaries who had left it.   But Archbishop
Whitgift's firm policy met with its due
reward.   The obstinate Puritans within the
Church were deprived, and the remainder
took a more moderate tone.   The covert
establishment of the Genevan " Book of Discipline,"
and its administration through the Presbyterian
" classis," as a secret supplement to the Church system,
ceased until its revival under Cromwell.

Separatists plot against the life of Elizabeth.

Annoyance of the Puritan leaders.

Archbishop Whitgift's firm policy and its results.

Archbishop Whitgift's leaning to Calvinism has been
exaggerated.   His " Nine Lambeth Articles " were, as
Dr. Frere calls them, " a compromise," and a modification of the extreme language of those who drew them
up.   The Puritan attempt to give them equal authority
with the Thirty-nine Articles is in itself a sufficient
witness to the fact that the Thirty-nine Articles are not
Calvinistic.   On March 24th, 1603, James I. peaceably
succeeded Elizabeth.   The hopes of the " foreign Protestant " party within the Church rose high, but James
had bitter experience of Scottish Presbyterianism.   He
had come to see that the maxim " No Bishop, no King "
expressed the political aspirations of the Puritan Party,
and the maxim was verified within fifty years ; for the
martyrdom of Laud, and the consequent temporary
overthrow of the Church of England, was speedily
followed by the imprisonment and subsequent martyrdom of King Charles I.   The Puritan or " Nonconformist " party within the Church immediately
approached King James, and presented the " Millenary

Petition," with the extravagant "claim," as Dr. Frere calls it, "that it represented the wishes of one thousand ministers" (p. 294). Dr. Hook, the old-fashioned moderate Anglican, uses stronger language than Dr. Frere. He calls it "the great lying petition—called the *Millenary Petition*—although only signed by seven hundred and fifty ministers." *(Lives of the Archbishops*, vol. x. p. 179.) It contained the usual objections of Hooper and the Marian exiles to the Cross in Baptism, the Ring in Marriage, Confirmation, the use of the Surplice, the terms "Priest" and "Absolution," bowing at the Holy Name and the reading of Lessons from the Apocrypha. The "foreign Protestant" party went further in canvassing for more signatures. They expressed a desire for further reform, "agreeable to the example of other Reformed Churches." They desired to substitute the polity of Geneva and Zurich for the polity of the Church of

The Hampton Court Conference. England. James, with Bishop Bancroft as his chief adviser, met them at Hampton Court on January 14th, 1604. The Puritans gained nothing by their efforts. A few minor changes were made in the Prayer Book, and the addition of the portion of the Catechism which deals with the Sacraments was also made, to their great discomfort, because of its Catholic teaching. After the death of Whitgift, Bancroft became Archbishop of Canterbury in 1604. He carried on Whitgift's work from a higher standpoint of Churchmanship. Clarendon (vol. i. p. 36) says that Archbishop Bancroft could have checked the coming Puritan Revolution, had he lived. He did most valuable constructive work, which made Laud's subsequent efforts to restore true Church life possible, and modern Church historians have begun to recognise his real greatness, (*vide The Reconstruction of the English Church*, by Professor Usher). The acute and well-balanced mind of Mr. Wakeman recognised the Hampton Court

Conference as the parting of the ways between
Puritanism and the Church.

"The Hampton Court Conference marks the end of
the first great effort of Puritanism to obtain
Mr. Wakeman's
summary of the
Hampton Court
Conference. ascendency over England.   It entered on
the struggle with great advantages . . .

But as, year by year, it developed on its
own lines, it became increasingly evident that it was
impossible to combine a Calvinistic Church theology,
resting on the doctrine of election, with the Catholic
Church theology, resting on the doctrine of Baptismal
Regeneration.   Still more impossible was it found to
combine a Calvinistic system of Church Government,
resting upon a *classis* of Presbyters as the centre of
authority, with the system of the Catholic Church
which made the Bishop the unit of Government and
the source of jurisdiction.   Because the struggle broke
out about dresses and ceremonies, men have jumped
to the conclusion that dresses and ceremonies were
the cause of the struggle.   History tells a very
different tale.   Dresses and ceremonies are in themselves indifferent.   As the visible expression of
doctrine they are in the highest degree significant.
The Puritans objected to the cap and surplice, because
to them it meant the continuity of the Church, its
claim in England to be the heir of the Church of
Athanasius and Lanfranc.   They refused to use the
sign of the Cross in Baptism, because to them it
meant the doctrine of Baptismal Regeneration.   They
rejected the Ring in Marriage, because to them it
seemed to assert the sacramental character of the rite.
They demanded the abolition of Confirmation, because
they did not believe that it was a means of grace.
They endeavoured to introduce the Book of Discipline,
because they desired to undermine and destroy the
authority of the Episcopate. . . .   Arguments there
may be to show that Puritanism is better than the
Church—there are none to prove that the two systems

were compatible with one another. The English Government and the English nation had to choose between them, and the Hampton Court Conference marks the choice which they made." (*History of the Church of England*, p. 354.)

This lucid summary of the issues of the controversy is specially valuable for the purpose of this book. In former chapters the theological standpoint of the Puritan, or "foreign Protestant," theology, as it appears in the English Church to-day, has been definitely set forth. Its doctrinal agreement with "foreign Protestant" theology has been plainly manifested. It embodies an alien system of religion, which is *inherently incompatible* with historical Christianity, as embodied and taught in our formularies. The "foreign Protestant" party have admitted this incompatibility in their own publications. In the *Christian Observer* for 1845 (p. 126) the following passage occurs: "There are essentially *two Churches* in our Church, *and they cannot exist together*." This is a self-evident fact. It is also true that its adherents of to-day do not make the same demands as its adherents made at the Hampton Court Conference—demands which were carried to their logical completeness in the Puritan victory under Cromwell, when the Hierarchy was abolished and the Prayer Book proscribed by law. It is also true that our modern "militant Protestants" do not demand the abolition of the Hierarchy or the establishment of Presbyterianism in its place. They have ceased to object to the surplice, although some of them still adhere to the use of the gown in the pulpit. They do not object to the "Sign of the Cross" in Baptism, although they object to its use as a token of private devotion, or even as an architectural decoration. They have quietly dropped the ceremonial objections

Marginal notes:
This summary is valuable.

Puritan and Catholic Theology are *inherently incompatible.*

Altered standpoint of Modern Puritans within the Church.

of the Puritans, except with regard to the Ornaments Rubric, on which subject they vehemently re-echo the

Our "Foreign Protestant" partisans have become "Conformists." Puritan objection to the Vestments which was disregarded by the Bishops at the Savoy Conference in 1661. They have become "Conformists" instead of "Non-conformists" of Hooper's type. But their "Conformity" at the present day by no means involves their repudiation of Hooper's theology. As "Conformists" they inculcate the Puritan theology and the tenets of "foreign Protestantism" generally, on different and

They use wiser methods than their Puritan predecessors. wiser lines than their predecessors in the sixteenth and seventeenth centuries. They tried Prayer Book Revision on Protestant lines in the nineteenth century and failed. They do not fight the Hierarchy, but have attempted to capture it by political means, as was the case with the Protestant Bishops appointed by their influence in the "sixties" by Lord Palmerston. They have used political weapons at elections and have struck at their theological opponents by means of Parliamentary debates. They have resorted to mob violence and aggressive invasions of peaceful parishes. They have used great bitterness of speech and unscrupulous methods of controversy. But their masterpiece of wisdom in controversy has been their attempt to prove

They claim that their Protestant interpretation of our formularies is the only tenable view. that the Prayer Book and Articles are on *their* side and that the Church of England is a *Protestant body*. Their attack upon the Catholicity and historical continuity of the Church of England is directed upon the inner lines of its citadel, whilst the Puritans of the seventeenth century attacked its outer defences. Suppose the Puritans at Hampton Court and at the Savoy Conference had said "We accept the Hierarchy, but we reserve to ourselves the privilege of denying its necessity or efficacy. We accept the Prayer Book, but we will find ingenious methods for disusing such parts of it as we do not believe in. We will accept *everything on paper* and then we will enter upon a polemical campaign to evacuate the Church system of its true meaning, and we will fill the ranks of the Hierarchy and Clergy with men specially trained to our own views, who will brand all others who hold true Prayer Book views, as Romanising traitors or imperfect Christians." It would have been a very ingenious and clever plan of campaign. But it would not have worked in the seventeenth century. Men's methods in those days were too primitive and direct. But this plan of campaign has worked well in the nineteenth century. The good fruits of religious toleration have by very over-ripeness decayed into the evil fruits of "Universal Comprehensiveness" and consequent religious anarchy. And the modern representatives of the Puritans of the seventeenth century now tell Catholic Churchmen that *And that the Catholic interpretation is treasonable.* the Protestant interpretation of the Prayer Book and Articles is the only tolerable and reasonable one and that the Tractarian revival of the forgotten Catholic theology of the Caroline divines is treason to the Church. This is the practical standpoint of the writers we have been criticising in the previous chapter.

The seventeenth century "Puritan within the Church" said at Hampton Court, "We *They accept the formularies by reading into them their own interpretation of them.* cannot tolerate the Prayer Book and the Hierarchy." The modern "Puritan within the Church" says, "We have no quarrel with the Hierarchy or the Prayer Book. It is easy for us to read our *own* meaning into the book, and take our *own* line with the Hierarchy. And we have the additional satisfaction of stigmatising as traitors all those who are loyal to the true meaning of the formularies."

The fierce and stern invective of the old Puritans is much to be preferred to the suave intolerance of their

modern representatives and to the absolute self-con-
fidence with which they condemn all who
attempt to dispute their exclusive claim to
interpret our formularies in accordance
with their views.   Certain proven facts are
at variance with this "exclusive claim" which our
modern Puritans believe themselves to be justified in
making. Bishop Ryle did not "untie" all the "knots"
which hindered the completeness of the "victory on
paper" of militant Protestantism. Mr. Dimock did not
succeed in convincing any reasonable person that Laud
and the Caroline divines did not teach the Real
Presence just as clearly as Dr. Pusey and Canon
Liddon did.   There are still to be found persons who
will dispute the claim of Dr. Griffith Thomas to set
forth *The Catholic Faith*, and there are still theologians
enough left to demonstrate that Bishop Moule and
Bishop Drury do not represent "English Church
Teaching" in the volume which they have put forth
under that misleading title.   This modern Puritan
claim to exclude from the category of loyal Churchmen
all those who decline to accept the Puritan interpretation of our Hierarchy, Sacraments and formularies is,
in its special way, just as arrogant as any
claim put forth at Hampton Court and the
Savoy Conference by the Puritans of the
seventeenth century. It is a curious ecclesiastical phenomenon of the nineteenth century, and it is
now necessary to trace very briefly the way by which it
came about. The Puritan party, after Hampton Court, had to wait till the Battle of Naseby
before they could put down the Hierarchy
and the Prayer Book by main force.   Their
modern successors, even in the midst of nineteenth century tolerance, inaugurated a policy of persecution which resulted in the imprisonment of five Clergy
of the Church of England who opposed their views
and declined to accept their Protestant and Erastian

This exclusive interpretation cannot be admitted.

This claim is as arrogant as seventeenth century Puritanism.

The Victorian persecution reflected the spirit of Crom-well's Puritan revolution.

conception of the law of the Church and the ceremonial of the Book of Common Prayer.

Our historical presentment of the influence of the alien "foreign Protestant" party in its various stages between the Hampton Court Conference and the Public Worship Regulation Act of 1874 must necessarily be much condensed.

An epitome of Puritan history.

The first stage in the progress of Puritanism resulted from the acute political instincts of its leaders. The personal characters of James I. and Charles I. were very different from the arbitrary strength of their Tudor predecessors. The mantle of the Tudor despotism sat uneasily on their shoulders, and they substituted for the inherent Tudor masterfulness the doctrine of a Divine Right of personal government, to be exercised apart from any consideration of the individual strength or weakness of the Sovereign. James I. was shrewd enough to see that the religious republicanism of the Genevan discipline, with its "parity" of ministers, would bring *political* republicanism in its train as its logical outcome. His watchword, "No Bishop, no King," was an instance of his political sagacity, which caused the Church to lean upon and support the Monarchy. The Puritan leaders saw their opportunity. The nation had acquiesced in the personal government of Elizabeth, because she was a woman and a Tudor. But James I. did not possess her powers of masterful and unscrupulous diplomacy, and the English people were ripening for a revolt against absolutism. The King helped the Church against the Puritans, and the Puritans eagerly retaliated by heading the popular party in their opposition to the Church and the Monarchy. Archbishop Bancroft had established new ideals in the Church. Bishop Andrewes restored the Catholic theology of the

Contrast between the Tudors and the Stuarts.

The Stuarts relied on the Divine Right of Kings.

The Puritans became champions of political freedom.

And opposed the Church and the Monarchy.

Church of England and displaced the predominant Calvinism. The Puritanical leanings of Archbishop

Catholic ideals and theology restored by Bancroft, Andrewes, and Laud.

Abbot were neutralised by Laud, who had banished Calvinism from Oxford, as Andrewes had from Cambridge. Charles I. succeeded his father in 1625, and Laud preached the Coronation Sermon next year.

Soon after this he became virtually Prime Minister, and, in 1633, Archbishop of Canterbury.

Charles I. made Laud Archbishop of Canterbury.

Laud carried the Catholic theology of Andrewes into practical effect. He restored the outward decency of worship and enforced discipline and order with a strong hand.

Laud's policy.

He used the Royal authority to effect his objects, *but he was no Erastian.* Erastianism really means the subjection of the Church to the world power. In Laud's day the Puritanical House of Commons, with their perpetual attacks upon the Church, represented the world power, and he used the Royal Authority to combat it, for the sake of the peace and order of the Church.

Laud first dealt with the Puritan doctrine. Their ineffectual attempt to legalise the Calvinistic

Laud's " Declaration " on the Articles.

" Lambeth Articles " led them to attempt to read a Calvinistic sense into the Thirty-nine Articles, as their Protestant successors do to-day. Laud drew up the Royal Declaration, which is still prefixed to the Articles in our Prayer Book. This Declaration

The " literal and grammatical sense " upheld the Catholic interpretation against the Puritan.

said : " No man hereafter shall draw the Articles aside in any way. No man shall put his own sense or comment to be the meaning of the Article, but shall take it in the *literal* and *grammatical sense.*" This is what Newman did in the famous " Tract Ninety," which raised such a storm in the early " forties." The masterly Treatise of Bishop Forbes expanded Newman's work, and we owe the Catholic interpretation of the Articles to Laud's bold policy in asserting their " literal and grammatical sense." In a former chapter we have considered briefly their true position and its limitations of authority. But, limited though the Articles are by the Creeds and the theology of the Prayer Book, it would have been a fatal blow to the theology of the English Church if the Puritans had been Professor able to fasten their own meaning upon them Mozley on Laud's " De- instead of their " literal and grammatical claration." sense." Professor Mozley well says : " That our Articles have not a Genevan sense tied to them, and are not an intolerable burden to the Church, is owing to Laud. He rescued them from the fast tightening Calvinistic grasp, and left them, by his prefixed *Declaration*, open. Laud saved the English Church. . . . He stopped her just in time, as she was rapidly going down hill, and he saved all the Catholicism which the reign of Genevan influence had left her. That we have our Prayer Book, our Altar, even our Episcopacy itself, we may, humanly speaking, thank Laud. The English Church in her Catholic aspect is a memorial of Laud." (*Essays*, vol. i. pp. 227-228.) Bishop Ryle made a curious blunder about this *Declaration* of Laud's.

He devotes chapter iv. of his *Knots* Bishop Ryle's *Untied* to an attempt at fastening a Puritan blunder about Laud's gloss upon the Articles. He quotes Laud's " Declaration." *Declaration*, and then says : " Admirable words these ! Well would it have been if the unhappy Monarch who put forth this *Declaration* had afterwards adhered more decidedly to the doctrine of the Articles, *and not ruined himself and the Church by patronising and supporting such men as Archbishop Laud* " (p. 88). It is evident that the late Bishop Ryle did not in the least understand the history and origin of the *Declaration* and its obvious purpose. But the The House of House of Commons did. They looked upon Commons the *Declaration* as the doctrinal condemna- attacked it in the Puritan tion of Puritanism, and they passed a furious interest. counter-resolution. They were ready to

abolish the Prayer Book, as things were, and the
Declaration only fanned their fury against it.   One of
the main charges against Laud at his trial was that he
The " Declara-   wrote this " Declaration."   The author has
tion " formed   before him, as he writes this page, a copy of
one of the chief
charges in   the first edition of Prynne's account of
Laud's trial.   Laud's trial called *Canterburies Doome*.   It
was published by the authority of the " Long Parliament " in 1646, and was intended to pave the way for
the judicial murder of King Charles I., which took place
three years afterwards.   Allusions to this masterpiece
of controversial malignity are frequent, but few have
read it through.   On p. 160 Laud is ac-
Prynne's   cused of allowing the Jesuits to bring in
malignity.   *Arminianism*.   To Prynne and his Puritan
friends any opposition to Calvin's " Five Points " was
Popery in disguise.   It did not matter to them that
Arminius himself was a Dutch Protestant.   Any
favourer of his doctrines was a veiled Papist.   To
teach as the Fathers of the Church taught on the
mysterious subject of Election was rank Popery to
Prynne and his friends, who denied that Sacraments
conveyed grace.   We have already seen that Bishop
Ryle's Calvinism caused him to deny " sacramental
grace."   The *Elect* can do without it as they are preserved by "grace indefectible."   The *Reprobate* cannot
receive it, as they are already doomed to eternal per-
dition, and are, *ipso facto*, incapable of receiving grace.
For opposing this unchristian and wicked theology
Laud was condemned to death.   The other issues of
Prynne con-   his trial were side-issues beside this domin-
sidered the   ant issue.   " This Jesuiticall Prelate," says
" Declaration " a
proof of Laud's   Prynne, " abusing both the Parliament and
" Jesuitry."   his Majesty, to set up Arminianism more
securely, projected a new way of advancing it.   To
which end he procured His Majesty by a printed
Declaration prefixed to the Thirty-nine Articles (compiled by himself and other Bishops, of which the most

part were Arminians) to prohibit all unnecessarie disputations, altercations, or questions to be raised which might nourish faction both in Church and Commonwealth. And that no man print or preach to draw the Article aside any way, but shall take it in the *literall* and *Grammaticall sense*. By colour and abuse of this Declaration all Bookes against the Arminians were suppressed . . . on the contrary those of the Arminian confederacy were advanced, and freely tolerated to vent their Erroneous Tenets everywhere " (p. 161).

Prynne also accuses Laud because he answered the

Laud saved the Catholic sense of the Articles.

attack on the " Declaration " by the House of Commons, by stating that laymen have no authority in matters of doctrine, and that (with regard to the "literal sense" of an Article or Canon) " it is lawful for any man to choose what sense his judgment directs him to, so that it be a sense *secundum analogiam fidei*, and that he hold it peaceably, without disturbing the Church " (p. 164). Laud's breadth of view concerning subscription to the Articles was fatal to him. The Commons' "resolution" demanded subscription *according to a Calvinistic gloss*. Thus Laud saved the Catholic sense of the Articles, and gave his life for his work.

Sanguis martyrum semen ecclesiæ was never a truer

The effect of the martyrdom of Laud and Charles I.

maxim than in the case of Laud and Charles. We must rapidly summarise. The " Long Parliament " met on November 3rd, 1640, and sat till Cromwell dissolved it to set up a military despotism in 1653. Laud was

Summary of events.

committed by Parliament to the Tower on December 18th, 1640. He lay a close prisoner during the first period of the Civil War, until March 13th, 1644, when his trial began, which lasted till July 29th of the same year. The skilled malevolence of Prynne and his false witnesses could effect nothing to warrant a sentence of High

Treason.   So the trial was dropped, and a special
" Bill of Attainder" was rushed through the Commons
sentencing the innocent Primate of All England to be
hanged, drawn, and quartered.   Six Presbyterian
Peers formed the " House of Lords " which passed
this infamous Bill, which was, of course, *illegal*
without the consent of the Crown.   The Commons
violently insisted upon the indecency of hanging the
Archbishop.   The Scottish Presbyterians had promised
to help the Puritan cause if Episcopacy and the
Prayer Book were abolished, and Prynne's following in
the Commons thought that the public hanging of
Laud would further their plans.   Ultimately the

Martyrdom of Laud.

sentence was changed to beheading, and
on the 10th of January, 1645, Archbishop
Laud won his martyr's crown.   In 1643
Parliament abolished Episcopacy, and used the Epis-

Abolition of Episcopacy.

copal revenues for carrying on the civil
war against the King.   In the same year
Parliament ordered the convening of the Westminster

Westminster Assembly and abolition of the Prayer Book.

Assembly for the purpose of establishing
Presbyterianism on the Scottish model,
and drawing up a " Directory of Worship "
to supplant the Book of Common Prayer.
The Assembly was instructed to follow the discipline
of "foreign Protestant" Churches, and its " Confession
of Faith," as we have already seen, reflected " foreign
Protestant" theology.   The Westminster "Directory of
Worship " superseded the Prayer Book by Act of
Parliament on January 4th, 1644, and the use of the
Prayer Book was made a " penal offence " on August
23rd of the same year.   King Charles I. was sold by
the Scotch to Cromwell and the Parliament in 1647,
after the ruin of his cause by his defeat at Naseby.

Martyrdom of Charles I.

Cromwell's army dominated Parliament,
and, by its power, he procured the trial
and condemnation of the King, after
Charles had definitely refused to purchase his life

by consenting to abolish Episcopacy. His judicial murder on January 30th, 1649, was thus a true "martyrdom," or witness-bearing, for the Church, despite his errors in "King-craft," which must be set down to the difficult times in which he lived, and the relentless ferocity of his Puritan and Republican enemies.

England a Puritan Republic.

England thus became, for the time being, a Puritan Republic. The triumph of Presbyterianism was brief. Cromwell's army were mainly Independents or "Brownists," and the military despotism which he set up tolerated all kinds of sectaries except Quakers. Roman Catholics and Anglicans were vigorously forbidden to exercise their religion. But the civil despotism and religious anarchy came to an end at the Restoration of the Church and Monarchy in 1660, which very soon followed the death of Cromwell in 1658 and the abdication of his son Richard in 1659. The Bishops who survived the Puritan Revolution at once resumed their jurisdiction, and Juxon, who had attended Charles on the scaffold, became Primate. Charles II. desired a policy of toleration. The Parliament would have none of it. They ordered "the Solemn League and Covenant," which bound England and Scotland to a common Presbyterian polity, to be publicly burnt by the common hangman. But the Presbyterians and Independents still persevered in their policy. They met the Church leaders in the Savoy Conference in 1661, and practically reiterated the Puritan demands at Hampton Court.

Cromwell's Independents rule the Country.

The Restoration of 1660.

The Savoy Conference.

The last stage of the English Reformation was reached by the revision of the Prayer Book in 1662. About six hundred changes were made, and nearly all of them in a Churchly and Catholic direction. The theology of Laud and Andrewes was more powerful an influence

The Prayer Book of 1662.

after their death than during their lifetime.   On
S. Bartholomew's Day, 1662, all Ministers
The ejected who would not accept the Prayer Book
Ministers. were ejected, just as Cromwell had ejected
the Church Clergy.   Only eighteen hundred in all
were ejected for Non-conformity, a far less number
than the Clergy dispossessed by Cromwell.   The
lawful Clergy in many cases came back to their old
parishes, but a number of Puritanical Clergy conformed, to become the nucleus of the " Conforming "
Puritan party within the Church.   The demands of
the Puritans at the Savoy Conference would have
destroyed the historical continuity of the Church.

The English people have been unjustly credited
with steadiness of character.   But the verdict of
history shews that they are subject to sudden fits of
unreasoning passion and panic.   The Restoration
Parliament was more violent in restoring the Church
than the Bishops and Clergy thought
The Revolution prudent.   Under James II., the Parliament
of 1688 was the
triumph of rapidly became Whig-Erastian.   The Revo-
Erastianism. lution of 1688 was in some respects a
worse blow to the Church than the Puritan Revolution,
because its effects dominated the policy of the State
towards the Church up to the date of that culmina-
tion of Erastianism, the Public Worship Regulation
Act of 1874.   The ejection of the · Non-Jurors robbed
the Church of the best part of its Catholic element,
The " Conform- and the " Conforming " Puritans strength-
ing " Puritans
divide into the ened their position.   Their party bifur-
" Broad " and the cated into two distinct divisions at the
" Low Church "
parties. close of the seventeenth century, namely,
the Puritanical party and the Latitudinarian.   The Catholic-minded clergy of the Restoration
were, for the most part, men of learning and ability.
Macaulay's false The picturesque historical mendacity of
estimate of the Macaulay poured scorn on these men, but
Restoration
Clergy. he viewed them through Whig-Erastian

spectacles. The names of Pearson, Cosin, Barrow, South, Ball, Beveridge and Ken alone suffice to adorn this period of our Church History. But they were neither Whigs nor Erastians. The Non-Jurors thought of other things besides refusing allegiance to William III. The Usurper was a convinced Calvinist, who speedily abolished Episcopacy in Scotland, and, in 1689, moved Tillotson and other Latitudinarian divines to undo the work of the Savoy Conference. Their revised Prayer Book would have imperilled the Apostolic Ministry of the Church, and destroyed its Catholic character. Convocation was bold enough to reject the proposed revision, for the Non-Jurors left much of their influence behind them. This influence was distinctly manifested in the refusal of the Convocation of Canterbury to permit the phrases " Protestant Religion " and " Protestant Church " to be applied to the Church of England in a formal Address from the Clergy to William III., on the express grounds that the term " Protestant " was not applicable to the Church of England. (Lathbury's *History of Convocation*, p. 331.)

The Non-Jurors.

The abortive Revision of 1689.

A brief explanation of the " Latitudinarian " wing of the Puritan party within the Church is here necessary. It began in Laud's day with Chillingworth and Hales of Eaton. Chillingworth was a Roman Catholic converted by Laud. When he produced his misleading *dictum*, " The Bible, and the Bible only, is the religion of Protestants," it is impossible to avoid wishing that Laud had left him where he was. He was no Calvinist, and Hales was likewise an Arminian who rejected Church principles and Calvinism alike. Hales desired the elimination of all Catholic doctrine from Church services, so that Arians and Catholics should worship together. Cudworth and the Cambridge Platonists did not go so far as this, but their

The rise of the Latitudinarians.

influence was in the direction of an undogmatic Protestantism.   The Erastianism of Hobbes, who held
that the State ought to define the belief of the
Church, was an influence which more or less infected
them.   They were the forerunners of the school of Dr.

Arnold of Rugby, Archbishop Whately
Their Whig-Erastian policy. and Archbishop Tait.   Their ideas of
Churchmanship exactly fitted in with the
Whig-Erastian policy of the Revolution of 1688, and
they did their best to suppress what was left of the
Catholic element in the Church after the secession of
the Non-Jurors.   The brief revival of sound Church-
manship in the reign of Queen Anne was soon
Its triumph at the accession of George I. quenched by the predominance of Whig-
Erastian principles at the accession of
George I. in 1714.   Toland and the English
Deists influenced Germany, and their ideas laid the
foundation of German Rationalism.   Waterland and
Bishop Butler successfully combated the rising tide of
Waterland, Butler, Law and Hoadly. infidelity, but Walpole's policy, which
upheld Bishop Hoadly's mingled Ration-
alism and Zwinglianism, by suppressing
Convocation and refusing to promote any of the
Clergy who adhered to the Catholic teaching of the
Prayer Book effectually crushed it for nearly one
hundred years.   Hoadly was opposed by William Law,
whose *Serious Call* was the means of converting
John Wesley.   The "conforming" Puritans of the
Loss of spiritual religion by the Separatists. early eighteenth century had become as
"savourless salt."   The "Nonconformists,"
who had now become "Separatists," had
lost the subjective personal religion of their immedi-
ate predecessors—a generation which had produced
Baxter's *Saints' Rest,* and Bunyan's *Pilgrim's Pro-
The intellectual Puritans adopted Unitarianism. gress.*   The intellectual Puritans of the
Cromwellian Revolution followed Milton
in his Arian, or rather Socinian, views.
Sir Isaac Newton and John Locke were

practically Unitarians; and the "Salter's Hall" controversy showed that Unitarianism had become the heir and lineal descendant of the "Nonconformity" ejected in 1662. Dr. Waterland's great controversy with Arianism within the Church resulted in a victory which was more than controversial. There was room for a revival of personal religion, which came from the Wesleys and Whitfield. The Wesleys were Arminians, and Whitfield and his friends restored Calvinism, and the revival of religion which they preached was real, so far as it went. It was religion of a subjective and emotional type, with a vivid and real grasp of certain Christian verities. But the leaders did not "prophesy according to the proportion of the Faith"; they had no realisation of the *objective* side of religious truth. They did not teach that the Church is a visible polity, and they disregarded the Apostolic Ministry and the Sacraments of which it is the appointed guardian. The Church of England had been so long the slave of the State and the instrument of the Tudor and Stuart policy of religious uniformity that it ceased to appear to be what it really was and is, the Catholic Church of the English people.

The Wesleys and Whitfield revive personal religion.

The defects of this subjective revival.

Effect of the Tudor subjection of the Church by the State.

In the Introduction of this book the piety and good works of the eighteenth century "Evangelical" leaders was noted and commended. They owed their chief impulse to the Wesleys and to Whitfield. Romaine, Venn, Newton and Cecil did much to revive personal religion in England. Cowper, the poet, and Wilberforce, amongst laymen, exercised a powerful influence. Balleine's "History of the Evangelicals" gives a vivid picture, on the whole, of these men and their influence, although it is somewhat coloured by his manifest

Piety and good influence of the early "Evangelicals."

hero-worship.   A truer estimate is to be found in
Blunt's estimate Blunt's *Dictionary of Doctrinal and His-*
of their   *torical Theology.*   " Of the doctrine of this
theology.   school it may be said that, regarding
Redemption and the natural state of fallen man, they
held the tenets common to Luther, Calvin, and
Zwingli.   Luther's doctrine of Justification by Faith
was put foremost.   The doctrine of Free Grace was
much insisted on.   The necessity of an experience of
religion was taught, by which was meant that men were
to judge themselves, not by the testimony of a good
conscience, but by their feelings and an inner sense of
God's love and favour.   In this was made to reside
the proof of conversion to God, and a sense of sudden
conversion, as from a state of utter irreligion to an
assurance of forgiveness, was very commonly required.
Calvin's doctrine of Election and Predestination was
received; an Augustinian phase of belief looked coldly
on. . . Baptismal Regeneration was held in abhorrence,
and with Justification Baptism was held to have
nothing at all to do.   The statement of the doctrine
of the Holy Eucharist could not be distinguished from
Hoadly's, but, practically, the far greater devoutness
of the Evangelicals invested this Sacrament with
greater sacredness then did their doctrine.   As to the
constitution and order of the Church, the Evangelicals
were Episcopalians by habit, and so far as *Episcopacy*
consented to be subservient to their view of the
Gospel.   The Liturgy was little more than tolerated.
It was a current opinion that Dissenters from the
Church of England were the salt of the land. . .   This
doctrine is connected with the Latitudinarian theology
by the link of (Archbishop) Leighton, whose works were
again and again reprinted at the rise of Evangelicalism.
It was, thus, the zeal of Whitfield and Wesley that
re-animating the remains of the Foreign Reformed
Theology, and assimilating with it the better teaching
of the Latitudinarians formed the Evangelical School.

In neither of these sources was the true sacramental doctrine to be found " (p. 257).

It was admittedly difficult for the early Evangelicals to realise that the Church of England in the eighteenth century was a living and visible portion of the *One Holy Catholic and Apostolic Church*. The Non-Juring tradition had perished. The defeat of Charles Edward in 1745 had killed it politically. And the severe persecution of the ancient Episcopal Church of Scotland, on account of its link with the Non-Jurors, tended still further to obscure what remained of the Catholic teaching of the Caroline divines. But the saintly Bishop Wilson (and in a lesser degree, Bishop Horsley and clergy of the type of Jones of Nayland) maintained the Catholic tradition of doctrine, so that it never quite died out. Wesley's schismatic and invalid consecration of Coke, as "Bishop" for America, found its Churchly and lawful parallel in the consecration of Dr. Seabury as the first American Bishop by the Bishops of the despised and persecuted Scottish Church on November 14th, 1784. But the main feature of the early "Evangelicals" was their gentle and tolerant temper, which formed a marked contrast to their Puritan predecessors and their "militant Protestant" successors. They did not aspire to capture the Church of England. Their outlook was as narrow as their theology. "Preaching the Gospel" was their leading idea, and they did not concern themselves about the forgotten doctrines of the Prayer Book, or the constitution of the Visible Church, so long as the Anglican "Establishment" permitted them to use her pulpits to disseminate their views. They did not desire to dominate the whole ecclesiastical situation, and were content with toleration and a general acceptance of things as they found them. Their successors were not content with anything short of domination, as the next chapter will show.

Feebleness of the Catholic tradition in the eighteenth century.

Bishop Wilson and others maintained it.

CHAPTER VII.

INFLUENCE OF " FOREIGN PROTESTANT " THEOLOGY IN
THE CHURCH OF ENGLAND IN THE NINETEENTH
CENTURY.

THE nineteenth century has witnessed a conflict of
ideals within the Church of England and
its daughter Churches, which has brought
about difficulties greater than any it
has been previously called upon to face.
The twentieth century may see the solution of some of
our most pressing problems, but it is impossible to fore-
cast the future.   The main conflict of to-day is between
the ideal of a creedless invertebrate Christianity, which
loosely binds together in one communion men of
opposite and mutually destructive beliefs, and an
honest acceptance of the " literal and grammatical
sense " of our formularies.   There must be
of necessity varying types of thought, and
minds of a subjective, and of an objective,
tendency.   And these variations of type have always
existed in the broad and tolerant unity of the Holy
Catholic Church.   But the Anglican Communion will
cease to be Catholic, and will thereby forfeit its title to
the allegiance of believing Catholics, if it permits such
a conflict of ideals to be perpetuated within its borders
as will destroy its corporate witness to the
Revealed Truth of God.   The very *idea* of
Revealed Truth is *lost*, if portions of the

[marginal notes:]
Conflict of
ideals within
the Church of
England.

Legitimate
variations of
type.

Denials of the
Faith cannot be
tolerated.

Catholic Faith are regarded as open questions. The Protestant assertion of the " Real Absence " and the Protestant denial of Baptismal Regeneration cannot honestly be tolerated in a Church whose formularies teach the exact opposite, especially when the Protestant party claim the right to interpret those formularies in their own exclusive way, and to make their denials and assertions in the face of Scripture and history. The " Virgin Birth " of our Lord and the literal fact of His Resurrection and Ascension cannot honestly be denied, or even regarded as open questions, in a Church whose formularies directly assert these central facts of the Catholic Faith.

Sunt certi denique fines. *Defective* beliefs, whether in the direction of Protestantism or Latitudinarianism, can be tolerated so long as they do not pass into absolute *negations* of Catholic truth, as taught in our formularies. The Church can well tolerate a *minimising* theology on certain points, so long as it does not venture into the region of specific denial of some essential part of Revealed Truth. But militant Protestantism, and certain phases of so-called " Liberal" theology, categorically deny Revealed Truth as expressed in the Catholic Creed and our Anglican formularies. We are face to face to-day with these denials, and it is futile to under-estimate their disruptive force, and to minimise the anarchy to which they have reduced the *Eccelsia Anglicana.* They are the direct heritage of " foreign Protestant " theology, and its baleful influence upon the Church of England is clearly manifested by them.

(margin: Defective beliefs need not pass into specific negations.)

(margin: Foreign Protestant theology has produced specific denials of the Faith.)

In the early part of the nineteenth century the " Evangelicals " won influence and popularity. But they gradually lost their religious simplicity, and mingled their piety with polemics. Dean Church was

(margin: Dean Church's view of the decadence of the later Evangelicals.)

one of the clearest thinkers and wisest theologians of the nineteenth century. His cast of mind resembled Butler's, and his dispassionate judgment of the "Evangelicals" in 1833, when the Catholic revival began, is well worth recording. "It was the second or third generation of those whose religious ideas had been formed and governed by the influence of teachers like Hervey, Romaine, Cecil, Venn, Fletcher, Newton, and Thomas Scott. . . . But the austere spirit of Newton and Thomas Scott had, between 1820 and 1830, given way a good deal to the influence of increasing popularity. The profession of Evangelical religion had been made more than respectable by the adhesion of men of position and weight. Preached in the pulpits of fashionable chapels, this religion proved to be no more exacting than its ' High and Dry ' rival. It gave a gentle stimulus to tempers which required to be excited by novelty. . . . The circle of themes dwelt on by this school in the Church was a contracted one, and no one had found the way of enlarging it. . . . It too often found its guarantee for faithfulness in jealous suspicions, and in fierce bigotries, and at length it presented all the characteristics of an exhausted teaching and a spent enthusiasm." (*The Oxford Movement*, pp. 11-13.)

It is impossible to find space for a summary of the Catholic revival. Historians like Dean Church and Mr. Wakeman leave no room for lesser minds to cover the ground which they have so brilliantly and thoroughly occupied. The present writer is concerned with some forgotten facts and episodes of the last seventy years which will show how the alien influence of foreign Protestantism fought against the revival of Prayer Book teaching and Catholic theology, both from the Protestant and the Latitudinarian side. Dean Church speaks of Keble's " looking with great and intelligent dislike at

No space to tell the story of the Revival of 1833.

the teaching and practical working of the more popular system which, under the name of Evangelical Christianity, was aspiring to dominate religious opinion, and which, often combining some of the most questionable features of Methodism and Calvinism, denounced with fierce intolerance everything that deviated from its formularies and watchwords" (*Ib.* p. 21). It is the story of this "*fierce intolerance*" which forms the subject of this chapter. It is as unpleasant to describe as it has been unpleasant to discover the taint of "foreign Protestant" error—and error held with a presumptuous dogmatism—in the books of the modern writers which have been criticised in the preceding chapters. But it is a false optimism to disregard unwelcome facts and ignore the inner causes of disunion. *The Tracts for the Times* and their authors were fiercely attacked by the Evangelical leaders and their press. *The Christian Observer*, their chief organ, said, in 1848, of the "Tractarians": "There is hardly a single individual in the whole party, from the highest to the lowest, that has the slightest claim to the character of a well-read theologian; and the great majority are young men of the most superficial attainments." This ludicrous assertion was made when Pusey, Keble, Marriott, and other men of wide theological learning, were the leaders of the Tractarians. Well might the Broad Churchman afterwards known as Dean Alford of Canterbury observe: "As to all the opponents of the *Tracts* which I have seen, their spirit is so un-Christian, their ignorance so truly barbarous, and their theological systems so discontinuous and inconsistent with themselves, that I have never been able to read many pages of their writings without indignation." (*Life of Dean Alford*, p. 133.)

Fierce intolerance of militant Protestantism.

The Protestant attack upon the Tractarians.

Dean Alford's condemnation of it.

It may be noted here that Mr. Balleine, the modern champion and the enthusiastic historian of the Evangelical party, virtually accepts the thesis of this book on the theology of himself and his friends as the correct one. He begins his History with the words : "Evangelical Churchmen trace their pedigree to the Puritans, the Reformers, and the Lollards, to all within the National Church who have learnt to love a simple worship and a spiritual religion." (*History of the Evangelical Party*, published 1908, p. 1.) The implication that Catholics do not love " a simple worship and a spiritual religion," is characteristic of the unbalanced partisan. The severe simplicity of a Carthusian Mass finds its parallel in the early Eucharist of many a stately Parish Church and simple little Mission chapel. And the monopoly of " spiritual religion," which is the common heritage of millions of Roman, Greek, and English Catholics, does not lie with the Protestant party in the Anglican Communion, or with the non-Episcopal bodies outside its pale. " Spiritual religion," in a lesser or greater degree, is the common heritage of all sincere believers in the Incarnation and Atonement of our Lord. It is wider than Mr. Balleine's party, and it does not aptly harmonise with their exclusive claims and narrow partisanship. But this by the way.

Mr. Balleine's curious assumption of a Protestant monopoly of spiritual religion.

Militant violence of the Record newspaper.

Their chief organ in the Press was the *Record* newspaper, which was founded in 1828. Its editor, Alexander Haldane, was a militant Protestant of so bitter a type that the Evangelical Archbishop Sumner used the words " the conduct of the *Record* is execrable." Bishop Wilberforce of Oxford quoted these words of the Archbishop in an appeal he made to the *Record* on account of its violent attacks upon himself and Bishop Denison of Salisbury. The editorial reply was : " You firmly hold the doctrine of Baptismal Regeneration ; we as firmly believe that doctrine to be the tap-root of Popery, to constitute its very essence. We firmly believe that whoever believes in that doctrine is a Papist in reality, whatever he may be in name, *and that the salvation of his soul is thereby jeopardised.*" (*Life of Bishop Wilberforce*, vol. ii. p. 219.)

This *dictum* of the chief organ of the party expresses its determination to expel from the Church of England as " Papists in reality " everyone who believed in the Catholic doctrine of Baptism which the Reformers deliberately retained in the Book of Common Prayer. Dr. Pusey's great Treatise on Baptism, which was published in 1835 as one of the Oxford Tracts, had revived Catholic teaching on Baptism, and consequently evoked the bitter hostility of the ultra-Protestant party. Loyal Evangelicals, like Melvill, openly testified to the dishonesty of the extreme men of their party in the face of the plain teaching of the Prayer Book. But the protest of the few loyal Evangelicals was of no avail. The great bulk of the party followed the extremists, especially in the controversy about Tract 90, which appeared in March, 1841. It is impossible to summarise this great controversy, the pith of which was the return to Laud's Declaration " that the Articles were to be taken in their literal and grammatical sense " apart from conventional interpretation and Protestant glosses. Chapters xiv. and xv. of Dean Church's " Oxford Movement " deal with the matter fully. The opposition to Tract 90 was the result of Protestant ignorance and bigotry. Mr. Close, of Cheltenham (afterwards Dean of Carlisle), said: "When I first read No. 90 I did not then know the author; but I said then, and I repeat here, not with any personal reference to the author, that *I should be sorry to trust the author of that tract with my purse.*" (*Oxford Movement*, p. 259.)

This Evangelical leader, who was known as the

[marginal note: Attack on Tract 90.]

[marginal note: Controversial virulence of Dean Close.]

Protestant Pope of Cheltenham, published a sermon called "The Restoration of Churches, the Restoration of Popery." His followers preferred "preaching houses" to Churches, and realised with him that the restoration of our glorious mediæval Churches from whitewash and "pewdom" would mean the recovery of higher ideals of worship. So far he was right, but his allusion to the author of Tract 90 was an

Mr. Baptist indecorous personality. It might be
Noel's lines in thought that the utterances of the *Record*
The Guardian. and the future Dean of Carlisle represented the furthest limits to which savage intolerance could go. But they seem almost temperate compared with some lines written by Mr. Baptist Noel "to a Youthful Anglo-Catholic" and published in *The Guardian*. One verse of this effusion ran :—

> By the prayer in which thy heart
> Ne'er consents to take a part :
> By the heaven thou canst not gain :
> By the hell of endless pain :
> Turn thee from thy follies quick,
> Youthful Anglo-Catholic !

They drew from the gentle Bishop Walsham How a

Bishop Walsham letter couched in language perhaps the
How's con- strongest and most indignant that he ever
demnation of used. "Have you read Mr. Baptist Noel's
them. rhymes in *The Guardian* ?" he writes : " I can hardly conceive anything so horrible being believed, much less expressed . . . . They would disgrace a Mohammedan, and coming from a professing Christian they make one shudder. Read them line by line and think of their meaning, and ask yourself if you ever saw in print anything so fearful, so almost Satanic. My first thought when I read them carefully last night was, 'His delight was in cursing, and it shall happen unto him : he loved not blessing, and it shall be far from him.' My next, 'That it may please Thee to forgive our slanderers and to turn their

hearts.' Not that I identify myself in any way with the party he attacks; but if there be a love for the Cross and a voluntary taking it up day by day; if there be an ardent and over-strained searching after truth; if there be hours and hours of earnest and absorbing prayer; if there be a quiet hope and looking for a better country, it is to be found in that party. . . God forgive the man that could write the line, ' By the heaven thou canst not gain.' What is all this, but in the words of David, ' cursing and lies'? " *(Life of Bishop Walsham How*, pp. 38-40.)

We have already seen that " foreign Protestant " theology rejected the Sacrament of Confirmation, and that the minimising view of it, which has been put forth by Dr. Griffith Thomas and others, is contrary to the teaching of the Prayer Book. In 1843 a beneficed clergyman, Mr. Head, published a violent attack on Confirmation, in response to an official Circular, issued by the Bishop of Exeter, dealing with Confirmation. Mr. Head's Protestantism was imprudent in its violence. He said: " As I am pledged by my ordination vows to banish and drive away all erroneous and strange doctrine, I do hereby decline and refuse to give any countenance whatever to the Office of Confirmation, and instead of recommending the perusal of that Service to the young people of this parish, I warn them all to beware, in the Name of God, of *the erroneous and strange doctrine* which it contains." This was a little too much for Bishop Philpotts, and he cited Mr. Head for depraving the Book of Common Prayer, and won his case. His success in vindicating the Doctrine of Confirmation was a distinct vindication of Prayer Book teaching against militant Protestantism.

The agitation against the Tractarians increased in
Violence of agitation against Tractarians. violence. It is impossible to compress its details within the limits of this chapter. Suffice it to say that Newman's secession in 1845 drove the Catholic movement out of Oxford into

the country. The movement ceased to be academic,
and became practical. The forgotten Catholic teaching
of the Prayer Book was revived in town and country
parishes, and the younger clergy restored the ceremonial of Andrewes and Laud so as to teach by the eye
as well as by the ear. On Easter Day, 1851, the Rev.
T. Chamberlain, of S. Thomas's, Oxford, wore a

Restoration of
Eucharistic
Vestments in
1851.

chasuble at the Altar, the first restoration
of the Eucharistic Vestments since 1662.
That historic chasuble is now a treasured
possession of S. Saviour's Cathedral at
Maritzburg. The South African Church also possesses
Keble's Library, besides the personal link with the
Tractarians afforded by its first Bishop, Robert Gray,
the "Athanasius of the South." The attack on the

Dr. Arnold
attacks the
Tractarians.

Tractarians was twofold. Dr. Arnold, of
Rugby, furiously assailed them in the
Edinburgh Review, and Mr. Tait, of Balliol,
who afterwards as Archbishop of Canterbury was
responsible for the Erastian " Public Worship Regulation Act " of 1874, was the leader of the attack on
Tract 90. The Latitudinarians, or as they preferred
to call themselves " Liberals," were just as vehement
opponents of the revived Catholic teaching as the
militant Evangelicals of the Stowell and McNeale type.
In chapters iii. and iv. we have already shown that the
Court of Arches vindicated the Catholic doctrine of

Mob violence
of the Militant
Protestants.

Baptism and the Holy Eucharist. We have
now to deal with the mob violence and
aggressive methods of the militant Protestants. We do not wish to emphasise unduly the evil
methods employed and defended by people who were
carried away by party feeling. A physician registers
abnormal symptoms in diagnosing a disease. In telling
the evil and disgraceful story of the Victorian persecution, we have only space to record the abnormal
symptoms of the spiritual disease of "militant
Protestantism," without recording the normal symptoms,

whereby many of its supporters showed themselves better than their creed. There is no space here to record the good deeds of the party, which have already found a most eulogistic chronicler in Mr. Balleine, to whose pages we refer our readers. Tractarianism stirred up all their fighting qualities. Their supremacy had been challenged, and they fought for it with any weapon that lay handiest. Very often they did not stop to think of the true bearing of their actions. In 1849 the Irish Church Mission Society was founded to

Blasphemous outrage upon the Blessed Sacrament by the Irish Church Mission Society.

proselytise the Roman Catholics in Ireland. Meetings to support the movement were held in England, and at one of these meetings the Protestant party began those blasphemous outrages upon the Blessed Sacrament of the Altar which they subsequently openly defended. It is difficult to write temperately on a profanity so vile, and an outrage so horrible, as the exhibition at one of the meetings of this Society of a "Consecrated Host" surreptitiously obtained from a Roman Catholic Church for the purpose of mockery and derision. The seventeenth century Puritans in

A logical result of the teaching of the "Real Absence."

their worst days of iconoclastic fervour avoided such a blasphemy as this. (See Proby's *Annals of the Low Church Party*, vol. i. p. 513.) And this evil deed bore its evil fruit in later years, and showed to what lengths the theology of the "Real Absence" could impel persons who were deemed, in other ways, to be respectable citizens. A rapid view only is possible of the blasphemy and profanity of the mob which drove Mr.

Blasphemous profanity at S. George's-in-the-East.

Bryan King from S. George's-in-the-East in 1860. Bishop Tait did nothing to check the rioters, and the Government allowed the riots to continue till the Rector resigned. Mr. Bryan King was what would now be called a moderate

Anglican. He received the following letter which points to a secret organisation of violence :—

A threatening letter. " I hereby warn you that unless you desist from your hellish and Popish practice and teaching in our Parish Church I shall take foul means to prevent your doing so. I am one of a secret society which has sworn to see your downfall. I am, etc., *A Protestant.*" This letter shows that some persons of education incited and probably paid the rioters, as was

The Evangelicals did not disclaim the deeds of the rioters. distinctly proved in 1877, when similar riots took place at S. James's, Hatcham. The responsibility for the S. George's riots was not disclaimed by the leaders of the Evangelicals. The Rev. James Hilliard, Rector of Ingoldsby, openly defended the rioters in a letter to *The Christian Observer*, and that magazine, as the leading organ of the Evangelicals, said in its issue of March, 1860, " The respectable church-going people of England will not feel that *justice has been done* if the rioters are

Their organ, the Christian Observer, defended the rioters. punished before the Romish exhibitions have been suppressed. They are afraid that, *if order be restored*, Tractarianism will be allowed to triumph at S. George's-in-the-East, and of two fearful evils *they prefer the least.*" Could shameless cynicism further go ? The evil of hooting and yelling in the House of God, so that not a word of the service could be heard, songs in chorus howled by the mob, cushions and hassocks hurled at the altar, and the chancel and choir stalls invaded by the rioters, so that the clergy and choir were forcibly extruded from their seats ; all this profanity was, to *The Christian Observer*, a *less evil* than the triumph of what, to put it on its lowest level, was an earnest effort to render the services of the Prayer Book in the beauty of holiness, and in decency and order. And

Dr. McNeile's violent language on Confession. the militant Protestant leaders used an incredible violence of language. Dr. McNeile, of Liverpool, had inaugurated this

controversial fury at an earlier period.   Preaching at
S. Paul's, Liverpool, on December 8th, 1850, he used
the following words with regard to the use of Private
Confession and Absolution which the Prayer Book,
which he had sworn to accept and use, enjoined upon
him.   He said: "I would make it a *capital* offence to
administer confession in this country.   Transportation
would not satisfy me, for that would merely transfer
the evil from one part of the world to another.
Capital punishment alone would satisfy me.   Death
alone would prevent the evil."   This ferocious utterance, which is worse than anything Prynne said of
Laud, appears in the report of his sermon in the
Liverpool Mercury.   It was of him, when in after
years he became Dean of Ripon, and in his old age
felt bound by law to wear a cope in the Cathedral, that
the witty Bishop Samuel Wilberforce said (when he
heard of the Protestant Dean's dilemma) :

> " And Zion in her anguish
> With Babylon must *Cope*."

It was natural to expect that the violence of the
militant Protestants would lead the clearer heads of
the party to see that violence by itself
The Protestant
demand for
Prayer Book
Revision.
would defeat its own ends.   Their thoughts
went back to the Puritan demands at the
Savoy Conference and they began to demand " Prayer Book Revision " on the Whig-Erastian
lines of 1689.   They knew that the Prayer Book of
1662 is the stronghold of the theology and ceremonial
which they detested as " Tractarian."   They believed
that they had crushed the Catholic movement, and
they thought that the time was ripe for some constructive Protestant work in the way of Prayer
Book Revision.   In 1833, and again in 1840, the
" Evangelical" *Christian Observer* had expressed a
desire to revise the Prayer Book in the interests of
Protestantism.   The C.M.S. in 1849 had obtained
Archbishop Sumner's consent for an expurgated

Prayer Book for use in native missions. In 1854 Lord Robert Grosvenor (afterwards Lord Ebury) and some leading Evangelical Clergy, formed the "Prayer Book Revision Society." Its objects were officially set forth as follows:

Its specified objects.

I. *Priest.* The substitution of the word "minister," or "presbyter," for the word "priest," whenever the officiating clergyman is intended.

II. *Ornaments Rubric.* "That the Rubric commonly called the 'Ornaments Rubric' be expunged from the Prayer Book, and some plain direction substituted."

III. *General Rubrics.* "Such alterations as may avoid undesirable repetitions and make the services more edifying and elastic. A Revision of the Tables and Kalendar."

IV. *Athanasian Creed.* "That the public recitation of the Athanasian Creed be no longer imperative."

V. *Communion Service.* "Removal of a few phrases which have been alleged to favour *priestly Confession and Absolution* and other unscriptural doctrines and errors."

VI. *Baptismal Offices.* "Removal of expressions which seem to assert spiritual regeneration as inseparably connected with Baptism. A review of the sponsorial system. The Church Catechism and Confirmation Service to be in harmony."

VII. *Ordinal and Visitation.* "The authoritative form of words accompanying the imposition of hands (*Receive, etc.*) to be rendered as in primitive times, and through long ages, in the language of prayer. The clause, *Whose sins thou dost forgive, etc.,* in the Ordinal, and the corresponding Absolution, '*I absolve thee,*' in the Visitation of the Sick to be omitted."

VIII. *Marriage Service.* "The alteration or omission of some passages at present unsuited for public reading."

IX. *Burial of the Dead.* "Modification of the Rubric respecting those who die unbaptised, and expressions which seem to imply the salvation of everyone over whom the service is performed."

X. *Commination.* "Omission of the Curses and accompanying exhortations."

These demands for drastic changes in a Protestant direction involved a far lower doctrinal level than that touched by the Prayer Book of 1552. These Revisionists traced their spiritual pedigree to Hooper in the main points. Their attack on the Athanasian Creed is paralleled by the desire of Dr. Griffith Thomas to omit the Rubric directing its recitation, as the Irish Church has done. (*Catholic Faith*, p. 430.) This shows that the Evangelical "left wing" has lost its hold upon definite dogma, which the Puritans of the seventeenth century rigidly maintained. The Dutch Reformed Communion in South Africa represents seventeenth century Puritanism, and at a recent Conference on religious education with representatives of the Anglican Church, the Dutch "Moderator" laid upon the table the Athanasian Creed in Dutch, with the words "This is our Faith." There is much more hope in finding some common basis of co-operation with foreign Protestantism of this definite and dogmatic type than with "Evangelicals" within our own borders, who dislike the Athanasian Creed, and whose self-esteem leads them to imagine that they, and they *only*, represent the true tradition of Anglican theology and ceremonial, and that all others must be cast out of the Church of England. The demands of the Prayer Book Revision Society were fairly complete. They included the Puritan demand at the Savoy Conference for the abolition of the Ornaments Rubric, which the Bishops then refused. The doctrine of Baptismal Regeneration, and of the

(marginal notes: Their extreme Protestant tendency. / Their attack on the Athanasian Creed. / Dishonesty of the demands of the Prayer Book Revision Society.)

Sacerdotium of the Christian Priesthood were to be banished from the Book of Common Prayer. If the supporters of this Society had been members of some religious body outside the communion of the Church, and if their demands had been made as *conditions* to enable them to join the Church, they would at least have been honest and intelligible. But they came from those who were within the Church. They came from beneficed clergy who held their benefices upon the express condition of their unfeigned assent and consent to the doctrines of the Anglican formularies. The demands which they made involved drastic and fundamental changes in the doctrines of the Church of England which would have utterly destroyed its Catholic character, and reduced it to a level with other Protestant sects. It was no case of a re-adjustment or an enrichment of the formularies on certain points. It was a deliberate attempt to " Protestantise " our formularies in the interests of a party of Protestants who felt that they could not honestly use them without violence to their own convictions. Men who find themselves in such a position as this ought to seek their remedy in secession. Their fellow-religionists in Scotland boldly took this line at the " Disruption " from the Established Kirk in the early " forties." They had no doctrinal reasons for secession, such as were alleged by the " Prayer Book Revision " party within the Church of England. They went out upon the question of Erastianism, and showed unflinching zeal and courage in so doing. The " Prayer Book Revisionists " showed neither and, when their movement failed, took the line of attempting to drive all who did not think as they did out of the Church of England. Canon Battersby of Carlisle and other beneficed clergymen joined the " Revision Society " and began an active campaign to further its objects. They did not apparently consider

Questionable position of the beneficed clergy who belonged to it.

that their advocacy of such drastic changes rendered
their own position as beneficed priests a very questionable one, as they all held their benefices upon the
condition of declaring their " unfeigned assent and
consent " to that very Book of Common Prayer which
they desired to alter in its fundamental doctrines.
One of these clergy, the Rev. J. C. Proby, addressed a
published letter to Bishop Sumner of Winchester, in
Strange conduct of one of them in submitting to Anabaptism. which he stated that " Baptismal Regeneration," which he called, " a tradition of
the Fathers, revived in the Church of
England *and not known elsewhere*," must
be removed from the Prayer Book. Mr. Proby's
ignorance of the Roman and Eastern teaching on
Baptism is manifested by his use of the phrase " not
known elsewhere." But he was more logical than his
fellow Revisionists. He was re-baptised by immersion
in the river Itchen by a Baptist minister, and Bishop
Sumner, although himself an Evangelical, felt bound
to take some steps against this flagrant act of heresy
and schism. Mr. Proby was suspended from his
benefice for three years. But at the expiration of his
sentence he still continued to hold office as a beneficed
Priest of the Church of England, and the Evangelical
Mr. P. Gell on Revision. party, as a whole, seemed content that he
should so remain. In 1860 the Rev. Philip
Gell, incumbent of St. John's, Derby, a
well-known leader of the " Revisionist " party in
the Midlands, published a bulky pamphlet called
" *Thoughts on the Liturgy ; the difficulties of an honest
and conscientious use of the Book of Common Prayer,
considered as a loud and reasonable call for the only
remedy—Revision.*" It might have been thought that
" *the difficulties of an honest and conscientious use of
the Book of Common Prayer* " might best and most
honestly be solved by secession, as Bishop Cummins
and his followers thought in 1873. But Mr. Gell
preferred to hold his benefice, which compelled him,

as a legal condition of its tenure, to use a Book which

Mr. Gell's four heresies of the Prayer Book. he alleged to be *heretical*. Mr. Gell's pamphlet stated that the Book of Common Prayer taught *four leading heresies*.

I. " Auricular Confession and Priestly Absolution."

II. " The supposition of power to give the Holy Ghost by Episcopal hands to every ordained Priest."

III. " The doctrine of the Real Presence in the Holy Communion."

IV. " Baptismal Regeneration."

Mr. Gell's offence in publicly stating that four plain doctrines of the Prayer Book were *heresies* was of course as flagrant a *depraving of the Book of Common Prayer* as the offence of Mr. Head in attacking the doctrine of Confirmation. If the Bishop of Exeter was able to win his case against Mr. Head in 1843, the Bishop of Lichfield, had he taken proceedings, would have been equally successful against Mr. Gell in 1860. Mr. Gell was, of course, theologically accurate in stating that the Prayer Book distinctly teaches these

Mr. Gell's attack on the Prayer Book preferable to the usual non-natural interpretation of its doctrines, four Catholic doctrines which he calls heresies. He is thus a useful witness from the Protestant side against the non-natural interpretations of the Prayer Book which have been put forth by the late Bishop

Ryle, Bishop Moule, Bishop Drury, Dr. Griffith Thomas and Mr. Dimock, who is the worst offender of all, because he obscures plain issues with a show of learning. The " Revisionists" were bold enough in

Bold disloyalty of the Revisionists. their disloyalty. One of them, the Rev. R. Bingham, published an expurgated Prayer Book of his own devising, under the arrogant title of *The Prayer Book as it ought to be.* In 1867 the Rev. the Hon. E. V. Bligh, published a letter to Lord Derby, the Prime Minister, demanding from the Government the excision of certain passages in the Prayer Book which, in Mr. Bligh's opinion, "were derived from Popery of the darkest ages."

In 1860, Lord Ebury moved for Prayer Book
Revision on the lines of his Society, but
Prayer Book
Revision in the failed to carry his motion in the House of
House of Lords. Lords. In 1880 he brought in a Bill to
remove the Absolution from the Visitation of the Sick
and the omission of the words " Whose sins thou dost
forgive," etc., from the Ordinal. He had no sense of
humour or he would not have made the statement
that the Prayer Book sanctioned " a system alien to
the doctrine and practice of the Church." He apparently forgot that the Church sanctioned the Prayer
Book of 1662 as the *formal expression* of its doctrine
and practices. But his Bill did not pass. On May
Mr. Glyn desired 9th, 1882, the Prayer Book Revision
the omission of Society held its Annual Meeting. At this
" consecration " meeting the Rev. C. J. Glyn made the
in the Holy
Eucharist. astounding statement that, in his opinion,
"a great deal of harm had arisen from the *consecration*
of the elements (i.e. in the Holy Eucharist). He
believed that for one hundred years that was not
allowed in the Church." Whether his mind was confused about the omission of the " manual acts" in
1552 we cannot tell. At any rate, his words show an
ignorance equalled only by that of the
Curious blunder Privy Council in the *Westerton* v. *Liddell*
of the Privy
Council on the case in 1857, where the judgment solemnly
same subject. and publicly affirmed that in the Prayer
Book of 1552 *the prayer for the consecration of the
elements was omitted.* This case was of considerable
importance otherwise. It interpreted the Ornaments
Rubric in accordance with its plain meaning, although
the question of Vestments had not yet been raised.
One of the Judges who sat in the case remarked to a
friend, " We have just given the clergy authority to
wear the Eucharistic Vestments if they like. *It is to
be hoped they won't find it out.*" But they did find it
out, and not for the first time, for the Vestments had
been restored at S. Thomas's, Oxford, in 1851.

The "Revisionist" movement did not meet with the success which its promoters expected. In 1865, its supporters merged their efforts, which were honest, so far as their admission went that the plain words of the Prayer Book contradicted their views, into a new departure in the Protestant "plan of campaign" against the Catholic teaching of the Prayer Book. It was a complete and dishonest *volte face*. The men who had been clamouring for a Revision of the Prayer Book, because it taught Catholic doctrines, which Mr. Gell and others called "heresies," suddenly turned round and professed loyalty to the Prayer Book upon the basis of their own "non-natural" and forced interpretation of it. They accused the Tractarians and Ritualists of disloyalty to the Prayer Book, and lawlessness, for obeying the Ornaments Rubric by restoring the Vestments which it legally and undoubtedly ordered. They formed a Society for the avowed extermination of Catholic doctrine and ceremonial within the Church of England, which was named the "Church Association," and which, after a career of unsuccessful persecuting intolerance, still survives in a condition of ignominious suspended animation.

Failure of the Revision movement.

A new plan of campaign.

The Revisionists pose as Prayer Book champions against the Tractarians.

They found the Church Association.

It began with an imposing list of Vice-Presidents which included the Marquis of Westmeath, five Earls, six other Peers, four Deans, three Archdeacons, and five Members of Parliament.

Archdeacon Prest, one of its three Archdeacons, was a better lawyer than his fellows. He urged the support of a Bill before Parliament to abolish the Eucharistic Vestments, because (to use his own words) "Vestments were clearly sanctioned by the law, and therefore the sooner the law was altered, in order to put in the

Legality of the Vestments undoubted.

position of wrong doers those clergymen who wore the Vestments, the better." (*Church News*, May 8th, 1867.)

Six eminent barristers gave an opinion that the Ornaments Rubric meant what it said, and that therefore the Vestments were legal. In 1908 a Committee of five Bishops submitted a learned, exhaustive and unanimous Report to the Upper House of the Convocation of Canterbury to the same effect. But the Church Association did not care a jot for the existing law of the Church. They put forth as their chief object " the suppression of all ceremonies, vestments, and ornaments " which had dropped out of common use, however legal they were. They published an " Address to the People of England " in which they said that " if a clergyman calls himself a sacrificing Priest, the case is clear, we can see what he is ; he is not a Pastor of the Reformed Church of England ; *he is a Priest of the Church of Rome*. He must be treated as such. . . . . Such persons must be treated as men having the plague. They must be put in quarantine, lest they infect us." It did not apparently strike the noble Lords, Members of Parliament, Deans and Archdeacons who were jointly responsible for this Circular, that it was ludicrous as well as uncharitable. The doctrine of the Christian Priesthood is held just as tenaciously by the Eastern Church as by the Roman Catholics. To call a clergyman who held the Catholic doctrine of the Priesthood a " Roman Priest," just because he held what Roman Catholics, Easterns and Anglicans hold in common, savours of theological ignorance and illogical absurdity. The Church Association raised a fund of £50,000 for their legal expenses in prosecuting the Catholic clergy. The Rev. A. H. Mackonochie, Vicar of S. Alban's, Holborn, had begun

Marginal notes:

The Church Association address the " People of England."

The Address was malicious and uncharitable.

Church Association raise £50,000 for prosecuting Ritualists.

a noble work in one of the most neglected districts

Prosecution of Mr. Mackonochie. of London.   He taught the Catholic Faith by the eye as well as by the ear in perfect loyalty to the Book of Common Prayer. His great spiritual work amongst his own parishioners attracted outside attention.   He carried out the full ceremonial enjoined and permitted by the Ornaments Rubric and consequently he was singled out for *His prosecution became persecution.* attack.   Dr. Tait, then Bishop of London, had been a strong opponent of the Catholic movement since the " forties," when he joined in the denunciation of Dr. Newman's famous " Tract 90."   He readily acceded to the prosecution of Mr. Mackonochie, and the case against him, in varying forms and before different Courts, continued until the Archbishop of Canterbury (Dr. Tait) on his death-bed, in 1883, asked Mr. Mackonochie to resign S. Alban's, and an exchange with Mr. Suckling, the Vicar of S. Peter's, London Docks, was effected with the consent of Bishop Jackson of London and with the assent of the Archbishop.   But the Church Association was not satisfied with the Archbishop's legacy of peace.   Its authorities immediately took *He resigned S. Alban's and was driven out of S. Peter's.* proceedings to deprive Mr. Mackonochie of his new benefice.   Rather than embarrass the poor parish of S. Peter's, Mr. Mackonochie resigned and with the Bishop of London's approval became curate to Mr. Suckling in his old parish of S. Alban's.   But the strain of incessant persecution for sixteen years, coupled with the strain of the spiritual charge of a large and poor parish, completely exhausted Mr. Mackonochie's *His breakdown and tragic death.* physical and mental powers.   He broke down utterly and became mentally incapable of discharging his office as a Priest. He was still able to attend Divine Service, and the Peace of God was upon his soul.   He was staying with some friends in Scotland, and one day wandered off for a long walk, as his custom was. He was overtaken by a snowstorm and perished from cold and exposure. The responsibility for his mental break-down and comparatively early death must in justice lie at the door of his persecutors.

Other cases of attack on Catholic ritual occurred which centred as a whole upon an attack against the following usages :—I. The Mixed Chalice. II. The Eucharistic Vestments. III. Wafer Bread. IV. The Eastward position of the Celebrant. V. Altar Lights. VI. Incense. All these were condemned by the Privy Council in the Purchas and Ridsdale Judgments. The numerous cases and their issues cannot readily be summarised in the very brief space at our command. It must suffice to say that the Court of Arches in most cases vindicated the historical continuity and Catholicity of the English Church by declaring the impugned ceremonial to be legal. The Privy Council, which never had jurisdiction in matters ecclesiastical or spiritual, declared, in successive—and in some cases contradictory—judgments, that all the Six Usages which have been mentioned above were illegal. One of the Judges, as a Barrister, had given Counsel's opinion (on a case stated by the English Church Union) to the effect that the use of the Vestments, which he subsequently condemned as a Judge, was undoubtedly lawful. In the Ridsdale Judgment Chief Baron Kelly, who sat as a member of the Privy Council in the case, published his dissent from the judgment of the majority of the Judges, and openly stated that the Privy Council's condemnation of the Vestments and other Catholic usages was " an iniquitous judgment, the result of policy and not of law." In 1874 Archbishop Tait passed the " Public Worship Regulation Act " for the purpose, as the then Prime

The Protestant attack upon the Six Points of Ceremonial.

The Privy Council, an unlawful Court, condemns them all.

Chief Baron Kelly condemns the Ridsdale Judgment.

The Public Worship Regulation Act and the " Mass in Masquerade."

Minister cynically observed, " of putting down
Ritualism and the Mass in masquerade." This Act
destroyed the ancient spiritual jurisdiction of the Court
of Arches, and substituted for it a new Court, framed
by the sole authority of Parliament, apart from any
Church authority, or even consultation with
the Convocations. The new Court was presided over by a State-appointed Judge, and
the curious choice was made of Lord Penzance, an
ex-Divorce Court Judge, by way of further emphasising
the un-Churchly and Erastian character of both the new
Court and its new Judge. The late Bishop
Merriman, of Grahamstown, said to the
author of this book that " the Bishops of
England had placed their croziers in the hands of an
ex-Divorce Court Judge," and the fearless old Bishop
repeated this remark in the face of Archbishop Tait at
the Croydon Church Congress of 1877. The Catholic
Clergy naturally declined to submit to the authority of
this new Court. The *consensus* of " Church and
Realm " is necessary in the Church of England as the
very condition and foundation of the relations between
Church and State, which is commonly known as
" Establishment." The Government dared not have
forced a new State Court to deal with ecclesiastical
matters upon the " Established " Presbyterian Kirk of
Scotland. The sturdy Presbyterians of
Scotland have never tolerated the interference of the State in their internal affairs.
But the Government was ready enough to force a new
State Court upon the Church of England, because its
corporate life had been so weakened by the strife and
internal disorder caused by the alien influence of
foreign Protestantism. The Protestantism that was
violently hostile to State interference in Scotland
was ready to welcome State interference in England
as a ready weapon against the Catholic
traditions, usages and doctrines of the
Church of England. But the Clergy who

Lord Penzance
supersedes the
Dean of Arches.

Bishop Merri-
man condemns
the P.W.R. Act.

A new State-
made Court.

Which the
Clergy were
bound to resist.

were attacked were bound in conscience to resist State-made ecclesiastical law. Dr. Pusey well called it " Un-law," and it was speedily made evident that resistance involved imprisonment. In 1877 Lord Penzance's Court condemned the Rev. A. Tooth, Vicar of S. James's, Hatcham, for wearing the Vestments and other Catholic usages. Mr. Tooth took no

Mr. Tooth's resistance ends in his imprisonment.

notice of the judgment which he could not have acknowledged without violation of his Ordination vow binding him to the *consensus* of " Church *and* Realm." The usurped and unlawful authority of the " Realm," or State, acting *per se*, committed him to prison for contempt of Lord Penzance's Court on January 22nd, 1877. A Protestant mob disturbed the services of S. James's and riots continued after Mr. Tooth's release and subsequent resignation in 1878. The disgraceful outrages of the Protestants at S. George's-in-the-East were repeated, and it was discovered that some of the rioters were actually paid to create disturb-

Mr. Dale's imprisonment.

ances in the House of God. The Rev. T. Pelham Dale, Rector of S. Vedast's, in the City of London, was marked down for attack by the Church Association for inviting the congregation of S. Alban's, Holborn, to attend S. Vedast's during the six weeks of Mr. Mackonochie's suspension in order that they might receive the Blessed Sacrament. Mr. Dale wore the Eucharistic Vestments and used Altar Lights. He was condemned by Lord Penzance, and in October, 1880, was committed to prison. A specially disgraceful feature of this case was that the Church

Malversation of Trust Funds to pay Protestant legal expenses.

Association made use of charitable Trust Funds, left for the poor of S. Vedast's parish, to help them to meet their law expenses. The Rev. S. F. Green, Vicar of S. John's, Miles Platting, near Manchester, was con-

Mr. Green's imprisonment.

demned by Lord Penzance on similar charges in 1879. He was pronounced.

"in contempt," and imprisoned in Lancaster Castle on March 19th, 1880. His case was aggravated by the grasping procedure of the Church Association in exacting from him the costs of their prosecution. The bailiffs were put into his vicarage, and his wife and family were turned out. His books and furniture were sold under distraint, and part of the law costs he had to pay were the expenses of hired witnesses who were sent to his church to Protestant hired spies. spy upon his actions at the altar and report to their employers thereon. This profane indecency was carried on in other cases by the Church Association, and it was justly rebuked as indecent by Archbishop Benson in his Judgment in the Lincoln case. The sale of his goods did not satisfy Mr. Green's persecutors. He remained in prison for over eighteen months, and was not released till November 4th, 1882. Bishop Fraser of Manchester illegally intruded curates into Mr. Green's parish during his imprisonment. One of these schismatic clergymen, the Rev. R. Pym, afterwards became Bishop of Bombay, and embroiled his Diocese with an attempt to crush the teaching and ritual of the Cowley Fathers, who were doing a splendid and devoted missionary work.

The Rev. R. W. Enraght, Vicar of Holy Trinity, Bordesley, Birmingham, was tried in Lord Mr. Enraght's imprisonment. Penzance's Court on August 9th, 1879, upon the usual charges. Special stress was laid upon his use of wafer bread, and the horrible profanity which we have already chronicled in the case of an "Irish Church Mission" meeting was repeated. The foreign Protestant theology of the "Real Absence" lay behind what will The Bordesley Sacrilege. always be remembered as the "Bordesley Sacrilege." A sacrilegious and ignorant man was bribed to go up to the Altar and secrete the Blessed Sacrament of the Body of Christ. It was taken into Lord Penzance's Court as an "exhibit" to be used in evidence at Mr. Enraght's trial. Lord Penzance was too ignorant to realise the blasphemous profanity which he authorised. Bishop Philpotts of Worcester was appealed to, as Mr. Enraght's Diocesan, to stop the outrage. He did not believe in the Real Presence, and showed himself utterly regardless of the feelings of those who did. He took no action. The Birmingham Protestants who were responsible for the outrage "gloried in their shame." When an appeal was made to them they made the following reply: "The Committee repudiate the idea of outrage and blasphemy charged upon the act of securing an illegal wafer for inspection, and regard it rather as one of loyalty to the Church and patriotism to the State. They rejoice in it and its results." Their conduct showed the true bearings of the foreign theology of the "Real Absence." Such a wave of indignation swept over England, in which decent and reverent people of all kinds united with Catholic Churchmen, that Archbishop Tait was forced to take action. He removed the Blessed Sacrament from the custody of Lord Penzance and reverently consumed It in his own private Chapel. The last of the imprisoned priests was Mr. Bell Cox of S. Margaret's, Liverpool. Bishop Ryle naturally allowed Lord Penzance to commit one of the best priests of his Diocese to prison. His position in this matter was logical enough. He originally belonged to the Church Association. But the other Bishops who did not exercise their veto upon the prosecutions acted upon the principle of obliging an intolerant faction. Bishop Ryle, as a militant Protestant himself, acted according to his convictions and deserves more respect than the other Bishops who allowed their clergy to be imprisoned. Liverpool,

The Protestants "glory in their shame."

The sacrilege was a logical consequence of the "Real Absence."

Imprisonment of Mr. Bell Box of Liverpool.

Bishop Ryle was responsible for this.

since Dr. McNeile's days, has been a centre of Orange
Protestantism and of a policy of intolerance, which was
manifested a few years ago in a deliberate attempt to
capture seats in Parliament for Protestants pledged to
evict all Catholic clergy from the Church.   But the
imprisonment of Mr. Bell Cox did him no harm in
Liverpool.   A few years back the Liverpool Protestants returned him at the head of the poll in the
School Board Election.

A few incidents of a different character may now be
mentioned.   Bishop Baring of Durham, in
the year 1867, deprived the Rev. the Hon.
F. R. Grey, Rector of Morpeth, of the office
of Rural Dean for the offence of wearing a black stole
with three crosses embroidered on it.   This manifesta-
tion of childish and ludicrous partisanship did Mr.
Grey no harm, but when the Bishop, in 1876, refused
to license any curate to assist Dr. Dykes of S. Oswald's,
Durham, the outcome of this evil episcopal
intolerance was the untimely death of Dr.
Dykes from overwork.   The loss to the
Church of this faithful priest and most skilled and
churchly musician must be laid at the door of Bishop
Baring.

Bishop Hamilton of Salisbury was originally an
" Evangelical."   He learnt to add to his
subjective devotional religion the full
Catholic Faith.   He felt it his duty to
deliver a "Charge" to his Diocese in which he, fully
and fearlessly, explained the Catholic doctrine of the
Holy Eucharist.   His " Charge " is still one of the best
and clearest expositions of the subject
which we possess.   A Bishop is naturally
more exposed to criticism than a Priest, and
seventy of his clergy protested against his
teaching to the Archbishop of Canterbury.   There

Bishop Baring's Protestant intolerance.

Its result in the case of Dr. Dykes.

Bishop Hamilton's Charge.

Protest against his teaching the Real Presence.

was a lay protest as well and Bishop Hamilton was

His death.   furiously attacked by Protestant peers in
the House of Lords. The " Charge " was
delivered in 1867, and the consequent controversies
certainly shortened the good Bishop's life. He died in
July, 1869.

There is just space here to record a noble protest

Mr. Ormiston's   made by the Rev. Daniel Wilson, an
indecent con-   Evangelical of the older and more devout
duct at
S. Alban's,   type, against the conduct of the Rev. J.
Holborn.   Ormiston, a prominent member of the
" Church Association," who presented himself to Mr.
Mackonochie, at S. Alban's, Holborn, as a person
desirous of making his confession. Mr. Ormiston then,
in a loud voice, broke into a tirade against Catholic
practices and against confession. Of course this outburst was stopped, but before Mr. Ormiston left the
vestry he profanely requested Mr. Mackonochie to give
him absolution. This profane impertinence was justly
rebuked by the Bishop of London, who directed Mr.
Ormiston to make an apology to Mr. Mackonochie. To

Protestant   trace the various Protestant outbursts of
agitation against agitation against the Sacrament of Penance
Confession.   would fill half this volume. It began with
the revocation of the licence of the Rev. A. Poole,
curate of S. Barnabas, Pimlico, by Bishop Tait in

Mr. Poole's   1858 for the offence of hearing Confessions
Case.   and ministering Absolution, as the Prayer
Book enjoins and directs. It was continued
at intervals until 1877, when the storm burst with full

"The Priest in   fury because of a privately printed manual
Absolution."   of moral theology called " The Priest in
Absolution." This manual was brought to
public notice by Lord Redesdale in the House of Lords,
and at this time it was openly alleged that it had been
stolen from a clergyman's study for controversial
purposes. The manual was private, and not for the lay
public, just as certain medical books are not intended for

general and indiscriminate circulation amongst persons
who are not medical men. Moral theology
Necessity of
moral theology. is just as necessary for the clergy as special
medical books are for physicians and
surgeons. The pathology of spiritual disease must be
studied by the clergy just as carefully as medical men
study the pathology of physical disease. If Lord
Redesdale had complained to the House of Lords that
certain medical books were to be suppressed as unfit
for general reading and had said that doctors had no
business to write any treatises on disease which were
unfit for the perusal of a girl of fourteen, he would have
only made himself supremely ridiculous. But because
he attacked certain of the clergy for circulating
privately amongst themselves a book to help them in
dealing with certain forms of spiritual disease, Lord
Redesdale was actually thanked for his action by
Archbishop Tait. The controversy gradually died
down, with the result that more people than ever
resorted to Confession. There is much in the old
adage that " Truth shines the more it is shaken." And
Trial of the   certainly the public controversy on this
Bishop of   subject did much to dispel a widespread
Lincoln.
                  ignorance. It is not necessary to do more
than mention the trial of the Bishop of Lincoln in
1892, and the vindication of certain essential points of
ceremonial in the Judgment delivered by Archbishop
                  Benson of Canterbury in that case. Nor is
The Kensit
outrages.   there space to mention in detail the Kensit
                  outrages and disorders of the year 1898,
which were continued in subsequent years. We may
conclude this chapter by quoting the judgment of the
Church Quarterly Review upon the Victorian persecution : " The *immoral period* (in the history of
The " Church   Protestantism within the Anglican Church)
Quarterly   is a harsh title, but really some things have
Review."
                 occurred that seem to justify it. What is to
be said about that ugly story of Charities at S. Vedast's

Church being used to pay expenses incurred by the Church Association against the Rector ? What of that monstrous utterance that Private Confession, so obviously enjoined under certain circumstances by the Church of England, should be made punishable by death ? What of the strange story, authenticated beyond a doubt, of a Low Church clergyman describing himself anonymously as a *great and good* man ? What of the Bordesley Sacrilege, which one would have thought likely to shock even those who regard the Holy Communion merely as a commemorative act, but which was actually defended by men who are rightly described as *glorying in their shame ?* What of those organised bands of ruffians whom honest men, to say nothing of professing Christians and Churchmen, ought to have blushed to own as allies, but did not ?" (*Church Quarterly Review*, January, 1890, p. 312.) No one could accuse the *Church Quarterly Review* of being a partisan publication. Its judgment upon the evil details of the Victorian persecution is impartial and final.

CHAPTER VIII.

The Story of the Cumminsite Schism.

It is a relief to turn away from the unsavoury episodes of the last chapter to record the
The American Church.
history of a body of honest, logical and consistent Protestants. The American Church was deprived of the Episcopate before the Revolution, because of the Whig-Erastian policy of the Hanoverian Kings and their advisers. Consequently the Church was face to face with a struggle for existence when the United States were severed from the Mother Country.

In Virginia, and other Southern States, the Church was " established " in pre-Revolution days.
Virginian Churchmanship.
It consequently reflected the Whig-Erastian Protestantism of the early eighteenth century. In the New England States, where Puritanism was a dominant and intolerant power, the handful of Church people had to justify their Churchmanship.
Bishop Seabury and the strong Churchmanship of the North.
They got a firm grip of true Church principles, and at the close of the eighteenth century they were the salt of the American Church. Bishop Seabury, who was consecrated by the Bishops of the Scottish Church, as the first American Bishop, in 1784, was a firm adherent of the type of Churchmanship evolved in the North. To him the American Church owes her beautiful and Catholic Eucharistic Office, and his influence caused the

rejection of the Protestant revision of the Prayer Book, known as the "Proposed Book" of 1785.

The "Proposed Book" of 1785. This attempt at revision on Protestant lines was mainly owing to the influence of the Virginian clergy and laity. The Protestant traditions of certain Southern dioceses survived the great Civil War of Secession, and therefore we are not surprised to find Dr. George David Cummins, who was consecrated Assistant Bishop of Kentucky on November 15th, 1866, a strong and determined Protestant controversialist. He had much more scholarship and learning than Bishop Ryle and the usual type of "militant Protestant" clergy in England. He never descended to the depths of controversial vulgarity and profanity which characterised the extreme members of his school of thought in England. He was an honest and, in many respects, an able man.

Bishop Cummins a strong Protestant.

He was true to his convictions.

He was too honest to remain within the communion of the American Church when he found out that its formularies did not agree with his views. He did not carry on a Protestant agitation *inside* the American Church with a view to alter its formularies to suit his own opinions, and to extrude all those who did not agree with him. He did not call those who held by the formularies dishonest traitors, as his co-religionists in England did. He took the "Old Catholic" movement in Germany as his model, and determined to found what he called a "Reformed Episcopal Church" to do the work against the sacerdotalism and sacramentalism of the American Church which Dr. Dollinger was attempting to do against the Church of Rome. The immediate cause of his secession has been already mentioned in the Introduction of this book. Bishop Cummins claimed the right to disregard the protest of the Bishop of New York against his action in taking part in an

His secession was the result of his controversial honesty.

His controversy with the Bishop of New York.

Inter-denominational " Communion Service" held at
New York by the "Evangelical Alliance," of which, as
we have already seen, Bishop Moule of Durham was a
member. Bishop Cummins saw clearly that he could not
honestly act as he had done in the Diocese of New York
without adopting one of two courses. He could either
express regret at his schismatic action in the Diocese of
New York, or secede from the Church altogether. He
chose the latter course, as being the more straightforward and honest. He did not abuse the American
Church. His letter of resignation, addressed
to the Bishop of Kentucky, and dated
November 10th, 1873, was simple and
dignified in its absence of bitterness and recrimination.
He said : " As I cannot surrender the right and privilege
thus to meet my fellow Christians of other Churches
around the table of our dear Lord, I must take my
place where I can do so without alienating those of my
own household of faith. I therefore leave the communion in which I have laboured in the sacred
ministry for over twenty-eight years, and transfer my
work and office to another sphere of labour." Bishop
Cummins did not desire to " alienate those of his own
household of faith." He did not call those
who held by the formularies in which he
disbelieved *traitors* to the Prayer Book and
Articles, as the Church Association did. He did not
venture to say that his own Protestant standpoint
within the American Church was the only tenable one.
Rather than cause faction and strife he seceded, like an
honest Christian gentleman, which the chastened and
courteous tone of his letter shows him to have been.
No greater contrast can well be imagined
than that between Bishop Cummins and
Bishop Ryle of Liverpool. We may deplore
the views of Bishop Cummins and his followers, but
we cannot help contrasting with admiration the honesty
and courtesy of these men with the polemical virulence

His letter of resignation.

Its reasonable and courteous tone.

And absence of controversial virulence.

of such men as Dr. McNeile, Dean Close, and their followers, who were responsible for the Victorian persecution.

There were no outbursts of vulgar Protestant fanaticism in America. Such manifestations would be quite impossible in any of the British Colonies or Dominions where people have learnt to differ in matters of religion without abusing each other. It is true, of course, that some friction occurred in Natal when Dr. Colenso turned the orthodox clergy out of their churches. But even Sydney Orangemen have hitherto refrained from the public indecencies of riots such as militant Protestantism engineered at S. George's-in-the-East and at S. James's, Hatcham. The crude violence of Mr. Kensit and his "Wyckliffe" Preachers would be impossible in any civilised country excepting England.

No Protestant mob violence in America or in the Colonies.

Bishop Cummins conducted all his proceedings in decency and order. He summoned his followers to a Council in New York, which sat on December 2nd, 1873, and set forth the following "Declaration of Principles."

Orderly procedure of Bishop Cummins. His first Council.

I. "The Reformed Episcopal Church, holding *the faith once delivered to the Saints*, declares its belief in the Holy Scriptures of the Old and New Testaments as the Word of God, and the sole Rule of Faith and Practice ; in the Creed *commonly called the Apostles' Creed ;* in the Divine institution of the Sacraments of Baptism and the Lord's Supper ; and in the doctrines of grace substantially as they are set forth in the Thirty-nine Articles of Religion."

Its "Declaration of Principles."

II. "This Church recognises and adheres to Episcopacy, not as a divine right, but as a very ancient and desirable form of Church polity."

III. "This Church, retaining a Liturgy which shall not be imperative or repressive of freedom in prayer, accepts the Book of Common Prayer, as it was revised, proposed, and recommended for use by the General Convention of the Protestant Episcopal Church, A.D. 1875, reserving full liberty to alter, abridge, enlarge, and amend the same, as may seem most conducive to the edification of the people, *provided that the substance of the faith be kept entire.*"

IV. "This Church condemns and rejects the following erroneous and strange doctrines as contrary to God's Word :

"First, that the Church of Christ exists only in one order or form of ecclesiastical polity.

"Second, that Christian ministers are *priests* in another sense than that in which all believers are *a royal priesthood.*

"Third, that the Lord's Table is an altar on which the oblation of the Body and Blood of Christ is offered anew to the Father.

"Fourth, that the Presence of Christ in the Lord's Supper is a presence in the elements of Bread and Wine.

"Fifth, that Regeneration is inseparably connected with Baptism."

The next work of Bishop Cummins was the revision of the Prayer Book on Protestant lines. The aims of Lord Ebury's Society found their fulfilment in this American revision. The Second Council of the "Reformed Episcopal Church" met at New York in 1874, and as a specimen of the changes carried out it may be noted that the words "Seeing now, dearly beloved brethren, that this child is regenerate" were omitted, and the clause *He descended into hell* was omitted from the Apostles' Creed. A proposal was made to adopt the "Nine Articles of the

His revision of the Prayer Book on Protestant lines.

He carried out Lord Ebury's views.

Evangelical Alliance " (to which allusion has already

The Third Council of the Reformed Episcopalians revised the Articles in 1875. been made in a previous chapter), but the majority decided to alter the Thirty-nine Articles in a Protestant direction. A committee of " Doctrine and Worship " was appointed to amend the Articles, whose report was adopted and carried by the Third Council of the " Reformed Episcopalians " which met at Chicago in May, 1875. The agreement of these " Cumminsite "

These Articles agree in doctrine with Bishop Ryle and his followers. Articles of Religion with the statements of the late Bishop Ryle, Bishop Moule, Bishop Drury and Dr. Griffith Thomas has already been carefully noted in a previous chapter. The fact that the " Reformed Episcopalians "

This Protestant revision of the Articles proves their Catholic interpretation. found it necessary to " Protestantise " the Thirty-nine Articles is evidence enough that Tract Ninety has done its work. The Articles are distinctly capable of a Catholic interpretation, if they be taken as Laud's Declaration takes them, and as Bishop Forbes' great work on the Articles takes them,—in their " literal and grammatical sense." Bishop Cummins and his followers naturally

Bishop Cummins expected strong support in England. thought that their movement would receive strong support in England. They were honest in seceding themselves, and they had read the violent polemics of the militant Protestants in England. Surely the men who had been denouncing Baptismal Regeneration and preaching the " Real Absence " would gladly join them. They hoped for a secession of at least a third of the Church of England. Their expectations were natural, but they

His disappointment and its causes. did not recognise the curious mental processes of English Protestants. In the first place the " militant Protestant " party did not like to follow an American lead. Their insular pride caused them to despise the logical honesty of the " Cumminsites." They clung to the endowments and privileges of the " Establishment." They desired to drive out the whole Catholic school of thought, and capture the " Establishment " for themselves. Their leaders made no secret of their aims in this direction. So that when Bishop Cummins "consecrated" a Bishop

He consecrates a " Bishop " for England.

for the " Free and Reformed " Church of England, the "militant Protestants" gave him the cold shoulder. Bishop Cummins was too tactful to send an American. He chose an English clergyman, who had resigned his benefice and seceded from the Church on account of the Bennett judgment, which vindicated the doctrine of the Real

His choice of Dr. Gregg.

Presence. The Rev. Dr. Gregg, the clergyman chosen by Bishop Cummins, had been Vicar of East Harborne, near Birmingham, till his secession in 1877. The author of this book had

His honest secession.

a slight acquaintance with him, and he gave the impression of being an honest man, with the courage of his convictions. After his so-called "consecration," " Bishop" Gregg showed a good deal of energy. His position, from a moral stand-

His moral standpoint.

point, was infinitely more logical than that of the late Bishop Ryle and other Bishops of similar views, who remain within the Church of England whilst their theology and beliefs are really those of Bishop Cummins and "Bishop" Gregg. The secessionist Bishops certainly occupied a higher moral platform than their co-religionists of the

Failure of his mission.

" Establishment," with their Palaces, large incomes, and seats in the House of Lords. The poor and humble " Reformed Episcopal " Bishop who was trying his best to induce his Protestant co-religionists in the " Establishment " to be honest men and follow his own example, was

Mr. Balleine rejoices thereat.

bitterly disappointed. And Mr. Balleine, the historian of the Evangelical party, glories in the fact that the " Reformed Episcopal " effort came to naught in England. After speaking of " the brilliant tactics of the Ritualists,"

he says, " No doubt Evangelicals made a hundred
And considers it mistakes, but this must be said in their
honourable for favour—*they never dreamed of deserting*
militant Pro-
testants to abide *the ship,* even when she seemed to be
in the Church
of England. driving straight upon the rocks. Though
the great secession of the Scotch Evangelicals (1843) and the formation of the Free Kirk was
a precedent that could not be disregarded; though
every Nonconformist newspaper was loudly urging
them to come out, though the Reformed Episcopal
Church, a small American body, ordained a Bishop
for England, and made desperate efforts to win over
many congregations—through all these trying and
disheartening years hardly a man left the Church."
(Balleine's *History of the Evangelical Party*, p. 233.)

Although the conditions of life in " the ship of the
And endeavour Establishment " have been too pleasant
to capture her and favourable for the militant Protestants
by mutiny. ever to dream of deserting her, they have
never ceased from their efforts to capture her by
mutiny. And the twentieth century sees the mutiny
still carried on by the Latitudinarian wing as well as
by the Puritan wing of the party.

But it is necessary to deal with one very important
point before closing the story of the
The validity of " Cumminsite " schism. Bishop Cummins
the " Cum-
minsite" ordina- was a validly consecrated Bishop. The
tions.
question is, did he convey the grace of
valid ordination, or consecration, to the " Priest " he
purported to ordain or to the " Bishop " he
Careful investi- purported to consecrate? The American
gation by the
American Church very carefully investigated this
Church.
crucial question, and decided that all the
ordinations and consecrations which Bishop Cummins
performed were invalid and utterly null and void.
The conclusions of the American Church upon this
subject were officially laid before the Lambeth Conference of 1888, and formally endorsed by it.

The main reasons for this decision are as follows:

I. " That there was not even a pretence of
Its decision of ordaining and consecrating a Bishop in the
their invalidity meaning and *intention* of the Ordinal.
and its reasons. We do not, of course, mean in this to
affirm that *secretly* held and unexpressed *intention
not* to do what the service purported to do, would
invalidate the act. In this instance, the purpose *not*
to do what the service purported to do was openly
declared. Under such circumstances, if the Ordinal
were used, the use of it was nothing short of a
mockery." (*The Lambeth Conferences*, p. 360.)

It may be noted here that the Lambeth Conference
The Lambeth accepted the conclusions of the American
Conference of Church as expressing the Catholic doctrine
1888 endorses
the American of " Intention."   The   secret   and   un-
decision. expressed misbelief of a Bishop consecrating,
or ordaining, does not invalidate his act from lack of
intention. He may not realise in his own mind the
fulness of Catholic doctrine upon the Sacrament of
Holy Orders. But provided he has the *intention of
doing what the Church does* (*intentio faciendi quod
Ecclesia facit*) his act is valid. But Bishop Cummins
Bishop Cum- did not intend to do what the Church does
mins did not in the act of consecration. He was quite
intend to do
what the Church honest about it. We have seen how Dr.
does. Griffith Thomas and other writers of his
school of foreign Protestant theology have denied the
Apostolic Succession in their published writings.
Bishop Cummins denied it in his public action, which
He purported was a far more open and straightforward
to " consecrate " course than theirs. On December 13th,
Dr. Cheney.
1873, he went through a form of public
imposition of hands whereby he declared Dr. Charles
His sermon E. Cheney to be a " Bishop " of his
declared his lack " Reformed Episcopal Church." His sermon
of intention. on the occasion was published, and

in it he declared openly his Protestant opinions on the Christian ministry. He declared that he did *not* intend to make Dr. Cheney a Bishop of the Catholic Church. He denied that the Episcopate was a distinct *Order* in the Church. He said "Bishops are not the successors of the Apostles. Holy Scripture contains not a suggestion that others could ever perpetuate their office in the Church. The Episcopate is *not* the depository of the Faith. The Episcopate is *not* an ordinance of Apostolic institution." In his second so-called "Consecration" of Dr. Nicholson on February 24th, 1876, Bishop Cummins was "assisted" by a Methodist Episcopal "Bishop," one Methodist minister, and two Presbyterian ministers. He thus logically and honestly carried out the foreign Protestant theology of Holy Orders in an open manner. Bishop Cummins never meant to convey the Apostolic Succession, and he said quite plainly what he meant.

His denial of the functions of the Catholic Episcopate.

His honesty in declaring that he did not intend to convey Catholic orders.

II. The second reason why the American Church disallowed the "consecrations" performed by Bishop Cummins was that both Dr. Cheney and Dr. Nicholson were deposed priests. The case of Timothy Aelurus (fifth century) was cited. In connection with this case the Bishops of Cappadocia Secunda in their reply to the Emperor Leo I. stated that a priest who had been deposed was excluded by ecclesiastical law from being consecrated to the episcopate. (See Labbe and Cossart's *Concilia*, vol. iv. col. 956.) The deposition of Dr. Cheney forms an important ecclesiastical precedent. He was Rector of an influential parish in Chicago, where his extreme Protestant views were supported by a large and wealthy congregation. The Bishop of

Deposed priests are incapable of receiving consecration.

The deposition of Dr. Cheney for denying Baptismal Regeneration.

Illinois (Dr. Whitehouse) took proceedings against him for depraving the Book of Common Prayer. He wilfully and deliberately omitted the words *Seeing now that this child is regenerate* in the Baptismal Office. This flagrant act of disloyalty was more outspoken than

The Bishop of Illinois before the Supreme Court.

the conduct of an English clergymen of extreme Protestant views, who used to say the words in question, and then say in a whisper *which I do not believe.* The Bishop cited Dr. Cheney before his Diocesan Court, and deprived him of his benefice as Rector of Christchurch, Chicago. He was encouraged by his congregation to resist the Bishop's sentence, and the matter came before the Supreme Court of Illinois. An attempt was made to

Clear statement of the Judge in refusing to deal with Church doctrine in a Civil Court.

make a second "Gorham case" of it, and Dr. Cheney desired to argue the question of Baptismal Regeneration before the Civil Court. But the Judge stopped the theological argument very promptly. He used some memorable words on the occasion. "Freedom of religious profession and worship," said the Judge, "cannot be maintained if the Civil Courts tread upon the domain of the Church—construe its Canons and Rules—dictate its discipline and regulate its trials." (*American Law Reports*, vol. xi. p. 95.)

The case showed the true relation of the Church to the Civil Power.

These sound principles exactly define the true relation of the Church and the Civil Power. The Church, as an independent spiritual corporation, must be free to exercise her own discipline upon her own members. She is, from the civil point of view, a voluntary

The Church, as a voluntary Society, must be free to exercise her discipline.

society whose members are bound by her rules of membership, just as in ordinary life the members of a club must abide by the rules of the club they have joined if they are to partake of its privileges. The Judge, in the case of the Bishop of Chicago *v.* Dr. Cheney, had to ascertain who had the right of

occupation and use of the Church buildings of the
The Civil Court parish of Christchurch, Chicago, which
has to see that were legally vested for the use of the
the discipline of American Church. He therefore caused
the Church is
civilly protected. Dr. Whitehouse to prove that he was the
lawful Bishop of Illinois, and that Dr. Cheney had
taken the usual oath of canonical obedience to him.
By this oath the Judge held Dr. Cheney to be bound.
He had been tried and condemned in the Spiritual
Court of the diocese for depraving the Prayer Book.
The Civil Court could take no cognisance of the
doctrinal issues involved. All it did was to affirm
that Dr. Cheney could not use Christchurch because
the fabric and Church property belonged to a body
whose rules he had broken and whose authority he
had defied. This famous case forms a precedent for
all parts of the Anglican Communion which are
happily freed from the disabilities and entanglements
of the State connection. If the Chnrch of England
could deal with her militant Protestants as the
American Church has done, there would be peace.

CHAPTER   IX.

THE " LIBERAL " OR LATITUDINARIAN WING OF THE FOREIGN PROTESTANT PARTY.

WE have already briefly noted the rise of the Latitudinarian side of Protestantism within the
Church of England. The Whig-Erastian
policy of the eighteenth century favoured
its development. The agitation of Archdeacon Blackbourne and others against subscription
to the Thirty-nine Articles by the clergy was part and
parcel of the same policy. The ideal of
these men and their followers was to
eliminate the Athanasian Creed, and with
it all the definite teaching of the Prayer Book and
Articles upon the Trinity and the Incarnation. We
need not deal in detail with the Deist and Arian controversies of the first half of the eighteenth century.
The anti-Christian leaders of these wearisome and
heretical logomachies formed the left wing of the
Latitudinarian party. We have already
also seen that Dr. Arnold and the Latitudinarian Archbishop Tait vehemently assailed the Tractarian leaders from their own standpoint
of anti-dogmatic Protestantism. Dean Stanley of
Westminster Abbey was another Latitudinarian leader,
with an amiable temperament, coupled with an
inherent dislike of any definite Christian
teaching. When the revision of the
authorised version of the Bible was undertaken in the "seventies," the New Testament Company

Marginal notes:

Whig-Erastian policy of the eighteenth century.

Agitation against subscription to the Articles.

Latitudinarian attack on the Tractarians.

Dean Stanley and the West-minster scandal.

of Revisers included scholars from various religious bodies including Mr. Vance Smith, a Unitarian minister. Dean Stanley invited the whole body of Revisers, including the Unitarian, to a corporate communion at the Abbey. It took place in the Chapel of Henry VII., and the Unitarian communicated with the rest. The admission of unconfirmed schismatics was a distinct violation of the rubric in the Book of Common Prayer, but the admission of the Unitarian was a scandal of the same character as the admission of a Jewish Rabbi would have been. Dean Stanley took the same advantage of the exemption of the Abbey from episcopal jurisdiction as Dean Armitage Robinson did in using, in our own day, a mutilated version of the Athanasian Creed, or as Canon Henson has done in preaching heretical sermons in the Abbey for which he would have been amenable to the Bishop of London's jurisdiction had he preached them in his Church of S. Margaret's, Westminster. There was a vigorous and determined protest against Dean Stanley's action, but his privileged position was unassailable. The exempt jurisdiction of the Abbey is one of the open sores of the Church of England as an Establishment.

Curious position of the Abbey as an exempt jurisdiction.

Advantage taken of this by Dean Stanley and others.

It is unnecessary to do more than summarise the controversy concerning the volume called "Essays and Reviews." It was condemned by the Convocation of Canterbury, and two of its authors were brought to trial for heresy. The usurped jurisdiction of the Privy Council was as successfully exercised to shield the Latitudinarians from condemnation as it had been to excuse Mr. Gorham for denying Baptismal Regeneration. The book is forgotten, although its authors sowed the dragon's teeth whence sprang the multitudinous host of modern Latitudinarian heresies. A South African

The "Essays and Reviews" case.

writer may naturally be expected to say some-
The Case of
Dr. Colenso. thing about the Colenso case.   Dr. Colenso's
heresies mainly concerned the doctrine of
the Trinity, the Incarnation, and the Sacraments.
His curiously uninspiring form of " Higher Criticism "
of the Old Testament evoked the comment from his
friend Professor Maurice that he evidently considered
history to be based upon arithmetic.   His theories on
Its real issues. the Pentateuch formed only a side issue of
the case, and Bishop Gray very carefully
avoided any assertion of verbal inspiration or any
condemnation of criticism, as such, in his Judgment.
He condemned Dr. Colenso's Kenotic theory of our
Lord's ignorance as Man as being a form of Nestorianism.   The author may be permitted to refer here to
his *Life of Dean Green* of Maritzburg. (*Longman's*
2 vols. 1908.)   These volumes contained a detailed
history of the whole case, and a full explanation of its
origin and subsequent results.   The Colenso Judgment
is still in force as part of the " case-law " of the South
African Church, and it is worth careful study from the
fact that, in condemning a false " Liberal Theology,"
it carefully guards the true " Liberalism " of the
Catholic Faith.   The present day phase of "Liberalism"
has received a strange stimulus from a similar move-
"Modernism"
within the
Roman Church. ment within the Roman Catholic Church,
which is known as "Modernism." This
movement has naturally fallen under the
condemnation of the Vatican because it is funda-
mentally hostile to the Faith of the historic Creeds of
Christendom.   Men like the Abbé Loisy have gradually
severed themselves from historical Christianity and
have adopted some of the wildest theories of modern
anti-Christian German criticism with regard to the
authority and accuracy of the Gospel narratives.
Dr. Cheyne, amongst Anglicans, has acquired an
Dr. Cheyne and
the Anglican
" Modernists," unenviable notoriety for the perverted anti-
Christian bias of his theories of Biblical
criticism.   His theories have very naturally

landed him into a position of negative creedlessness, and the only positive element in his teaching consists of denials of the root-facts of historical Christianity. Certain persons, who do not usually concern themselves with the diagnosis of error, were seriously shocked and alarmed at the fact that Dr. Cheyne, notwithstanding his negations, was yet a Canon of Rochester, and administered the Holy Communion when he was in residence. It is difficult to under-

His responsibility for Unitarian views in the "Encyclopædia Biblica."

stand how a man who had made himself practically responsible for Dr. Schmiedel's denial of the "Godhead of our Lord," in the *Encyclopædia Biblica*, could use the Anglican Office (which contains the Nicene Creed) at the altar of an English Cathedral without grave dishonesty. Is it not dishonest for a person who does not believe in the careful and accurately worded dogmatic statements of the Nicene Creed, to use that Creed at the Altar as an officiating Priest? Such a priest would seem to be performing the central act of Christian worship with " a lie in his right hand." And this is not the only case. In 1910 a book was published by G. Bell & Sons, called the " Confessions

" The Confessions of a Clergyman."

of a Clergyman." On p. 144 the writer says: " I am not called upon to disclose my identity when such a disclosure would not tend to my own good or the good of others." The author tells us (p. 24) that he is a beneficed priest of the Church of England, but that he thinks it better to

Its author an Arian denier of the Trinity.

stick to his benefice although he has lost his faith. Possibly the book might be put aside as an abnormal and freakish development. But the attitude taken up with regard to it by a Church paper so influential and so widely respected

Strange attitude of the *Guardian* on this book.

as the *Guardian*, must justify some examination of a volume which the *Guardian* calls " an honest and outspoken presentation of the attitude of many Broad Churchmen," and evidently regards as a typical utterance of the so-called " Liberal Theology." The *Guardian* even goes further, and calls the author "a sane, manly, religious soul, with a dominant honesty of purpose." It is strange to find the *Guardian* calling a man " honest " who has become an Arian and yet expresses his determination of retaining his benefice. He says (p. 140) : " I am still in the active Ministry of the Church. I see no reason why I should sever this connection." His confession of Arianism is plain and open. He says (p. 139) : " I recognise Jesus as my Saviour. *But I do not recognise Him as my God.*" Thus he is relieved from what he calls (p. 131) *the burdensome, perplexing, and impossible dogma of the Trinity.* When Mr. Stopford Brooke found that he had ceased to believe in the Apostles' Creed, in its plain and natural meaning, he resigned his benefice, like an honest man. The strain of foreign Protestantism that has infected the Church of England is dishonest on its Latitudinarian side as well as on its Protestant side.

Honesty of Mr. Stopford Brooke.

The Church of England has to reckon with its foes on both sides, and her chief danger lies in the fact that her worst enemies are within her own borders, comfortably sheltered by the anomaly of a " comprehensive " ecclesiastical Establishment. The " Liberals " just now are more dangerous than the " militant Protestants." Their scheme of " Prayer Book Revision " is worse than the attempt of 1689, and they would retain less dogmatic truth than is retained in the " Cumminsite " Revised Articles and Prayer Book. Its leader in the Canterbury Convocation appears to be Canon Henson, who has skilfully utilised the immunities of his stall at Westminster to promulgate his special variety of Anglican " Modernism "

The evils of indiscriminate " Comprehensiveness."

Liberal scheme of Prayer Book Revision.

Canon Henson advocates it.

or "Liberalism." He has spoken of "the acute conflict between the modern intellect and conscience and the Prayer Book." He has denounced "the arbitrary and irrational emphasis laid on the letter of the ancient Creeds." (*Liberty of Prophesying*, p. 8.)

Attack on the Athanasian Creed. He objects strongly to the Creed commonly called "Athanasian." The failure of Archbishop Tait's efforts to get rid of this Creed in the "seventies" and the subsequent failures of similar and more recent agitations in the same direction do not deter our "Liberal" Revisionists. The South African Church is happily so bound by its constitution that it has legally "estopped" itself from following the Church of England if any alterations or omissions are made in the text of the Creed. The success of the Revisionists in England in this direction would only build up a wall of separation between the Mother Church and the Church of South Africa. But such an argument as this would not touch them in the least. Their "Liberalism" is far too narrow and insular to make them consider for a moment the attitude of the Anglican Communion, as a whole, towards Revision. They point to Ireland and America, and say that South Africa has no right to take a different line. Canon Henson in the same book

Liberal denial of the Virgin Birth. relegates our Lord's Birth of the Blessed Virgin "to the region of *religious opinion*" (p. 86). And when Bishop Gore put pressure to bear upon Mr. Beeby, a beneficed Priest of his Diocese, for denying the Virgin Birth, Canon Henson openly supported Mr. Beeby against his Bishop. But there are yet lower depths than those sounded by Canon Henson. Another Revisionist, Mr.

Mr. Garrod's attack on Christian ethics. H. W. Garrod, says (with regard to the "Modernist" denial of our Lord's Second Advent to Judgment by Professor Inge and others): "Criticism of Christianity upon the ethical side has scarcely yet begun. I do not see how we can

escape the necessity of wholly revising our view of
Christian ethics.   Christ's main apocalyptic idea
dominates His moral teaching." (*The Religion of All
Good Men*, p. 152.)   Apparently Mr. Garrod desires to
abolish the Sermon on the Mount as well as the
Creeds.   He says, very truly, "We cannot abandon
Christian dogma and keep Christian ethics.

Christian dogma and Christian ethics must both disappear.

The ethics must go, as well as the dogma."
Mr. Garrod objects to our Lord's teaching
on renunciation of the world and on
chastity and purity of life.   He says : " The objection
of young men to Christianity is not intellectual but
moral " (p. 59).   He says that "the *world* and the
flesh are two things which mankind *will never consent
to do without*.   The instinct of the average man is
healthy, its cry is ever still, Give us the world and the
flesh, or we will smash every window in your palace
of painted superstition " (p. 143).   This frank confession of Pagan ethics is useful.   We are called upon
to revise the Prayer Book in the interests of the
world and of the flesh.   Possibly the majority of those
very respectable clergy who have been trying to revise
the Prayer Book temporarily will pause in their
efforts to make room for the latest ethics of Liberal
Christianity.   We know that they are not liturgical
experts, but at all events we may trust them as moral
experts, so far, at least, as a condemnation of Mr.
Garrod's ideas will carry them.

Inherent disloyalty of both wings of the foreign Protestant party.

We need not pursue this subject further.
We have shown the inherent disloyalty of
both wings of the foreign Protestant party
within the Church of England.

Room in the Catholic Church for the subjective as well as the philosophical temper.

There is room in the Church, as we have already
said several times, for a legitimate and
loyal subjective temper of mind.   There is
also room for the philosophic and intellectual temperament.   It cannot be forgotten that the Apostolic College numbered

S. Thomas in its ranks as well as S. Peter, S. John, and S. Paul.

But the Catholic Church has no room for such defective and negative teaching as we have been bound to examine and criticise in this book. The "Modernist" Broad Church-man of this type has no legitimate stand-ing ground within the Church of England any more than the "Wyckliffe Preachers" have.

But no room for the disloyalty which has been proved in this book.

Modern Liberal theology, in its nebulous creed-lessness, has no definite Gospel message for the heathen world. It cannot deal with Mahommedanism or Hinduism, for it is too vague to offer any definite dogma to counteract either of them. Its indefiniteness is the measure of its inefficiency.

Uselessness of Modern Liberalism in the Mission field.

It may be asked whether it is worth while to expose the errors and heresies which are so com-placently tolerated within the Church of England. It is worth while to make men think whether they are honest or not. The Church of England has suffered more than enough from vague and nebulous Churchmanship which in-volves membership without corresponding obligations. And the errors of foreign Protestant theology, alike in their definiteness and in their vagueness, have most seriously weakened the witness of the Anglican Communion in one special direction.

Uselessness of Church Mem-bership without obligations.

The so-called "Liberals" have fortunately left the missionary work of the Church to others. With the exception of Dr. Colenso, they have shown little or no interest in missionary work. And his failure in that direction is writ large in the history of the South African Church. The Latitudinarian side of Pro-testantism has no definite message for the heathen world. A nebulous creedlessness is as futile a weapon in the mission field as a feather boa against the sword of Islam, the powerful traditions of Hinduism, and

the negations of Buddhism. It would be a crime
against a very capable and noble portion of the human
race to bring " Modernist " missionaries to our South
African natives. And the militant Protestant influ-
C.M.S. sec- ence is just as bad. In India the C.M.S.
tarianism in and the S.P.G. have virtually created
India. rival sects. The native Christians who have
become disciples of the C.M.S. will not harmonise as
brethren with the native converts of the S.P.G.

Not long ago a ritual disturbance arose near
Madras when some C.M.S. native Christians emulated
the Kensit outrages and destroyed a stained glass
window in a church because it contained a figure of
our Lord. We have brought with us to India not only
the British flag and British justice of administration,
which are good things, but we have also brought with
us the wretched party divisions of the Church of
England, an inherently bad thing.

A man who has lived so many years out of England
A remedy sug- as the writer of this book has done has
gested by Canon no business to suggest remedies from his
Hobhouse. own outside standpoint. But the recent
Bampton Lectures of Canon Hobhouse at all events
seem to suggest a remedy.

And that remedy is the severance of the connection
The remedy, a of Church and State in England. It is
severance impossible to overstate the difficulties
between Church which would surround the details of such a
and State. severance. But certain facts would emerge.
People would have to be honest. The Church would
be purged of its Latitudinarian and militant Protestant
elements. And the faithful remnant would be able to
Its result a govern its own household and maintain
concentration of its own discipline. Surely this return to
forces and an
organised self- the primitive position of the Catholic
government Church before its entanglement with the
without
narrowness. State under Constantine would more than
make up for any loss of temporal prestige and worldly
power.

" Merses profundo pulchrior evenit "

would be the true motto of the *Ecclesia Anglicana*
when she emerged from the immediate consequences
of the reorganisation rendered necessary by her
severance from the State. She would lengthen her
cords, strengthen her stakes, and concentrate her
forces. Once more, in the closing words of this book,
would its writer repeat his conviction that there is
ample room in the Catholic Church for the subjective
as well as for the intellectual and philosophical spirit.
He has no desire to narrow the bounds of an honest
and definite adherence to the Catholic Faith as taught
in the Catholic Creeds. But the Anglican Communion
must shake herself free from an alien theology, hostile
in both its aspects to the Catholic Faith.

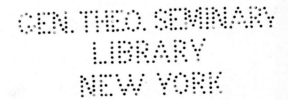

INDEX.

James Tilsed, Printer, High Street, Wimborne, Dorset.